The MUSEUM *of* LOST THINGS

ALSO BY SAM KEAN

Dinner With King Tut

The Icepick Surgeon

The Bastard Brigade

Caesar's Last Breath

The Tale of the Dueling Neurosurgeons

The Violinist's Thumb

The Disappearing Spoon

The MUSEUM *of* LOST THINGS

True Tales of Fabled Treasures, Legendary Cities, and
Mythical Creatures That Vanished From History

SAM KEAN

NATIONAL GEOGRAPHIC
WASHINGTON, D.C.

Published by National Geographic Partners, LLC

1145 17th Street NW Washington, DC 20036

Interior design: Lisa Monias

ISBN: 978-1-4262-2386-0

The authorized representative in the EU for product safety and compliance is Disney Trading B.V., Asterweg 15S, 1031 HL, Amsterdam, The Netherlands
email: DCP.DL-EU.bookscontact@disney.com

Printed in the United States of America

26/LSCH/1

"My name is Ozymandias, King of Kings;
Look on my Works, ye Mighty, and despair!"
Nothing beside remains. Round the decay
Of that colossal Wreck, boundless and bare
The lone and level sands stretch far away.

—"Ozymandias," by Percy Bysshe Shelley

CONTENTS

INTRODUCTION

Perhaps the single most common theme in all of history is *loss*. The loss of land, the loss of sacred relics, the loss of languages, of rights, of life—history groans with examples. That universal truth is the starting point for this book, which gathers together the world's most captivating tales about absence and explores what that means across the sweep of human history and the scope of human lives.

In these pages, you'll find everything from glittering biblical treasures to Leonardo's missing artistic masterpieces to subtler, quieter objects that nevertheless crack open the stories of our ancestors in unexpected and fascinating ways. You'll also encounter long-lost technologies and forgotten civilizations that we've only recently unearthed, as well as extinct wonders from natural history—species whose existence holds a mirror up to human evolution and human nature. Other treasures covered here aren't material items at all, but intangible aspects of a culture like its languages and religious rites—things that once filled people's lives with meaning and inspired the greatest societies the world has ever known, only to vanish like a breath on a cold winter's day.

Structurally, the book is organized by theme and spans a million years of Earth's history, from the days of our earliest ancestors up through the space age, with stops along the way in pharaonic Egypt, ancient Troy, Renaissance Italy, colonial Peru, and other milieus. In some cases, the loss at the core of each chapter resulted from villainy—theft, vandalism, genocidal madness. In others, the vicissitudes of time simply eroded something holy, year by year, until little more remained than the "vast and trunkless legs" of Ozymandias. In each instance, we'll learn why the loss occurred and how it might have been avoided—and perhaps gain insight into how we can avoid a similar fate for our own cultural heritage.

Many of the lost treasures here have been the object of obsessive and often foolhardy searches to recover them. These quests have consumed fortunes, ruined lives, and—most improbably of all—even succeeded on occasion. Other items remain missing despite our best efforts and will likely never be found.

In addition to the individual tales, this book explores the psychological fallout of loss. How do people and cultures deal with it? What does it do to our sense of identity and sense of self? Is recovery ever possible, or is loss permanent? Can loss even benefit us? In tandem, we'll explore how fragile history is—how easily things can be lost, and why we need to be careful when drawing sweeping conclusions about the past based on ancient discoveries that may not reveal the full truth about a culture or a period. For every object we find, millions of others remain missing, and some new discovery tomorrow could radically change our understanding of the past. (It's happened before.) This perspective will help us appreciate the history that we're making (and destroying) today, and how that process might influence the legacy of our own era.

Writing this book was humbling in many ways. As we'll see, certain aspects of modern life that seem ubiquitous and inescapable will likely fade to nothing in the future. Meanwhile, everyday items that we discard as trash could become the signature traits of our civilization (hello, chicken bones). Indeed, so much of what we cherish today will likely vanish—and it's this that connects us with the people of the past more profoundly than anything else. These are tales about things long lost. But they're tales about us, too.

CHAPTER ONE

LOST GRAVES

After amassing one of the largest empires in history, Alexander the Great died unexpectedly at age 32 in Babylon in 323 B.C. His retinue reportedly embalmed him with honey and spices and placed him in a golden sarcophagus draped with gaudy purple tapestries. But rather than let him rest in peace, his successors turned his body into a pawn in a power struggle so complex that George R. R. Martin himself would have been baffled.

Right away, Alexander's pregnant wife Roxana had another wife murdered, along with the woman's sister, and threw their bodies down a well. Alexander's generals dispatched Roxana in turn, as well as Alexander's half brother. Then the real mess began, as the military governors of the two dozen provinces of Alexander's kingdom began invading each other's territories. Seeking an edge in these wars, several went to pathetic lengths to portray themselves as Alexander's true heir. Some dressed like him or permed their hair to match his shaggy mane of curls. Others claimed he visited them in dreams, or commissioned fan-fic art of them fighting alongside him in battle. The general Ptolemy, who ruled Egypt, spread rumors that Alexander was his half-sibling.

Ptolemy also saw fit to seize Alexander's corpse. After the body had lain in state for a year, the governor-general of Babylon decided to transfer it to Alexander's homeland in Macedonia, a neutral site. But for some reason—perhaps a healthy bribe from Ptolemy—the funeral cortege swung well out of its way to Damascus, where Ptolemy's troops hijacked the sarcophagus and hightailed it to Egypt. The Babylonian governor invaded in retaliation; he knew what a potent symbol the body was. But he got bogged down crossing the Nile, at which point his own soldiers murdered him and turned for home. Ptolemy installed the sarcophagus in his palace and thereby legitimized his rule; he went on to found the dynasty that built the Great Library of Alexandria. Most of his rival generals met violent, unhappy ends.

For all the power accorded Alexander's corpse, however, we have no idea where it lies today. According to some traditions, it was buried in a mosque. Others hold that it was diced into bits and converted into magic amulets. Perhaps it burned in one of Alexandria's many riots. We just don't know.

Alexander is far from alone here. For every emperor or queen with a well-attested grave, dozens of others have vanished, and rediscovering their final resting place today—one tiny plot of dirt on the whole wide earth—seems impossible.

That hasn't stopped archaeologists from searching. Graves are arguably the single most important type of archaeological find. The burial process reveals details about the person's religion and worldview.

The bones can yield DNA or evidence of disease. Graves also contain treasures that provide insight into an era's art and technology. They're cornucopias of data.

All too often, though, sound archaeological reasons for hunting down a grave are a fig leaf for fanaticism. An obsession with some historical celebrity grips people, and they waste decades of their lives, and ruinous amounts of money, pursuing a phantom.

In 1809, a wide-eyed 11-year-old named Giovanni d'Athanasi arrived in Cairo to begin apprenticing in his father's shop. Raised on a modest Greek island, the boy had never seen such a bustling metropolis—much less the likes of the pyramids. The soaring monuments awed him, and he soon ditched his father's shop to become an interpreter for a British consul who funded archaeological treasure hunts on the side.

D'Athanasi also led sightseeing expeditions for foreign visitors. His nom de tour was Yanni, and he wore a sort of genie costume with a dark waistcoat, oversize fez, and ballooning pants tucked into stirrups. He had an ample belly, and a thick mustache and eyebrows. He proved quite popular and became a fixture of Egyptian archaeology.

The British consul's main treasure hunter was a six-foot-six-inch former circus strongman who could hoist 11 people into the air at once.* The carny proved equally headstrong, however, and the consul

* The strongman was Giovanni Belzoni. He discovered the giant Ramses the Great head now in the British Museum that inspired the poem "Ozymandias," by Percy Bysshe Shelley. "Look on my Works, ye Mighty, and despair!"

fired him after a dispute over some artifacts. Yanni leaped at the chance to take his place and hunt treasures himself. He soon scored a coup by finding the first-ever intact tomb of a pharaoh: Nubkheperre Intef of the 1500s B.C.

Yanni made his most important discovery in 1820: the tomb of Nebamun, who lived in the 1300s B.C. If you've never heard of Nebamun, don't fret; no one back then had, either. Nebamun worked in a temple in Thebes (modern Luxor) dedicated to the god Amun. Egypt was thriving at that time, wealthy and robust, and Amun was the preferred god of the ruling dynasty. The Temple of Amun was therefore a powerful institution, with scores of employees. Nebamun served as an accountant for the grains deposited there as taxes—a boring-ass middle manager. He'd be entirely forgotten today if not for his exquisite taste in art.

Sometime in middle age, Nebamun began constructing his mausoleum. Nowadays we think of mausoleums as somber structures, even a bit cold or forbidding. Not the Egyptians. People of Nebamun's class typically carved their final resting place into a hillside. At the far end, they'd sink a shaft and seal off the deceased's mummy. But out front, the tombs often had a cheery courtyard, and the walls inside were adorned with paintings. Rather than trudge through solemnly, families gathered there to feast, almost a picnic atmosphere. It was a place of joy, meant to celebrate the person's life.

To decorate his mausoleum, Nebamun hired a local painter. Archaeologists conjecture that the painter worked at the Temple of Amun, where Nebamun bumped into him. Regardless of how they met, Nebamun decided the man's art was just the thing for his tomb and hired him—possibly under the table.

To prepare a painting surface inside the tomb, the artist spread a paste of mud and chopped straw on the rough rock walls; he concealed that with smooth white plaster. He painted while the surface was still wet, fresco style. For pigments, he used black soot, red and yellow ochre, and finely ground blue and green minerals mixed with binders. He made brushes by chewing on rushes to fray the ends. Given the times—there was less of a cult of personality around artists then—no one today knows the painter's name or anything about him. Instead, he's simply known as the Michelangelo of the Nile. Nebamun's tomb was his Sistine Chapel.

The artist divided the tomb's walls into panels with separate scenes. Each one shows Nebamun participating in a different activity in the afterlife, and apparently the accountant planned to be busy: He's shown spearing fish, hunting waterfowl, raising cattle, hosting wine-soaked banquets with musicians and dancing girls, plus tending an estate with a pool and walled garden full of dates. The scenes paint an evocative picture of heaven.

But what raises them to the level of Michelangelo is the little artistic flourishes. You can see the shimmering scales on the tilapia in the marsh. In the garden, you can pick out which dates are ripest by their color and texture. A shirtless old man in one scene has flyaway hair and an outie belly button. Another scene shows a servant clutching a dwarf gazelle, and you can practically see it trembling in the man's arms. Tiger butterflies flit by, and a tawny cat flashes its whiskers as it snatches birds. Each vignette is a masterpiece of realism in an age when realism hadn't even been invented yet.

From the moment he broke into Nebamun's tomb in 1820, Yanni felt certain the paintings would fetch top dollar. Thanks partly to the Rosetta Stone, Egyptian goods were hot commodities at the time, and Yanni's boss the consul had good connections at the British Museum. Unfortunately, gangs of rival treasure hunters were prowling the hills around Luxor; fistfights sometimes erupted over prime sites.

Yanni's team therefore had to work quickly to remove the Nebamun paintings—too quickly. They selected a dozen of the best panels and pried them off the walls with hacksaws and crowbars. Several cracked and suffered damage.

In a shortsighted move, the British Museum then lowballed the consul, acquiring the paintings for just £2,000 ($150,000 today). It wasn't even enough to cover expenses. After the consul died, Yanni offered his services directly to the museum; the directors haughtily declined. The rejection insulted Yanni, who eventually cut ties with the museum. And no matter how much they begged, he refused to reveal the location of Nebamun's tomb to scholars who wanted to study the remaining paintings there. They could all go hang.

Although he built a decent career for himself, Yanni never made the big score he hoped for. Feeling his age, he quit Egypt in 1850 and moved to England to open a gallery, where he planned to cash in on his connections in the antiquities trade. Alas, the same British nobles who happily chatted with him on camel tours in distant Luxor wouldn't be caught dead with the swarthy Greek in a London drawing room, and the shop went belly-up. Yanni died in a poorhouse in 1854. He left no record of where to find the Sistine Chapel of the Nile.

A clue did emerge in 1890. That year, someone found a fragment of a Nebamun panel on the ground near a rugged, hilly necropolis called Dra' Abu el-Naga; it showed men netting quail. Yanni or a crewmate presumably dropped it while sneaking the panels away, in which case the tomb probably lies nearby. Unfortunately, a new village was erected over much of Dra' Abu el-Naga in the later 1800s, so there's no way to search for Nebamun without tearing down people's homes. Overall, two centuries of scouring the remaining hills has turned up no further trace of the unlikely connoisseur-accountant and his unknown masterpiece painter.

Around the time Nebamun was laid to rest, a new pharaoh took over: Akhenaten, who presided over one of the most tumultuous reigns in Egypt's history.

Akhenaten was a fascinating figure: the husband of Queen Nefertiti, the likely father of the future King Tut, perhaps the first monotheist in history. But his religious zeal doomed him. Dozens of gods had comfortably coexisted in Egypt for centuries, even if some (e.g., Amun) enjoyed more prominence. Suddenly, Akhenaten banned the worship of every other god except his favorite, the sun deity Aten. This decree shocked and angered his subjects. Rather than listen to them, Akhenaten doubled down and tried to eradicate all mention of other gods throughout his kingdom. He even sent his guards into tombs and temples to smash other gods' names.

One victim of this vandalism was Nebamun. Wherever his name appears on the panels in the British Museum, the hieroglyphs for N-E-B have survived, but the letters A-M-U-N have been destroyed. Imagine you're Nebamun's family, and you visit his mausoleum one morning with a picnic, only to find those brilliant paintings defaced. No wonder people hated Akhenaten.

Akhenaten's volatile reign caused an economic slump, and borderland provinces rebelled and broke away from Egypt. People naturally blamed this chaos on Akhenaten's heresies, and he left the kingdom in near shambles when he died around 1335 B.C. The line of succession gets fuzzy at this point, but within a few years, the nine-year-old King Tut assumed the throne.

For all his renown today, Tut was a nobody pharaoh—the Millard Fillmore of Egypt. He did reinstate religious freedom and restore the worship of the old gods. But the gods failed to reward him with a long, prosperous life—probably because Tut's parents were brother and sister, and he himself was sickly and weak. He died around age 19, having accomplished little of note.

And here's where things get interesting. Tut was interred in a puny underground tomb, hardly worthy of a pharaoh, even a minor one. The murals inside are also discolored with mysterious, coin-size blobs of brown mold. Apparently, Tut was buried in such a rush that there wasn't time to let the paint dry on the walls before sealing him up.

All of which has led some archaeologists to make a radical suggestion: that Tut's tomb was originally meant for someone else. The thinking is that Tut died so young and so unexpectedly that no mausoleum was ready for him. Scrambling to make do, his advisers took over some unknown person's tomb instead. Even more radically, a few archaeologists have floated the idea that Tut's body was laid to rest in Queen Nefertiti's tomb—and that Nefertiti's body is still down there, sealed off behind a false wall. In support of this idea, the archaeologists claim they can make out faint doorways etched into the walls of Tut's burial chamber.

To be clear, few archaeologists buy the Nefertiti theory, and recent studies using radar to probe the walls for hidden chambers have uncovered nothing. But the less radical idea that the tomb wasn't meant for Tut does seem plausible, albeit unproven.

Tut's restoration of the old gods did nothing to ease the hatred toward his father, and after his dynasty ended, the new ruling clan carried out a *damnatio memoriae* (damnation of memory) campaign, defacing statues and smashing any wall texts that mentioned Akhenaten. They aimed to wipe out all trace of the heretical pharaoh from the annals of history. This attempt failed, obviously, but there is some justice in Akhenaten suffering the same treatment that Nebamun did.

Tut got damned by association with his father, and within a century of his death, his pitiful burial site was forgotten. When flood debris swallowed the entrance, people let it remain there as punishment. Then workers excavating a grander tomb nearby dumped more debris on top. In fact, Tut's tomb got buried so thoroughly that even looters struggled to find it. As a result, while the more conspicuous monuments of other pharaohs got stripped bare over the next few millennia, Tut's tomb remained forgotten until 1922, when the intact treasures inside made him a worldwide sensation. By trying to erase Tut from history, his enemies ensured that this minor figure became the most famous pharaoh of all.

If archaeologists could vote on which lost grave they'd most like to find, Genghis Khan's would likely appear near the top of the list—in part to fact-check the gruesome legends surrounding his burial.

He was born in Mongolia around 1162, and supposedly emerged from the womb clutching a clot of blood in his fist. By all rights, the boy—whose original name was Temüjin—should have died young. His father, a nobleman in their tribe, was poisoned by a rival tribe when Temüjin was nine, and greedy schemers within his own clan banished the boy's family to the empty steppes, expecting them to starve.

Historical accounts describe Temüjin as overly sensitive, terrified of dogs and prone to crying. But he grew up fast. Even before adolescence, he'd already been enslaved (he engineered his own escape) and killed his older half brother. As a young man he discovered that soldiering suited him, and he ruthlessly eliminated all potential rivals among other nomadic tribes, until he was crowned Genghis

Khan—universal ruler—in 1206. His other nickname was the Disturber of the Universe. His warriors were bold and battle-tested, and when they stopped murdering each other and turned their attention outward, they proved unstoppable.

They favored blitzkrieg tactics, sweeping in on horses and bombarding the enemy with arrows. But they could be surprisingly patient, too, and perfected the art of siege warfare. One notorious siege involved the city of Merv, in what's now Turkmenistan. Merv was the Alexandria of its day: a desert oasis teeming with gardens and libraries, famous for its silks and refreshing melons. The Mongols couldn't resist it, and when the terrified artists and merchants inside surrendered after just six days of siege, a massacre ensued. "It was a memorable day for shrieking and weeping," lamented one chronicle. After burning Merv for good measure, Genghis Khan ordered his troops to count the corpses. There were 700,000.

Yet however crazy it sounds, life under Genghis Khan had its benefits. He allowed the conquered to worship whatever gods they liked, a rare example of religious tolerance. He introduced the idea of diplomatic immunity to facilitate negotiations, and outlawed torture during interrogations. He promoted free trade, and founded history's first international mail system. Over time, his empire also spread key technologies like the compass, abacus, printing press, and paper currency, as well as key social programs like universal education for children. No one was more ruthless when conquering (ask Merv). But if the vanquished people picked up the pieces and swore fealty afterward, life generally improved under Mongol rule.

Genghis Khan's realm stretched from Korea to the Caspian Sea, an area twice the size of the Roman Empire. (Under his successors, it grew to the size of Africa.) And he accomplished all this with an army of just 100,000 warriors—fewer people than some modern stadiums hold. Historian Jack Weatherford summed up his achievements thus: "[Imagine] if the United States ... had been founded by one of its illiterate slaves, who, by the sheer force of personality, charisma, and determination, liberated America from foreign rule, united the people, created an alphabet, wrote the constitution, established universal religious freedom, invented a new system of warfare, [and] marched an army from Canada to Brazil." Alexander, Julius Caesar, Napoleon—they weren't fit to carry Genghis Khan's saddle. If anyone in history deserved a grand mausoleum, it was him.

Genghis Khan wanted the opposite.

Despite all the blood they shed, the Mongols were oddly squeamish about discussing d-e-a-t-h, so beyond the year (1227), contemporary sources say little about how Genghis Khan died. As a result, rumors multiplied. One story claims he died after tumbling off a horse. Others have him struck down by lightning or an arrow to the knee during battle (at age 65, no less). One source swears he was trying to ravish a conquered queen who, anticipating the crime, concealed a blade inside her vagina that sliced lil' Genghis wide open. Regardless of the truth, his longtime wife Yesui dressed his body in a white robe, wrapped it in white felt with sticks of fragrant sandalwood, and clasped the shroud shut with golden straps.

What happened next is impossible to say for certain. But according to lore, Genghis Khan received probably the most outrageous funeral in history. After his wife bound him in white, a thousand soldiers took off on horseback to bury him atop a mountain. This cortege quickly turned into a rampage. To conceal their destination, the troops reportedly slaughtered every person they encountered on the 40-day journey, often with the cry "Go to the other world to serve our lord!" In some accounts, the soldiers killed every animal, too.

Based on other Mongol burials, they likely interred him 20 yards deep, with the body oriented north–south and the head facing east. They probably tossed some treasures in—gilded saddles, gold rings, pearls wrapped in silk—along with slaves, concubines, and horses. (One tale has the soldiers burying a live baby camel with him, either so its bleating would serve as a funeral dirge, or so the grieving mother could lead them back to the site if necessary.)

After filling the grave, Genghis's soldiers either diverted a river to conceal it or trampled the ground with a thousand horses to obliterate all trace. Then they resumed the merry rampage on the return trip, butchering every unlucky hunter or merchant who wandered across their path. To their surprise, the thousand soldiers were themselves slaughtered when they reached home, as a further guarantee of secrecy—and then those slaughterers were also slaughtered, to make doubly sure. Genghis Khan took privacy seriously.

We have no idea how much of that is true. But it hasn't deterred the hunt for the grave. To the contrary: The elaborate concealment has made the pursuit all the more enticing.

Four nations—Mongolia, China, Kazakhstan, and Russia—have claimed that Genghis Khan's bones lie within their borders. The strongest claim points to Burkhan Khaldun (God Mountain) in northeast Mongolia. Genghis Khan was born nearby, hunted there regularly, and worshipped the sky god Tengri there. He also once took refuge there while fleeing his enemies, and miraculously escaped. The mountain seemed charmed to him, and he'd mused during his life that it would make an ideal final resting place.

Strengthening the case for Burkhan Khaldun is the fact that later Mongol rulers proclaimed the land around the peak a forbidden zone and stationed a clan of ferocious guards there—the Darkhad, who murdered anyone who dared approach. (In exchange, the Darkhad paid no taxes and avoided compulsory military service.) Incredibly, the Darkhad kept this watch for 700 years, until the founding of the communist Mongolian People's Republic in 1924.

The republic was a puppet state of the U.S.S.R., and Soviet leaders had a schizoid attitude toward the Disturber of the Universe. On the one hand, they admired his ruthlessness and gazed longingly at all the territory he'd gobbled up. On the other, they feared his memory would stir up nationalist sentiments in Mongolia and spur a revolt against the hated communists. To forestall this, the Mongolian government banned the very mention of Genghis Khan's name. And to prevent Burkhan Khaldun from becoming a rallying point, officials fenced off a "highly restricted area" around the peak of 3,900 square miles (twice the size of Delaware), and parked a tank base at the site's entrance. The ban thawed somewhat after Joseph Stalin died in 1953, and one Mongolian official decided to celebrate the Disturber's 800th birthday in 1962 by putting him on a stamp. He overreached. Moscow ordered the man arrested, and he was chopped to bits with an axe.

After the republic collapsed in 1992, the restricted area devolved into a nature reserve with some public access. But the land near Burkhan Khaldun remains daunting to explore. It's one of the most desolate places on earth, with few roads and a population density down there with Greenland's. Centuries of vegetation growth have choked off many areas, and the clear parts are prone to flash floods. Temperatures can swing from 100 degrees in the summer to 50 below in the winter, so cold that even yaks drop dead.

None of this has stopped Genghis Khan obsessives from searching out his grave. They've suffered snakebites and frostbite and been left stranded when their vehicles tumbled off cliffs. One man spent 40 years crossing and crisscrossing and re-crisscrossing the slopes and died without finding a thing.

In 2010, a few archaeologists tried a new approach. They posted satellite images of the Burkhan Khaldun region online and recruited volunteers to scour them for bumps, depressions, and other features that might indicate graves. Ten thousand people spent approximately 30,000 hours (3.4 collective years) poring over 2,300 square miles. They flagged over a hundred spots worth checking out. While several proved inaccessible due to challenging terrain, 55 legitimate archaeological sites turned up among the rest, including megaliths, Bronze Age burial mounds, and an ancient city. But there was zero trace of Genghis Khan. One archaeologist lamented that it was like looking for a needle in a haystack, except you don't know what the needle looks like.

Call it Genghis Khan's final victory. The diverted river and trampling horses and the slaughter of all potential witnesses have succeeded in hiding him for most of a millennium now. His victims lay scattered across Eurasia, their skeletons long since ground to dust. But the bones of history's greatest warrior remain at peace.

Few kings in history have met an end as ignominious as Richard III. But before we get into that, there's one important matter to clear up: the whole Shakespeare thing.

For all the wicked delights of *Richard III,* the drama makes for poor history. Shakespeare portrays Richard as a bloodthirsty hunchback with a withered arm who's determined to seize the throne at any cost. Richard executes his brother, poisons his wife, and locks two innocent princes—his nephews—into the Tower of London and has them smothered in their beds to squelch their claim to the kingdom. The play is the apotheosis of the so-called three-*M* view of Richard's character: the malformed, murderous, Machiavellian tyrant. In this telling, Richard's eventual death at the Battle of Bosworth Field was divine justice—moral karma for his crimes.

In truth, people had divided opinions about Richard during his life. Contemporaries praised his piousness and generosity toward the poor. Even his enemies acknowledged his prowess on the battlefield. And far from Richard simply butchering his way to the top, Parliament passed a writ called the Titulus Regius to ratify his right to rule, a writ that won support from the English nobility and Church as well.

To be sure, Richard was no saint. Among other bad deeds, he seized the estates of widows and put at least one honorable man to death. Then there's the princes in the Tower. Richard's nephews were the sons of his brother King Edward IV. During Edward's reign, Richard clashed repeatedly with the boys' mother, Elizabeth Woodville, as well as her ambitious family.

After Edward died in April 1483, his 12-year-old son became Edward V, and Richard became Edward's Lord Protector. This left the 30-year-old Richard in a dicey position. As Lord Protector, he effectively ruled the realm—for now. But he knew full well that the queen and her Woodville relatives hated him, and would likely poison the king against him in time.

In May 1483, the young king and a Woodville uncle were traveling to London. Richard intercepted and arrested them, claiming—we don't know how truthfully—that the uncle had threatened Richard's life. He confined Edward to the Tower of London for protection. Sounds bad, but the Tower wasn't the gloomy dungeon most people think. It functioned more like a castle, with various government offices, and Edward could receive visitors there while preparations for his coronation proceeded. The queen also sent another son, age nine, to live under Richard's supervision in the Tower, which argues against the idea that Richard posed a danger.

Then a scandal broke. In June, a bishop claimed he had evidence that Edward IV had been betrothed to another woman before the queen. According to church law, that previous arrangement nullified his marriage to the queen and made their children illegitimate—and therefore ineligible to rule the kingdom. Richard, then, was the rightful monarch by default. He was crowned July 6, with the full, written approval of Parliament.

Another scandal sealed the twins' fate, it seems. In late July, Richard's ministers uncovered a plot involving several Tower guards who'd planned to start diversionary fires around London and spring the princes in the confusion. This would have seriously undermined Richard's power and could have led to his overthrow. The exposure of this plot shook the king, and he may have snuffed the princes out to quash a rebellion. If so, the decision certainly doesn't make Richard a hero. But perhaps fate forced his hand—it was "do or be done," as one historian argued. If nothing else, Richard was no worse than other monarchs of the time. It was an ugly era, full of ugly deeds.

After Richard secured his grip on power, one challenger to the throne remained: Henry Tudor, age 28. Henry's father was the half brother of a previous king (Henry VI), but only through their mother; he was not a descendant of the king, and reportedly came from bastard stock anyway if you traced further back. Worse still, Henry had spent his entire adult life in exile in France and was by all accounts a sniveling coward—contra the seasoned warrior Richard.

Still, the king of France, figuring he might as well sow chaos in a rival country, decided to give Henry 1,800 fickle French mercenaries—"the most unruly men that could be found," according to one source—to supplement the several hundred troops Henry had raised. The French king then put them on some ships and shoved them off toward England. *Good luck, kid.*

Upon landing, Henry learned that Richard had raised 8,000 soldiers and was marching to confront him. Henry begged for help from an enemy of Richard's, one William Stanley. Stanley agreed to gather some troops and accompany Henry to the battlefield, but he refused to commit to using them; instead, he'd wait to see how events unfolded before he did anything treasonous. Henry glumly acceded. By any reasonable expectation, Richard was going to rout him.

The two armies met at Bosworth Field on August 22, 1485. Richard slept poorly the night before, plagued by nightmares, but was in high spirits that morning, donning a crown-helmet and multicolored robe. He was 32 years old and was about to secure his kingdom for good. As for battle plans, Richard decided to linger with his cavalry behind the front lines and see how things progressed. Henry refused to get anywhere near the front and posted himself a mile back, almost too far to see what was happening.

Bosworth Field was paper-flat: an expanse of green with a marsh in the middle. Fighting began at midmorning when Richard's troops blasted their artillery. This left Henry's mercenaries trembling. But the French generals responded boldly. The English had the sun in their eyes and were half blinded. So despite the terror in their ranks, the generals ordered their troops to charge. They managed to surprise the English and outflank them.

In the melee that followed, Richard sniffed an opportunity. He rallied his cavalry, lifted his battle-ax, and countercharged—swerving right around the scrum in front of him. While Henry's troops were locked in combat, he would attack Henry himself. If he could capture or kill his rival, he could end the battle in a stroke.

When Henry saw Richard's cavalry thundering down, he leaped off his horse and practically tried to hide behind it. Luckily, his guards kept cool and deployed an innovative new tactic. They circled Henry, knelt on the ground, and angled their pikes in the air, raising a spiky hedgehog barricade around him.

Richard's cavalry blasted right through most of Henry's retinue, but slammed to a standstill against the circle of screaming pikemen. Still, Richard did not back off. He and his men began hacking their way toward the center, with Richard right there in the fury. He in fact killed Henry's standard-bearer and bulled his way to within yards of Henry himself.

But the delay cost him. Perched on a nearby hill, William Stanley had been watching with his troops. And when he saw Richard's cavalry get bogged down, a mile from any relief, he finally committed himself and charged.

The blast of his arrival knocked Richard's troops back. The king had no choice but to retreat a few hundred yards. He intended to regroup and return to the fight—except his horse blundered into the Bosworth marsh and tripped. Richard tumbled off, and Stanley's men swarmed him almost before he regained his feet. A few sword thrusts sliced through the strap of his helmet-crown, and several hard blows to his naked head followed. Richard expired in a heap, the last king of England to die on the battlefield. Henry Tudor, soon Henry VII, was the new king of England.

The battle dissipated quickly after that. Henry ordered Richard's clothes stripped off, and his nude body was flung over a horse. Henry's troops stabbed him in the bum for sport, then paraded the corpse into nearby Leicester in triumph.

During his soldiering days, the pious Richard had always ensured that his enemies received a proper Christian burial. The same respect was not accorded him. Three days after the battle, Henry's troops dug a pit in the churchyard of the Greyfriars monastery in Leicester and dumped Richard inside. No coffin, no funeral. The grave wasn't even large enough for his body; instead of lying flat, his head and shoulders were scrunched up against the dirt walls.

The propaganda against him began immediately. Henry declared that every soldier who'd fought for Richard at Bosworth was a traitor and would lose his estate—unless he could provide testimony that Richard had bullied him into enlisting. Dozens of men took the hint and began regaling the courts with all the supposed violence that Richard had threatened them with. These stories fed upon themselves, and with every passing year, the bogeyman of Richard grew uglier, more tyrannical, and more evil, until he'd devolved into a vile megalomaniac who could hardly get through breakfast without ordering somebody executed. (Never mind that Henry soon betrayed his own despotic side. He had one young prince murdered for being the son of Richard's brother George and therefore having a better claim to the throne—the very crime Richard allegedly committed against the princes in the Tower. Henry also tried to seize and destroy every copy of the writ of Parliament that had legitimized Richard's rule. He almost succeeded, but one slipped through.)

Before long, the tales about Richard grew truly wild. One "historian" charged that he'd stayed in his mother's womb for two years during her pregnancy and finally emerged with hair to his shoulders and vicious pointed teeth. He was hardly distinguishable from the Antichrist.

Meanwhile, Richard's pathetic grave vanished from memory. In 1538, Henry Tudor's son Henry VIII dissolved all the monasteries in England during a power struggle with the Catholic pope. The church of the Greyfriars monastery was torn down, and according to one account, a jeering mob—by now fully invested in the myth of the heroic Tudors—took advantage of Richard's unguarded grave to dig up his remains and toss them in a river. The monastery grounds later underwent renovations in Victorian times, by which point no trace of Richard's burial plot remained.

By the 1900s, however, something funny was happening with Richard. Shakespeare notwithstanding, a group of contrarian historians was trying to rehabilitate the king's reputation; they even founded an organization, the Richard III Society, to champion their cause. And in the early 2000s, one of their acolytes, the filmmaker and historian Philippa Langley, got a bee in her brain to find the old monastery grounds and recover Richard's skeleton. It was a daft idea, given the prevailing wisdom that Richard had been exhumed and tossed into a river centuries earlier. Even if that story were false, the Greyfriars grounds now sat smack in the middle of Leicester, an area jammed with stolid brick buildings. No one was going to tear them down on the off chance of finding some bones.

Langley nevertheless visited Leicester in 2004 to poke around. Tradition held that Richard's plot lay near a parking lot, next to a stone wall dating to medieval times. Langley bought a white rose to place as a memorial and visited the lot, eager to see the area through Richard's eyes.

But, squint as she might, she felt no connection to her hero; the place just looked like a parking lot. She left deflated. At that point, however, she noticed a second parking lot across the street. Ignoring the PRIVATE sign, she wandered in and looked around. The moment changed her life. "A feeling of raw excitement tinged with fear" washed over her, she said, and despite the sunshine, a shiver shot down her spine, and her skin rippled with gooseflesh. On a return trip, she even saw the letter *R* stenciled on the asphalt. It stood for *reserved,* but a single thought flashed through her mind: *Richard.* It all sounded pretty loopy, honestly, but she took it as a premonition. She hit the local archives and dug up some old maps. To her delight, one suggested that Greyfriars had possibly sat beneath the parking lot with the *R.*

Excavating beneath a parking lot would be far easier than beneath brick buildings, so Langley began organizing a campaign to dig. She met plenty of skepticism from professional archaeologists. ("Archaeology is not about going in search of a famous person," one sniffed.) But by early 2011, she'd raised enough funds for an initial survey with ground-penetrating radar. She hoped to map the buried monastery, plot out the most promising spots, and break ground by Easter.

Then everything fell apart. The radar survey detected no architectural features beneath the asphalt—nothing suggesting a monastery. Ground-penetrating radar can certainly miss things, but the news left Langley's funders skittish, and several dropped out. After all, was there any real evidence—beyond Langley's moment of clairvoyance with the *R*—that an actual king of England was buried beneath a parking lot?

Undeterred, Langley considered taking out a second mortgage to cover the funding shortfall. In the end, the Richard III Society pleaded with members to pony up, and dollars and pounds began dribbling in from as far afield as Australia. In all, Langley raised £33,000 for equipment and workers, and the dig was rescheduled to begin August 25, 2011, the 526th anniversary of Richard's initial interment. Langley took this as another omen.

On the first day of the dig, news crews gathered at the site to find medieval reenactors strutting around in tunics, armor, and hose—just the sort of circus atmosphere that makes professional archaeologists cringe. The £33,000 wouldn't cover the cost of tearing up the whole lot, so Langley's team planned to open three trenches and just hope they got lucky. Langley called it "a very expensive ... game of Battleship." Each trench ran 30 yards, and reached five feet deep. Langley insisted that trench number one cover the *R*.

Within an hour, they unearthed a wall of old yellow-white stone in that trench; the radar had indeed missed things. They also found two human leg bones close to where the *R* had been. More of the skeleton appeared to be buried in the vicinity. Still, there was no evidence the bones were medieval. In fact, examination of the wall revealed it to be Victorian—four centuries beyond Richard's time.

To Langley's irritation, the second and third trenches yielded more promising items, including a genuinely medieval wall, some silver halfpennies, and a tile decorated with an eagle. Eventually, some churchy artifacts did emerge from the first trench, including a piece of stained-glass window. But the news about the yellow-white wall just got worse. It turned out to be part of a privy; the soil beneath had even retained its stench. Langley felt miffed looking at the neighboring leg bones, as if the universe were mocking her: "A final resting-place next to a leaking Victorian lavatory is not fit for anybody, much less a king."

All in all, between the destruction of the medieval site and the remix in Victorian times, it proved impossible to untangle where exactly the Greyfriars' churchyard was. Still, on the dig's 12th day, the team decided to exhume the skeleton whose legs they'd found. Why not.

The exhumation started badly. Early that morning, an archaeologist was breaking up some soil with a mattock when she heard a *crunch*. She brushed the dirt away, and her stomach lurched to see that she'd just smashed into a skull. Puzzlingly, it was sitting much higher than the leg bones, as if the grave hadn't been large enough, and the person's upper body was scrunched against its dirt walls.

That wasn't the only oddity. Apart from the mattock hole, the skull had other gouges and wounds that, based on the encrusted dirt, seemed centuries old. That got everyone's attention. The teeth also belonged to someone in their late 20s or early 30s, and the spine, when uncovered, was twisted into an S-shape—a potential hunchback. The crew was dumbfounded. Although gut-punched at first, Langley couldn't help but gloat over the skeleton's proximity to the *R*.

A DNA test later confirmed it: 526 years after he'd disappeared into a pit, Langley's crew had found Richard III. The skull showed nine wounds from his last humiliating moments on the battlefield, and while it's impossible to know which blow killed him, one puncture wound that would have run through four inches of brain seems a likely culprit. As for the curved spine, a bone expert pegged it as scoliosis, a condition that can raise one shoulder up—a modest defect that later chroniclers twisted into a hunchback. Richard didn't have a withered arm, either. So much for Shakespeare.

In March 2015, Richard's bones were reinterred in an oak casket in Leicester Cathedral, with all the pageantry due an anointed king of England. It was a dignified end to a sordid tale.

In June 1941, Joseph Stalin ordered a team of Russian archaeologists to break into a sarcophagus in Soviet-controlled Uzbekistan. It contained the remains of Tamerlane the Great, a 14th-century general who was allegedly a distant cousin of Genghis Khan.

It's not clear what Stalin hoped to learn, but Tamerlane was one of the great military commanders of all time, and Stalin was obsessed with the man's exploits. So the archaeologists ignored the curse supposedly inscribed beneath the lid ("Whosoever opens my tomb shall unleash an invader more terrible than I!") and began picking through the dusty bones.

Three days later, Nazi Germany invaded the Soviet Union.

People in Uzbekistan still cite the story as evidence for why you should never ever open someone's tomb. And whatever stock you put in curses, it is a fair question to ask: Should archaeologists be seeking out, and opening, lost graves?

With Richard III, the answer seems obvious. He was thrown naked into a pit by his enemies without a Christian funeral, an outcome that would have horrified him. And while he was hardly a saint, given how dirty Shakespeare and others did him, it seems right to provide him with the burial he would have wanted.

Hunting for the tomb of Nebamun seems justified, too, given the chance to salvage the masterpiece paintings that remain behind. That's especially true because we can recover them without disturbing his mummy, which is safely sealed beneath the mausoleum.

Genghis Khan is a different story. He went to outrageous lengths to conceal his final resting place: No man in history ever wanted to be found less. And while the people of Mongolia idolize him—his likeness appears on everything from vodka to candy bars to currency—strong taboos about death persist there to this day. As a result, the Mongolian people are widely opposed to searching for his bones on God Mountain, and the government would never approve an excavation permit if they were found.

Archaeologists have made counterarguments here. This isn't some anonymous yak herder whose peace they'd be disturbing. It's Genghis frickin' Khan, and there's a clear historical interest in knowing more about him. Moreover, short of blocking off the whole mountain

Soviet-style, with tanks and machine guns, people are going to keep searching for the grave no matter what—you can't stop everyone. In which case, it would be vastly better for a respectable archaeologist to find it and ensure its security. We don't want some latter-day Yanni going in and stripping it bare, like so many other Mongol tombs.

Still, I'm not sure those arguments overcome the objections. As fascinating as it would be to find the mortal remains of the Disturber of the Universe, it's one lost treasure that should probably remain lost.

CHAPTER TWO

LOST CITIES

In 1876, archaeologist Heinrich Schliemann was excavating some graves in Greece when he discovered something stunning: a mummy with a mask of gold. The mask had a beaked nose, curly mustache, and jug ears. It looked like a real, recognizable human.

Schliemann peeled off the mask to confront the leathery visage beneath. After a solemn moment, he declared it the body of a legendary king from the Trojan War. As he soon announced to the world, "I have gazed upon the face of Agamemnon."

The tale was classic Schliemann. Captivating. Picturesque. And almost certainly horseshit. Schliemann did find a mummy and gold mask in those graves, but not together. Whoever the mummy was, he predated Agamemnon and the Trojan War by hundreds of years.

And while that line is Schliemann's most famous quote, there's no evidence he ever actually said it. He and his admirers had a disquieting tendency to exaggerate, romanticize, and fudge facts in service of his legend. Whatever made the best story became the truth.

But no one who's ever read a page of Schliemann's writing can deny how charming his lies are. As one biographer noted, he had "a canny sense of what the public wanted to hear" and gave them plenty of it: tales of plunder and woe, of lost tombs and epic battles with brave warriors and the maidens who loved them. Sigmund Freud sometimes daydreamed about living Schliemann's life, and he wasn't alone. Indiana Jones himself was modeled in part on Heinrich Schliemann.

Nowadays, Schliemann is best remembered for one thing: proving that the most fabled city in history, Troy, was not a figment of the poet Homer's imagination but actually existed. Despite that achievement, Schliemann remains radioactively controversial today, and not just for his exaggerations and untruths. As one scholar put it, "We may be grateful to Schliemann for plunging his spade into Troy ... But he tore it to pieces in snatching it from the earth." Other critics bluntly called Schliemann a "charlatan ... and imbecile." Another described his excavations as "the rape of Troy." Indeed, if Troy itself was once lost to history, the destruction of its remains at Schliemann's hands represents a second, deeper loss for archaeology—one all the more painful for being self-inflicted.

According to lore, the Trojan War began around 1200 B.C., when a prince named Paris absconded from Greece with a bride named Helen and brought her back to the magnificent walled city of his father, King Priam of Troy. The wronged Greek husband, Menelaus, rallied several other warrior-kings—Achilles, Odysseus, his brother Agamemnon—and sailed off to win her back. A decade-long war followed, until at last Troy fell.

Most of us associate this story with Homer and his *Iliad,* an epic poem composed in the 700s B.C. (Other names for Troy include Ilium and Ilios.) But in truth, the Trojan War was simply the backdrop for *The Iliad,* which opens nine full years into the fighting and focuses more on the personal clashes between the characters. In fact, several of the most famous scenes from the war never appear in Homer's poem. The Judgment of Paris, Achilles getting shot in the heel, even the most legendary moment of the entire saga, the stratagem of the Trojan horse—there's not a peep about them in *The Iliad.*

Most of these details appear instead in lost poems by other bards, collectively called the *Epic Cycle.* We know these poems existed because literary scholars from classical Greece either quoted or summarized them in their works. Had those summaries not survived, our knowledge of the Trojan War would be greatly impoverished. Luckily they did, and we wove them into the tapestry of Homer to produce some of the most beloved tales of all time.

But something funny happened to Troy over the centuries. In Homer's time, people considered the Trojan epics to be more or less straight history. They believed that Troy sat in what's now western Turkey near the Dardanelles Strait, a narrow sliver of water linking the Mediterranean Sea with the Sea of Marmara and the Black Sea beyond it. This strategic position allowed the city to amass great wealth and power by charging tolls on passing ships and controlling trade between Europe and Asia. People in Homer's day had even identified the supposed ruins of the city, and the very name of Troy stirred up the same echoes of sacrifice and courage that battles like Gettysburg and Agincourt do today.

This reverence continued into classical Greece, which began around 500 B.C. (The playwright Aeschylus once said that his own works were mere "crumbs from the great banquet of Homer.") During this era, temples sat where the war allegedly took place, and every heavyweight from Greek and Roman times stopped by to pay homage: Xerxes of Persia, Alexander the Great, Julius Caesar, and several Roman emperors after him. As late as the 300s A.D., the emperor Constantine considered building a new capital on the supposed site of Troy.

But classical Greece was also a skeptical age, steeped in philosophy, and despite the adulation of the masses, some of the more thoughtful types raised their eyebrows at certain passages in the poems: the invincible armor, the gods of Olympus plucking people off the battlefield. So in analyzing the works, these thinkers deemphasized the supernatural elements, even while honoring the history.

In later centuries, cynicism took root. Had the Trojan War really been so epic, so world-changing? Or had nostalgia and Homer's elegance seduced people into making far more of it than was warranted? Little by little, the old reverence decayed.

By the 1800s, most historians classified the Trojan War as fiction. And to be fair, they did have reasons to draw this conclusion. For one thing, Homer gets certain details wrong. The chariots he describes in such detail had wheels with eight spokes, as was characteristic of his time, but the Bronze Age chariots of Troy had four spokes. In another anachronism, the shield of Achilles in *The Iliad* famously bears an image of a Gorgon (perhaps Medusa), but such images did not appear on shields before Homer's day. Small missteps, perhaps, but telling: As scholars argued, if Homer got these little things wrong, could we really trust him on the big things? Oral histories were so flimsy, so corruptible anyway. Even more damning, archaeologists knew of no suitable ruins. If Troy was so grand, so mighty, where were its temples, its palaces, its fearsome citadel? Given this dearth of hard evidence, the conclusion seemed clear: Homer and the bards of the *Epic Cycle* had invented the entire war.

That's where things stood with Troy in 1822, when Heinrich Schliemann was born into a minister's family in northern Germany. For Christmas in 1829, his father gave him a book on mythology with a woodcut picture showing the hero Aeneas escaping the flames of Troy while carrying his father on his back. The picture fascinated young Heiny, who gaped at every detail and wouldn't stop talking about it. Someone, perhaps his father, gently suggested that the story wasn't real. But the boy crossed his arms and countered with a child's logic. If the war had never taken place, how could the artist have known what to draw? Troy *must* have existed.

Schliemann told this story often during his life, but it's almost certainly bogus. In truth, he was an indifferent student who showed no real interest in mythology or any other subject. And far from being kindhearted, his minister father was a petty despot who brazenly slept with maids and beat his mother, even during pregnancies. One day, the parish finally had enough. They surrounded the Schliemann home, banging pots and pans and smashing windows, demanding that Rev. Schliemann leave town. He refused, and Heinrich and the eight other Schliemann children were shunned as pariahs.

Schliemann escaped this chaos at age 11, moving in with an uncle, then became an apprentice to a grocer in a faraway town at 14. He spent five years (he claimed) toiling from 5 a.m. to 11 p.m. every day, packing the store's shelves with butter, liquor, sugar, salt, and potatoes. One magic day, the town drunk wandered in, a man from an elite family who'd fallen low. For some reason, he started reciting Homer in Greek. Schliemann froze in awe, spellbound at the beautiful phrases. When the recitation finished, he bribed the man with whiskey to do it again. This happened several more times, until the man presumably keeled over. It's a tale right out of Dickens, and probably about as true.

In 1841, at age 19, Schliemann lifted a cask of wine one day and felt something tear in his chest. He started coughing blood and shortly afterward decided to give up being a grocer. He settled on international trade as his new line of work and pawned his watch for a ticket on a steamship to South America—a voyage of 5,300 miles. He ended up 5,100 miles short. A storm sunk the ship off Holland, and he scrambled ashore. He faked an illness and malingered in a Dutch hospital to figure out his next move.

While in Holland, one of Schliemann's first genuine talents emerged: a knack for languages. He picked up Dutch, French, and English in cosmopolitan Amsterdam, partly by going to church in those languages and repeating the preachers' sermons under his breath. Over his lifetime, he added Arabic, Danish, Italian, Latin, Polish, Portuguese, Russian, Spanish, Swedish, Turkish, and Greek. Several times, he traveled to a country not knowing a word of the local tongue and learned enough within a few months to begin composing diary entries in the language. This is no tall tale, either. The diaries exist.

In 1846, the firm he was working for sent him to St. Petersburg to manage its Russian accounts. Soon after his arrival, he quit to spin off his own business, and made a killing.

He padded his fortune during the California gold rush. On the journey over from Russia, he stopped in Washington, D.C., where he claimed to have had a personal audience with President Millard Fillmore. In California, Schliemann realized (he did have a sharp business sense) that only suckers actually went prospecting in the hills. The real money was in "mining the miners" by selling them goods and services at wildly inflated prices. To this end, he opened a hotel and a bank and began buying gold dust. But after 12 months, he hightailed it out of California under a cloud of accusations, after supposedly skimming gold from shipments to the Rothschilds. No matter—he left America $2 million richer (around $80 million today).

Around this time, Schliemann—a balding, mustached man with crescent eyes and a wide forehead—decided to marry. Previously, he'd been engaged to a woman in St. Petersburg, but broke things off after he saw her flush with desire while dancing with a soldier at a ball. He decided to give her a second chance after California and penned a marriage proposal. Incredibly, to hedge his bets, he also wrote a letter proposing to one of her best friends. Obviously, the two women figured out what he'd done and grew furious. The second woman nevertheless accepted his proposal, and they entered a loveless, even hostile marriage, despite having three children together.

To add to Schliemann's woes, he no longer derived much pleasure from business. To be sure, he remained successful, and even vaulted into the realm of the megarich by profiteering on gunpowder during the Crimean War and speculating on railroad stocks and cotton during the U.S. Civil War. Ultimately, though, such success left him empty. And with his homelife in shambles—his wife barely spoke to him—he began traveling throughout Europe and attending lectures on Greek archaeology.

Schliemann initially embarked on this journey because European high society considered him a nouveau riche vulgarian, and he wanted to appear more refined. But he grew genuinely fond of the field—an affection that soon deepened into obsession. (His brother once noted with some bemusement how Heinrich seemingly fell in love with Cleopatra on a trip to Egypt, commissioning a mask of her face and hanging it near his desk to moon over.) Above all, Schliemann adored the legends of ancient Greece, venerating Homer the way some people do the Bible.

He took his first archaeological tour in 1868, visiting the swamp where Hercules slew the Hydra, then bouncing around to different places mentioned in *The Odyssey;* he was moved to weep, he claimed. He even tried excavating on Odysseus's homeland of Ithaca, and unearthed several funerary jars with ashes and human bones inside. He ended up breaking the pots while disinterring them, but was too overjoyed to worry about such details. He later gushed, based on zero evidence, that it was "very possible" he'd just uncovered the remains of Odysseus and Penelope.

Buoyed by this work, Schliemann decided to go looking for Troy. Despite the general consensus that the Trojan War was fiction, some scholars held out hope that the city itself once existed. Of those scholars, the far majority sited it in Anatolia, which was then part of the Ottoman Empire and now makes up the bulk of Asian Turkey. Specifically, they placed Troy at a mound in western Anatolia near the village of Pınarbaşı, a few miles from the sea. Still, many of those archaeologists never bothered visiting Pınarbaşı to search around or dig for evidence in support of their conclusion. They practiced a sort of theoretical archaeology, and weren't about to get their fingernails dirty. Schliemann, in contrast, did travel there; for all his faults, he never shied away from hard work.

But after poking around Pınarbaşı, Schliemann frowned. Unlike other ancient sites, he found no pottery fragments lying about, which made it doubtful anyone had ever lived there. Other details didn't add up, either. In *The Iliad,* Homer states that Troy had two springs nearby, one hot and one cold. In a hike around Pınarbaşı, Schliemann counted 34 springs, far too many. He also slipped a thermometer into some and recorded temperatures around 63°F—too tepid for a hot spring, too warm for a cold one.

In another passage of *The Iliad,* Achilles chases Hector around Troy, circling its walls three times. Schliemann gamely tried re-creating the scene himself by taking a lap around the Pınarbaşı mound, but found himself confronted with slopes of 65 degrees in spots. He nearly faceplanted descending one and ended up crawling on his knees. "Not even a goat," he concluded, could run down a slope so precarious. Given how precise Homer was with his landscapes, Pınarbaşı could not be Troy.

But there was another possibility. A handful of scholars sited Troy at a mound five miles north of Pınarbaşı called Hisarlık, the "place of fortresses." If belief in the Trojan War was marginal, then putting Troy in Hisarlık sat on the margin of the margin—not as crazy as believing in Atlantis, but not far off. These scholars had nevertheless converted a few enthusiastic amateurs to their cause, including Frank Calvert.

Although English, Calvert grew up in an expat family in western Anatolia. His older brother traded goods internationally and supported the family financially, freeing the more romantic Frank to dabble in archaeology. Perhaps not realizing how fringe the position was, Calvert decided that Troy had to lie beneath Hisarlık, and convinced his brother to buy some land that included half the mound. The brother apparently did this so Frank could farm the parcel and finally do something with his life. Frank had no intention of that.

However disdainful most scholars were, to an unbiased observer, the idea of linking Troy and Hisarlık had a lot going for it. Classical Greeks and Romans had placed Troy nearby, and built a temple to Athena there. Calvert certainly had nothing to lose in poking around.

Then disaster struck. His ambitious older brother gambled on some financial deals and lost. Unable to pay his debts, he filed fraudulent insurance claims for lost cargo and got busted, disgracing the family name. After going on the lam for five years, he was eventually sentenced to prison.

With the family's finances in ruin, Frank could not hire workers to dig at Hisarlık. Instead, he applied to the British Museum in London for a pittance grant of £100 (around $10,000 today). In return, he offered the museum every single artifact he unearthed. All Calvert asked, a little pathetically, was to be named director of this rinky-dink operation, so he could feel like a real archaeologist. Museum staff responded curtly. Perhaps they wanted to distance themselves from fringe ideas about Troy, or perhaps they didn't want to associate with scoundrels like the Calverts. Regardless, the British Museum told Calvert no. It proved one of the most shortsighted decisions in the history of archaeology.

Nothing if not determined, the 35-year-old Calvert undertook some small-scale excavations at Hisarlık in the mid-1860s, unearthing parts of a theater and the Athena temple, as well as artifacts. Farther down, he found pottery from the 600s B.C.—well short of Homer's Troy, but enough to kindle an interest to keep digging, if only he could find the funds.

Calvert often hosted European visitors traveling through Anatolia, and a few months after his brother's conviction in 1868, Heinrich Schliemann dropped by on his archaeological tour. The 46-year-old German was growing stocky by then, and was probably wearing his typical field attire of a straw sunhat and linen overcoat. Calvert showed him some vases and a bronze lion from his digs. Schliemann was impressed.

Hisarlık impressed him even more. The mound was roughly 200 yards wide and was surrounded, he later said, by lush green plains "embroidered with millions of flowers." More importantly, he found exactly the sort of gentle slopes on which Achilles might have chased Hector. The temple and theater that Calvert had excavated further stoked Schliemann's imagination. As for Homer's hot and cold springs, well, Hisarlık didn't have any springs. But Schliemann never let inconsistencies dampen his enthusiasm; he explained the lack away by hypothesizing that earthquakes or something similar had swallowed them. Regardless, when Calvert proposed a joint partnership to dig for Troy, Schliemann jumped at the chance. In extending this offer, Calvert perhaps calculated that he could play the German to his advantage—take the older man's money and preserve the glory of discovery for himself. The reality played out very differently.

Before Schliemann could start digging, he had a domestic matter to attend to. That Christmas, he made one last attempt to reconcile with his wife, telegraphing her that he was returning to St. Petersburg with armfuls of presents for their children. She responded by fleeing town.

At wit's end, Schliemann decided to end their marriage. Perhaps to avoid scandal in conservative Russia, he sought the divorce in a country with fewer scruples: the United States. Indiana in particular had liberal divorce laws, the Reno of its day. Still, to divorce there, Schliemann needed American citizenship, which required five years of residency. Schliemann had barely set foot there since the gold rush, but he took care of that pesky technicality by bribing a few schmucks to swear he'd been living in America for years. He bolstered his case by buying a home and a one-third interest in a starch factory (pocket change for him). Hoosier citizenship quickly ensued.*

* Unhappy about their state's reputation as the place where marriages went to die, Indiana legislators were attempting to tighten up divorce laws when Schliemann arrived. Panicked at this news, he hurried over to the statehouse and (he claimed) personally convinced several to change their position before a crucial vote. After the bill failed, its sponsors vowed to bring the measure up again soon and hammer it through. Stunningly, however, 41 legislators resigned the morning of the revote. Why? To avoid taking a public stand on the 15th Amendment, which outlawed attempts to deny Black people the right to vote. With the legislature in chaos, the divorce debate dissipated. Schliemann exulted.

The last obstacle to a divorce was convincing a judge that his wife was unreasonable—a wicked shrew, Schliemann claimed, whose refusal to join him in the land of the free and the home of the brave had shattered the family. When the judge asked for evidence of this, Schliemann presented letters that she'd allegedly penned, in Russian. The judge didn't speak the language, so Schliemann helpfully offered to translate them. Lo and behold, they proved his case in every particular. Schliemann got his divorce, then left scorch marks fleeing Indiana.

All the while, Schliemann was making arrangements to marry another woman. He'd written to an archbishop he knew in Greece, asking the cleric to help procure a new wife. The archbishop had just the person, 17-year-old Sophia Engastromenos. Schliemann refused her at first, claiming she was too young. But he wrote a second letter the next day, confessing the real problem: He hadn't slept with a woman in six years and feared he'd prove impotent, a humiliating prospect. But, ever resourceful, he added that he'd hatched a plan. He suggested—and remember, he's telling the *archbishop* this—that he would visit Paris after his divorce and test the ol' equipment out with some woman. (He doesn't specify whom, but given the circumstances, it was presumably a lady of the night.) If everything proved shipshape—and if Sophia would have an old coot like him—then he promised to marry her and treat her right.

Apparently, the woman in Paris did the trick. Schliemann and Sophia wed in late 1869.

With his domestic life back on track, Schliemann turned his attention to finding Troy. Despite Frank Calvert's hopes to run the dig, Schliemann shoved him aside and took over the operation. Excavating in the Ottoman Empire at the time required a permit, but Schliemann's crew broke ground at Hisarlık in April 1870 before he'd bothered securing one. The initial trench they dug disappointed him—"I only find trash," he moaned—but a second trench produced several nifty coins, figurines, and urns, plus five brick walls. Schliemann immediately declared them part of a temple mentioned in *The Iliad.*

The 1870 dig lasted just 12 days, after which Schliemann returned home to Sophia. He nevertheless bragged about his exploits in the newspapers—a dumb move, considering the lack of permits. Ottoman officials punished his impudence by purposely delaying his application to dig in 1871. Schliemann couldn't return to the field until October, and winter rains soon turned the site into a morass.

Encouragingly, though, his team did find some bronze axes and spearheads in the mud, plus jars with human bones. Unfortunately, it never occurred to Schliemann to record the strata or often even the depth at which artifacts appeared. Archaeology then was moving beyond the days of mere organized looting, but Schliemann remained unaware of more sophisticated methods of collecting data. As a result, everything he hauled away proved useless for historical analysis.

For whatever reason, the discoveries in 1871 convinced Schliemann that Homer's Troy lay at the very bottom of the Hisarlık mound. This was a regrettable assumption. As we now know, Hisarlık is a complex site, with 11 distinct layers of occupation running from 3500 B.C. to A.D. 1350. (In addition, in the 200s B.C., the Greeks occupying the land shaved off the top of the mound to flatten the hill before erecting a temple to Athena, which muddled the layers.) Homer's Troy, circa 1200 B.C., probably corresponds to layer VIIa,*

---

* Archaeologists initially identified nine layers at Hisarlık, from Troy I at the bottom to Troy IX at the top. Later work teased out two distinct layers within Troy VII, as well as an overlooked initial settlement beneath Troy I. Rather than create confusion by renumbering everything, archaeologists dubbed the earliest layer Troy 0 and split the seventh into VIIa and VIIb. The crucial layer VIIa is therefore the eighth up from the bottom.

nowhere near the bottom. But the bottom was where Schliemann was headed, ignorance be damned.

For the 1872 season, Schliemann hired 120 workers and gave them one order: Dig fast. A bulldozer could hardly have been less precise. One trench they opened stretched 87 yards wide, most of a football field. They removed 120,000 cubic yards of dirt overall, equal to 36 Olympic-size swimming pools. At that speed, the workers couldn't have documented their findings properly even if Schliemann had trained them to (which he didn't).

Topics of fundamental concern to archaeology—how buildings are constructed, how bodies are interred, how occupation layers change from generation to generation—were thrown by the wayside. Schliemann even purposely destroyed some discoveries. Upon finding one building, he merrily disregarded the clause in the permit that forbade the removal of any permanent structures and instructed his diggers to yank out the stones, like so many teeth, and send them tumbling down the mound. He'd seemingly channeled the gold rush mentality of scouring entire hillsides down to bare rock. All that mattered was reaching bottom.

Schliemann felt himself justified in July 1872, when his crew found the charred skeleton of a woman near the mound's bottom. At two other locations in that stratum, spots separated by 50 yards, they also found a ring and some gold beads. Close enough. Schliemann's imagination collapsed that distance to zero and said the jewelry must belong to the woman. She'd clearly scooped these treasures up while fleeing Troy, only to die horribly when a burning building collapsed on top of her. (You wonder what the seven-year-old Heinrich would have thought, considering his youthful protest that no one could ever just make up such a scene.)

Schliemann's shenanigans continued in 1873. His crew dug less aggressively that year (they could hardly have dug more aggressively), but the quality of finds was spectacular—at least in Schliemann's mind. A crumbling mudbrick structure jumped rank to become Priam's Palace, and an ambiguous gate in the city wall was brevetted into the famous Scaean Gate, where Paris killed Achilles and where Priam's people found the Trojan horse. Inside one building, Schliemann found a male skeleton in one corner and a bronze helmet with a regal plume-holder in another. Naturally, he declared the man a mighty warrior and placed the helmet on the skeleton's head in published accounts—even though expert analysis later revealed that the "helmet" was really a teapot, short and stout; it lacked a handle, but the "plume-holder" was its spout.

The teapot was actually a rare find at Hisarlık. Metal goods were scarce overall—worryingly so for Schliemann, given how much Homer prattled on about bronze this and gold that. But all those worries dissolved during the final two weeks of the dig, with the discovery that would make Schliemann world-famous.

Work on-site commenced each day at 5 a.m., with breakfast four hours later and lunch at 2:30 in the afternoon; they quit digging at sunset. Early on May 31, Schliemann was clearing the dirt around a copper vessel beneath "Priam's Palace" when he spotted a glint of gold buried with it. Not wanting to alert any workers—either because he feared they'd steal the gold for themselves or because Schliemann was supposed to split all artifacts with the Ottoman government, and he didn't want his men blabbing—Schliemann called for breakfast, even though it was far too early. His workers shrugged and wandered off to nibble bread and smoke. Meanwhile, Schliemann began hacking away at the ground near the vessel with a knife. What happened next, he said, was like a magic trick: piece after piece materialized from the dirt—vases, plates, goblets, and more. A stunned Schliemann summoned his wife Sophia from a rickety cabin nearby and had her stuff the items beneath her shawl to ferry them away. But Maccabees-like, more and more goods kept emerging. Daggers, spearheads, battle-axes. Bangles, earrings, diadems. Perfume jars, a gravy boat, even a cauldron. By now, his digging was undermining the palace wall—it seemed liable to topple onto him at any moment. But Schliemann didn't dare stop. He eventually unearthed around 9,000 items, all of which Sophia smuggled past the workers beneath her shawl. It was one of the greatest hauls in archaeological history. Schliemann dubbed it Priam's Treasure.

In case it's not clear, this was another one of Schliemann's tall tales, which he later recounted in a book. He did discover those 9,000 items, but not in one place and not at one time. Sophia hadn't been smuggling cauldrons beneath her shawl, either; she wasn't even in the country that day. After being called out for this lie years later, Schliemann shrugged. He'd been trying to get Sophia interested in archaeology and thought that including her in the story of Priam's Treasure would ignite in her the same passion for Homer that he felt. Besides, it was a good story.

Frank Calvert penned a more honest account of the excavations, based on what he'd observed on the days he could get over to his mound. Most of the time, however, he served as Schliemann's factotum—mending wheelbarrows, sorting mail, tracking down officials to sign permits that Schliemann wouldn't abide by anyway. Schliemann repaid Calvert's loyalty by violating the gentleman's agreement they had to split the proceeds from any artifacts that turned up, either concealing goods from him entirely or buying out the younger man's share of items at criminal prices, then turning around and selling them for 10 times more on the international market. Calvert's clever plan to exploit Schliemann had turned into Schliemann exploiting him. Calvert was especially vexed to read Schliemann's exaggerations and self-glorifying accounts in the press.

And worse was coming, because Schliemann soon engineered his biggest publicity coup yet. After excavating Priam's Treasure, he smuggled the items from Anatolia to his estate in Athens. There, he dressed Sophia up in the necklaces, earrings, and diadems—claiming they were Helen of Troy's own—and snapped a stunning photograph. The picture appeared in newspapers across the globe, beneath rapturous headlines about the once lost, now found riches of Troy. Choose whatever word you want: flabbergasted, gobsmacked, agog. People were all of the above.

The treasures seized the public's attention like nothing ever had before in archaeology, and like few things ever have since—perhaps only King Tut's tomb and the discovery of the *Titanic*. To be sure, scholars scoffed at Schliemann's boasts and harrumphed over the picture, pointing out that there was zero evidence linking the jewelry to Priam. Do you think anyone cared? As far as the public was concerned, Schliemann had found the lost city of Homer.

Scholars were right to be suspicious. Given that Schliemann found the hoard near the bottom of the mound, "Priam's" Treasure predated Homer's Troy by a thousand years. More damningly, archaeologists have never found anything even remotely as spectacular at any other site from that era. Again, while Schliemann probably did find all those artifacts in the mound, he likely found them in multiple locations and layers, then "salted" the spot under the wall to ratchet up the drama. But because he never admitted this, or kept any records that could untangle his lies, the treasures cannot shed much light on the civilizations that occupied the mound. Schliemann was reckless at the best of times. His stunt with Priam's Treasure is an archaeological crime.

And yet. Despite his lies, despite his despicable behavior, Schliemann really had located Troy. Some of the artifacts he found, however jumbled, were exactly the kinds of goods Homer describes. The buildings inside the mound, however battered in spots by Schliemann, were exactly the kinds of places where Priam and Paris and Hector would have lived and fought and died. Whatever his (many) failings, the amateur Schliemann had taken on thousands of better-heeled, better-read, and frankly smarter scholars—scholars who thought him a boorish ass and lying scoundrel—and proved every single one of them wrong. He never tired in pointing this out. It was the best story he ever told, and it was completely true.

Troy is not the only famous city in history to vanish. To satisfy an insatiable need for ivory, pearls, and especially black pepper, ancient Roman merchants sent half a million gold coins to India every year, mostly to the port of Muziris. This trade deficit made Muziris one of the richest cities on earth. But when the Roman economy buckled in the 200s A.D., Muziris's fortunes sank in lockstep, and people eventually abandoned it. It seemed as fictitious as Troy until archaeologists rediscovered it in 2004. Other mighty cities across the world have succumbed to desert sands, eroding coastlines, and ravenous jungles.

Lost cities figure heavily in myths, too: El Dorado, Sodom and Gomorrah, Shangri-la. And lest we forget, cities are disappearing today, right before our eyes. Venice floods dozens of times annually, and continues to sink lower each year. Ditto Ho Chi Minh City and Jakarta. We nearly lost New Orleans in 2005, and Miami and New York are under threat as well—not to mention San Francisco, which sits atop a geological fault line storing the equivalent of millions of tons of TNT. Let's hope that future archaeologists will search for our fallen skyscrapers with all the dedication of Heinrich Schliemann (albeit with a bit more scrupulousness).

After Troy, Schliemann dug at several other archaeological sites. Most importantly, in 1876, he discovered a mummy and golden mask at Mycenae* and allegedly "gazed upon the face of Agamemnon."

We now know that the mask predated the Trojan War by at least three centuries. Moreover, the circumstances of its discovery once again smell suspicious. The graves Schliemann excavated contained 44 pounds of gold—vastly more than any other graves from that era. And just like with Troy, Schliemann initially faced months of empty-handed frustration before suddenly discovering everything he was looking for, miraculously, during the last two weeks of the dig. Again, the mask and other gold items are almost certainly authentic, but he probably didn't find them in one place, much less in such a dramatic fashion.

Worse still for Schliemann's reputation, certain pots turned up alongside the graves.† These pots had distinct, stirrup-shaped handles; they were invented in the 1500s B.C. and were fashionable through the Trojan War era. At first, Schliemann thought nothing of them; they certainly stirred his soul less than the gold masks. But after returning to Hisarlık to dig years later, Schliemann found loads of the pots in certain layers of the mound—just not the layer where he'd supposedly found Priam's Treasure. The pots came from higher levels, which meant those higher levels were far more likely

---

* Despite all the riches there, Schliemann was crushed to find no writing at Mycenae—not even a tedious list of goods, much less the ancient accounts of the Trojan War he'd dreamed of. He considered the Greeks of the Trojan War the most illustrious heroes in history. Could they really be illiterate brutes?

† Notoriously, this pottery later inspired Adolf Hitler's choice of the swastika as the emblem of the Nazi Party. Swastikas were common symbols in ancient cultures, and Schliemann found numerous examples of them in the Hisarlık mound. Swastikas thereby became linked with the heroes of Troy in the German mind, and in choosing the swastika for the Nazis, Hitler was poaching their glory.

to be Homer's Troy. Among others, Frank Calvert had been trying to pound this fact into Schliemann's skull for years. Schliemann hadn't listened, but seeing the pots forced him to admit that he'd probably chewed right through the actual, real Troy in his race to the bottom of the mound years before. It was a painful moment. As one historian noted, Schliemann realized he'd "destroyed or thrown away many of the very buildings and objects for which he had been searching."

None of this, however, put the slightest dent in Schliemann's public reputation. In 1881, he gave Priam's Treasure to the German government, even though he had no legal right to do so. The publicity surrounding this gift ratcheted his fame to even higher levels. Before long, Schliemann's mansion in Athens became a tourist site in and of itself, largely for its connection to this Great Man. Learned societies across Europe invited him to give speeches, and the reception was always rapturous. "I am received in London," he once boasted, "as if I had managed to climb up to the Moon and there resuscitated the Library of Alexandria from its cinders." Cities sometimes shot off fireworks to greet him.

Schliemann died in 1890, thanks largely to his characteristic impatience. In mid-November that year, he underwent an operation to remove some bony growths from his ear canal that had rendered him all but deaf. The ear got infected, and Schliemann went stir-crazy sitting around the hospital. "I can't bear the loneliness," he wrote to a friend. Despite the stabbing pain in his skull, he discharged himself against his doctor's orders. He collapsed while taking a walk on Christmas Day in Naples, the infection having spread to his brain. He died the next day.

Schliemann got a tomb worthy of Priam or Achilles: a towering, multistory mausoleum decorated with marble pillars and friezes of scenes from *The Iliad* and *Odyssey.* One frieze also portrays Schliemann himself, standing alongside Sophia at Troy and reciting from a copy of Homer. An inscription reads, humbly, "To Schliemann the Hero." But a colleague named Wilhelm Dörpfeld supplied a truer epithet shortly after Schliemann's death, in the form of a double-edged comment: "Rest in peace. You have done enough."

Dörpfeld, an architect by training, took over excavating at Hisarlık in the 1890s. More than anyone else, it was he who sorted through the mess Schliemann left behind, and finally pinpointed the real Troy amid the strata. It's mostly the ruins he found, not anything uncovered by Schliemann, that visitors see at Troy today.

Despite Dörpfeld's work, a few grumpy scholars continued to doubt the existence of Troy for nearly a century—largely because the unearthed city still seemed too small, hardly worth Homer's time. But later excavations put the lie to that objection. Bronze Age Troy contained the biggest, stoutest fortress in the entire Mediterranean region, and its massive stone walls—12 feet thick, 27 feet high—show signs of repeated assaults. Moreover, in the 1990s, excavators began digging beyond the citadel and found a long defense ditch carved into the bedrock. It stretched a dozen feet wide and six feet deep, and enclosed a town of perhaps 75 acres and 10,000 people. Here, at last, was a city worth dying for.

Archaeologists now have a much clearer picture of the real Troy. Schliemann and his immediate successors tended to view the city as essentially Greek, and drew strong lines of continuity between Trojan and Greek culture. They weren't wrong in this: Troy did share affinities with Greece. But scholars back then had only spotty knowledge of the lands east of Troy, in wider Anatolia, where a powerful group called the Hittites reigned. And in light of modern knowledge, most features of Trojan society—the pottery, the mudbrick homes, the burial practices—far more closely resemble Hittite culture.

Further cementing this link, scholars have now deciphered clay tablets from Hittite sites that make suggestive references to kings, battles, and political strife in a city in western Anatolia called Wilusa—an echo of the alternative name for Troy, Ilios. One king mentioned in them is Alaksandu, or Alexander, an alternative name for the Trojan hero Paris, and there are references to battles between the Hittites and a group that most scholars think are Mycenaean Greeks. In all, while certainly a major city, Troy is probably more accurately thought of as a frontier outpost of the wider Hittite kingdom.

Archaeologists have also revised their views about Troy's downfall. The grandest iteration of Troy appears in layer VI at Hisarlık, the Troy of the massive citadel. But Troy VI seems to have been destroyed circa 1275 B.C. by an earthquake; it's a layer of crooked walls and half-toppled towers. Meanwhile, that city's successor, the diminished Troy VII, shows evidence of war: piles of burned wood, stores of arrowheads and sling stones, hacked-off bits of bodies. The best guess is that Homer, who lived centuries after Troys VI and VII, decided to conflate the two cities and set the battle that doomed Troy VII in the more distinguished Troy VI. Homer was first and foremost a poet, and even if an earthquake technically felled the latter, he knew its grandeur would better suit his purpose and better stir his listeners' hearts.

(Meanwhile, the other bards of the *Epic Cycle* might have kept an oblique reference to the earthquake, in the guise of the Trojan horse. In reality, the Greek army probably did not build a giant wooden animal with a secret compartment inside and trick the Trojans into dragging it into their city; I'd sooner believe that

Sophia Schliemann smuggled a cauldron under her shawl. But perhaps the Greeks blasted apart the walls of Troy with a siege engine or battering ram that looked like a horse or was decorated with horses, and then poetic license took over. Or perhaps the Trojan horse was an allegory. The Greek god of earthquakes was Poseidon, a deity who actively participated in the Trojan War. Poseidon is often portrayed driving a chariot pulled by horses, and the Greeks believed that the sound of the pounding hooves resembled a seismic rumble. Blaming a horse for Troy's downfall, then, might simply have been a poetic allusion to an earthquake.)

As for the war that led to Troy VII's downfall, it seems doubtful that the Greeks wasted 10 years of their lives because one of their buddies got cuckolded; even in an age that fetishized chivalry, you'd think one of them would have suggested, gently or not, that Menelaus get over it already. (Alternatively, you'd think the Trojans would have shoved Helen out the door and said good riddance.)

But perhaps we're being too literal in interpreting things this way. Saying "10 years" might simply have been shorthand for "a long time," the way that the Bible speaks of wandering in the desert for 40 years without being too precise. Or perhaps a showdown between the Hittites and Greeks had been looming for ages over the lucrative stretch of land that Troy occupied, and the loss of a bride was the precipitating event. In addition, according to Hittite records, multiple wars took place at Troy-Wilusa over the years. So perhaps Homer collapsed them all into one epic battle.

Regardless of the exact amount of truth in Homer—whether he telescoped multiple wars into one or nodded when describing exactly how many spokes a chariot wheel had—most scholars today believe that *The Iliad* and its *Epic Cycle* brethren point to at least some real, historical events and perhaps real individuals. That's a stunning turnaround from the days when everyone in the smart set viewed Troy as fictional. Usually, historians debunk things: They find some widespread, cherished belief and, killjoys that they are, pick it apart. Here, the opposite happened—and it all started with Schliemann. He always believed in Homer, and unlike those who merely bandied about theories from their armchairs, he got off his duff and started digging. He also had the personality and literary chops to make others believe, even if they had to correct his excesses. "If my memoirs ... contain contradictions," he once declared, "I hope that these may be pardoned when it is considered that I have revealed a new world of archaeology." (He was modest, too.)

I think of Schliemann as similar to one of his fondest admirers, Sigmund Freud. Freud got virtually every detail wrong about how the human mind works; his sheer consistency is remarkable. But he got One Big Thing right: that the subconscious drives human behavior far more than people ever suspected, an insight that forever changed psychology. Schliemann, too, made mistake after mistake, and even committed scholarly fraud at times by planting artifacts where they didn't belong. Plus, he often comes off distasteful in his personal life. Reading his biography, you're wowed one moment and cringing the next; as one exasperated historian admitted, "It is hard, and probably misguided, to develop a consistent attitude towards him." But no matter what, Schliemann found Troy, and even today it remains the most cited archaeological site in history.*

* The Trojan War is not the first recorded battle in history. In 1479 B.C., Egyptian scribes mentioned a victory over an army of Canaanites at a site in modern Israel called Megiddo—the biblical Armageddon.

Schliemann's work also stimulated further, and more careful, research in Greece and especially Anatolia. His successors in those regions would uncover wonders that not even his fertile imagination could have conjured up—especially one of them who, as we'll see next chapter, proved every bit as complicated and controversial, and every bit as steeped in scandal.

CHAPTER THREE

LOST PEOPLE

The moment the young woman entered the train car, archaeologist James Mellaart was bewitched. It wasn't because she was beautiful, although she was. It was the gold bracelet on her wrist. It looked like an ancient artifact, from the days of Troy. Why was she wearing it on a train?

It was spring 1958, and Mellaart was surveying some archaeological sites in western Turkey. He was 32 years old and recently married, a plump man with thick glasses and thick brown hair. The discoveries that would make him famous lay years in the future, but he burned with ambition. His obsession in life was Anatolia and its history.

In classical times, Anatolia had come under Greek and Roman rule, although Mellaart was sick to death of those eras, especially Rome.

(Whenever he found Roman artifacts at a dig, he'd toss them aside and mutter "F-R-M": filthy Roman muck. Although he didn't always say "filthy.") Instead, Mellaart revered the Anatolia of several thousand years B.C., and he longed to prove that the region had a history every bit as rich as that of Rome and Greece. Troy itself lay in Anatolia, so when the woman with the Trojan bracelet strolled into his train car and sat opposite him, Mellaart was transfixed. He screwed up his courage and struck up a conversation.

Her name was Anna Papastrati. She was around 20 years old and spoke fluent English. Mellaart pointed to the bracelet and they fell into discussion. She revealed that she had a whole heap of similar items at her house in İzmir on the Turkish coast, not too far away. Did Mellaart want to see them?

He did, badly, and agreed to accompany her home.

In İzmir, Mellaart and Anna took a ferry to her villa in a suburb across the bay. Night had fallen by then, and before they examined any artifacts, Anna insisted on splitting a bottle of wine over dinner, an intimate "tête-à-tête," Mellaart recalled. But if Anna wanted to linger and chat, Mellaart insisted on seeing the artifacts.

However put out, Anna rose, opened a nearby bureau, and began unwrapping the sheets of cotton inside, then laying the items that emerged on a table. Most were broken and still dirty or corroded from the ground. But Mellaart could not hide his astonishment. There were earrings, chalices, scepters, swords, and diadems, made of turquoise, amber, onyx, gold, and silver. A few items stood out. A silver bird vase with gold plumage. An ivory comb with carved dolphins. A dagger with a double-headed lion pommel. And most alluring of all, a gold statuette of a topless goddess holding her breasts—the sight of which must have left the atmosphere in Anna's home even more charged than before.

Anna said the treasures came from two royal tombs on a mountain spur overlooking Dorak, a town 125 miles east of Troy. They'd been unearthed secretly during the Greco-Turkish War of 1919, and she dodged Mellaart's questions about how her family had obtained them. He didn't press the matter; he feared spooking her and getting kicked out. He asked to snap some photographs instead. She refused this, but allowed him to sketch the goods.

By this time, it was quite late. Anna insisted that Mellaart spend the night with her. Mellaart hesitated. His wife would be furious about him staying with a strange woman. But his lust for archaeology got the better of him. Besides, it was just one night. He said yes—having no idea that that night would haunt him for the rest of his life.

Mellaart worked through the night, and much of the next day. Soon dusk was falling. Anna encouraged him to spend another night, so against his better judgment, he did. The same thing happened the next day and the next. Mellaart barely left the table, unwilling to waste a minute; when he ran low on cigarettes, Anna ran out and bought more. In all, he spent nearly a week in her home, fawning over the treasures while she fawned over him.

Archaeologically, the Dorak treasures were a bonanza. A few pots allowed Mellaart to classify the trove as belonging to the so-called Yortan culture, an enigmatic civilization that bordered Troy in ancient times. Before this, archaeologists had known about the Yortan people mostly through pots and graves. But the wrought-metal items and jewelry looked undeniably like goods from early layers of Troy, centuries before the Trojan War. At the table, Mellaart began to wonder whether the Dorak-Yortan culture might have influenced Troy, or even been the wellspring of Trojan culture.

Luckily—it was almost too much to ask for—whoever had excavated the graves had photographed the bodies inside, and even taken detailed notes. By the time Mellaart saw them, the photographs were fading, but they showed Yortan kings and queens lying on reed mats and woven carpets. One tomb even contained the skeleton of a pet dog, "lovingly provided," Mellaart later noted, "with its own stone bowl."

Mellaart lingered over two of Anna's items in particular. One sword had a line of nine ships etched into it, with oars and rectangular sails reminiscent of Jason and the Argonauts' legendary vessels. Dorak lay near a large lake, which connected via other bodies of water to the Black and Mediterranean Seas. The sword etchings, then, established the Dorak-Yortan culture as a seafaring one.

Equally fascinating was a sheet of gold stamped with Egyptian hieroglyphs; it formed a decorative cover for a throne. Mellaart could read hieroglyphs, and the message revealed that the throne was a gift from the Egyptian pharaoh Sahure, who died in 2477 B.C. Anna's trove also included decorated silver tubes that potentially contained Egyptian makeup—black eyeliner, red rouge, green eyeshadow.

Mellaart could hardly believe it. Archaeologists knew virtually nothing about the Yortan culture before. Now he had material evidence linking them to both Troy and Egypt, two iconic civilizations. What a coup! And it all resulted from his Hitchcockian encounter with a stranger on a train.

Mellaart ended the week exhausted, but joyfully so. Anna still forbade any photographs, though she promised to mail him some. Her behavior must have seemed cryptic to him, even suspicious. But upon leaving her villa, he slyly jotted down her address—217 Kazim Dirik Street.

Mellaart returned home to his wife and three-year-old son in Ankara, 320 miles distant, to await Anna's letter. A month passed. Although reluctant to, Mellaart reached out first. Did she have the photographs? Summer swept in and scorched the land, followed by the welcome cool of fall. Mellaart tried Anna a second time, then a third. Still no reply. Mellaart hesitated to keep writing; he'd sensed her skittishness and didn't want to drive her away. But every day saw him pacing and fretting, like a paramour over his beloved. Why hadn't she answered? Did he do something wrong?

In truth, Mellaart's anxiety here was only partly due to Anna. The rest stemmed from his background—especially his professional frustrations.

He was born in London to Dutch-Scots parents in 1925. During the Great Depression, they relocated to Amsterdam, where Mellaart's mother died. His art-dealer father remarried the family nanny, a woman Mellaart despised. He renounced his Dutch heritage after that and began looking to other cultures instead. After seeing a copy of the Rosetta Stone at age 12, he taught himself hieroglyphs, along with Greek and Latin. During World War II in Holland, to avoid getting conscripted into the occupying Nazi army, he spent his days hiding in a museum and gluing broken Egyptian crockery together.

During his undergraduate studies in England, Mellaart grew obsessed with the so-called Sea Peoples, a confederation of pirates who plundered and terrorized the eastern Mediterranean circa 1200 B.C. The Philistines of the Bible were one of these scurvy groups, and ancient Egyptian inscriptions mention others. But for the most part, who the Sea Peoples were and where they came from were complete mysteries.

Intriguingly, however, many archaeologists linked them to another cataclysm. Before 1200 B.C., several advanced civilizations were thriving in the eastern Mediterranean, including the Hittites in Anatolia and the Mycenaean Greeks of Homer's epics. And within a generation, every one of those cultures collapsed, plunging the region into darkness. Baffled, archaeologists have groped about for all sorts of explanations, including earthquakes, droughts, widespread riots, crop failures, and more. But some archaeologists blamed the Sea Peoples, whose raids perhaps inaugurated an era of anarchy and violence—so-called World War Zero.

As for the origin of the Sea Peoples, most archaeologists pointed to Sicily, Sardinia, or Greece; a few even linked them to the besiegers of the Trojan War, since the dates roughly line up. The young Mellaart, meanwhile, took the contrarian view that the Sea Peoples originated in Anatolia. To prove this, he accepted a 12-month fellowship in Turkey in 1951 and grew so enamored with the land that he stretched his £350 stipend over two years by being stingy, just to stay longer. He also fell in love with a Turkish excavator, Arlette, who was descended from the grand viziers (prime ministers) of the Ottoman Empire; one had signed the permits for Heinrich Schliemann to dig at Troy. Helpfully for Mellaart, Arlette had excellent connections among local archaeologists, including Max Mallowan, better known as the husband of Agatha Christie. In later years, the Mellaarts became close friends with the couple.

During the 1950s, Mellaart gained experience at digs in Palestine and Cyprus. He proved a divisive figure, loved and loathed in equal measure. Some colleagues considered him boorish, tactless, and overly hungry for publicity. Others basked in his presence, fondly remembering the long evenings at his home, where Mellaart swilled vermouth, smoked foul Dutch cigars, and cracked naughty jokes, sometimes in a Highland Scottish twang. No one, however, denied his talent as an archaeologist—especially his uncanny ability to know right where to excavate. He would stalk potential digs in baggy pants and a sweat-soaked khaki shirt, studying the landscape's ripples and rills. Then he'd stop and point somewhere. Inevitably, the best artifacts would emerge from that very spot; it was like archaeological dowsing. He also wrote up vivid accounts of his work, and wasn't afraid to draw bold, controversial conclusions.

Still, as a no-name junior archaeologist, he did face frustrations, especially when competing for grants. To his disgust, funders largely ignored prehistoric and Anatolian sites in favor of biblical or Greek ones—or, worse, FRM. In between his stints in Cyprus and Palestine, Mellaart hiked the Turkish countryside, sighing as he catalogued all the places he longed to dig someday, if only he had the money. But by 1958, he was no closer to finding the Sea Peoples than he'd been in 1951—nor to illuminating the rich history of ancient Anatolia in general.

Then along came Anna. Her Dorak treasures were everything he coveted. They tied the Yortan culture of Anatolia to Egypt and Troy, proving the importance of the region. And the sword with the etchings of ships proved that the Yortans were a seafaring people—perhaps even *the* Sea Peoples. The Dorak riches seemed certain to make his name as an archaeologist.

So where the hell was Anna? He wanted her permission to publish his findings, as well as the photographs she'd promised—photographs he'd need to convince other archaeologists how important the cache was. Her silence was driving him mad.

While awaiting her answer, Mellaart continued his wistful survey of Anatolia, looking for spots to excavate in an imagined future. One site in particular intrigued him: a grassy hill in south-central Turkey called Çatalhöyük.

Mellaart first laid eyes on Çatalhöyük (cha-tahl-HEW-ook) in 1952, calling it "a whopping great mound," 60 feet tall and a third of a mile long. He and two colleagues returned there in November 1958 to poke around more, with the colleagues scaling the hill and Mellaart wandering the perimeter.

On his circuit, his keen eye picked out several obsidian arrowheads—as well as traces of an ancient brick wall, scorched with black marks and exposed to the air by erosion. These artifacts weren't Roman muck: They looked far older, perhaps Neolithic. The thought thrilled him. The Neolithic era was the greatest, most consequential transition in human history, when our hunter-gatherer ancestors began settling down and living in one place. It's hard to overstate how big of a shift this was. Having a home base led to farming and organized religion, to technological innovations and the domestication of animals, to the world's first cities and centralized governments, and on and on. At the time, most archaeologists traced the origins of the Neolithic revolution to Mesopotamia in modern Iraq. No one imagined that Anatolia had anything to do with it.

Yet here Mellaart was, staring at a Neolithic wall. A moment later, he heard a shout and a stampede of footsteps. His colleagues were running pell-mell down the hill, clutching shards of pottery they'd scrabbled out of the dirt up there. One blurted out, "It's Neolithic at the top!" Mellaart boomed with laughter: "It's bloody Neolithic at the bottom, too!" In celebration, they went to their hotel and got roaring drunk. Çatalhöyük would soon make Mellaart the most famous archaeologist in the world.

The hotel bender must have been a welcome release for Mellaart; he'd been in a funk for weeks before that. Anna Papastrati had finally written him back.

Her letter arrived in October. Mellaart tore open the envelope, but it contained none of the photographs she'd promised. Instead, there was a curt note, clearly written by someone in pain: "Here is the letter you want so much." After granting him permission to publish, she wrote, "You were always more interested in these old things than in me." She signed it, "Love, Anna."

Were they lovers? It's not clear. But the letter stung Mellaart, who never saw or heard from Anna again.

Equally painful, without photographs, Mellaart could not publish anything about the Dorak-Yortan treasures in an archaeology journal. So as a consolation prize, he penned an article for the *Illustrated London News*. In writing it, Mellaart hoped to convince his peers of the links between Troy, Dorak, and Egypt, as well as drum up funds for digging elsewhere. To make the article more splashy, Mellaart took his sketches of the artifacts—many of which, again, were broken or crusted with grime—and had his assistants paint watercolors of what the treasures would have looked like shiny and new. He included the gold throne case covered in hieroglyphs and the sword etched with galley ships, as well as the statuette of the goddess clutching her breasts. In the meantime, he began shaping his notes into a scholarly treatise on Dorak, which eventually ballooned to 60,000 words.

The magazine article appeared in late 1959 and caused just the stir Mellaart had hoped for. He soon secured his first substantial grants for excavations. Unfortunately, the place the story caused the biggest stir was inside the Turkish government.

Turkey at the time was quite prickly about archaeological finds, for good reason. Centuries of looting and smuggling had robbed the nation of its cultural heritage; people still cursed Schliemann's name, and he was hardly the only offender. So you can imagine the government's alarm when it learned about the Dorak treasures in a magazine article. In addition, Mellaart's decision to sex up the illustrations and present the goods as pristine backfired. People saw the pictures and apparently assumed the goods *were* pristine; their worth was later estimated at £48 million (around $1.2 billion today). Turkish officials felt blindsided. Who was this Anna? How had she obtained the items?

Government agents demanded to see Mellaart. Unfortunately for them, the archaeologist was on leave in Great Britain then. But his place of employment, a British archaeology institute in Ankara, felt it had no choice but to give up Anna, and passed along her address, 217 Kazim Dirik Street. Agents in İzmir swept in to round her up. But when they arrived, they found something strange: 217 Kazim Dirik sat smack in the middle of a commercial district. There were no houses anywhere nearby.

At this point, the Turkish government—already paranoid about foreign archaeologists—began to wonder whether James Mellaart wasn't quite what he seemed. Was he protecting Anna, or perhaps playing another game? Officials wondered about Anna as well. Why would someone wear priceless gold artifacts on a train? And was it really a coincidence that she bumped into an archaeologist while wearing them? Was she an innocent naïf, or working on behalf of someone more sinister?

One of two possibilities seemed most likely: that Anna was tied up with a criminal scheme to smuggle Turkish treasures out of the country, or that her Dorak goods were simply too good to be true and were nothing more than illicit forgeries.

Most people who forge artifacts do so for money. Pots, statues, and ancient trinkets fetch good prices in the international art world, and the sheer amount of cash involved has proved irresistible for crooks. While firm numbers are obviously elusive, estimates claim that 90 percent of the goods in some markets (e.g., certain styles of Anatolian pottery) are fake. It isn't just vulgar rich folks getting ripped off, either. Curators at museums fall for forgeries all the time: A museum in southern France admitted in 2018 that more than half its art was fake.

Not all forgers covet money, however. Some manufacture religious relics to stir the faithful—the Shroud of Turin, splinters of the True Cross, even the "holy prepuce" (foreskin) of baby Jesus. In the 1500s, so many vials of the Virgin Mary's breast milk were circulating that John Calvin sneered, "Had [she] been a cow her whole life, she could not have produced such a quantity."

Similarly, some forgers want to kindle patriotism. In the early 1800s, Czech nationalists were struggling to keep their culture alive. Their language was being driven extinct by German, and unlike other groups, the Czech people had no myths or epic poems to rally around. Miraculously, in 1817 and 1818—the very moment they were needed most—a scholar discovered two lost sagas written in Czech. They portrayed the Czech people as wise, vigorous patriots willing to defend their homeland against foreign incursions. Philologists eventually exposed them as baloney, but everyday people drew strength from them and rebuilt a Czech identity that's still thriving today.

Then there were the Nazis. In 1892, excavators in Italy found a stunning example of Germanic art dating to the 500s: an eagle brooch covered in colored glass. When the Nazis later adopted an eagle as their symbol, the brooch was cited as proof of the technical genius of the ancient Germanic people, as well as a link between modern Nazism and the heroic past.

Forgers took note. In 1936, an art dealer made furtive contact with a historian of Aryanism and showed him another ancient eagle brooch, recently excavated in Czechoslovakia. This thrilled the historian. The Nazis had plans to annex the nation, and the brooch would help justify the seizure by demonstrating that Germanic people had roots there. The dealer arranged for a museum to display the brooch, to much acclaim. Predictably, more brooches soon turned up, some of which—what were the odds—had swastikas stamped into them. A few less oafish Nazis grew suspicious, however, and a chemist quickly found evidence of forgery on the brooches: file marks, modern chemical dyes. The art dealer maintained his innocence, but was sentenced to five years' hard labor for embarrassing the Reich.

In some cases, the motives for fraud remain mysterious. Before the Peking Man bones were unearthed in China (see chapter 5), the most famous hominin fossil in the world was the skull of the Piltdown Man, a supposed missing link from England. In reality, it consisted of an orangutan jaw fastened to a human cranium, artfully weathered and aged. Scholars still disagree about who concocted the fraud and why. As a gambit for fame? As a joke to humiliate a rival? We'll likely never know.

In some cases of fraud, the archaeologists involved almost willingly let themselves be duped—especially when the artifact "proved" a pet theory of theirs. In those cases, as one historian noted, the archaeologists became "victims and accomplices at the same time." Such might be the case with James Mellaart and the Dorak treasures.

In 1961, James Mellaart finally secured the grants and permits he needed to excavate the Neolithic mound of Çatalhöyük. He struck pay dirt immediately. Just two days into the dig, he uncovered an 8,000-year-old mural on a plaster wall. More soon emerged. These were the first paintings in history on human-made surfaces—the first canvases. And things only got better from there.

Mellaart showed that Çatalhöyük was arguably the first true city in history—four times larger than its contemporary Jericho—and a city unlike anything that exists today. At its peak, Çatalhöyük had perhaps 8,000 people, who lived in homes of adobe brick. These homes were packed together as tightly as molars, with no space between them, and no streets or public squares. People got from house to house by walking across their neighbors' roofs. And instead of using doors, they entered and exited their homes on ladders through skylights that doubled as chimneys. Çatalhöyük was a sky city.

The city thrived from roughly 7500 to 6000 B.C., with each generation building its houses on the rubble of the previous one's; this produced several archaeological layers, similar to Troy.

From all evidence, Çatalhöyük was determinedly, even ruthlessly, egalitarian. There were no palaces, no mansions, no government buildings or temples. Every home was roughly the same size, and each one served as a combination living space, granary, and shrine, complete with murals of vultures, leopards, and other beasts. Homes even served as cemeteries, with people burying their loved ones below their packed-earth beds. Some people snuggled up to sleep at night with the skeletons of 60 or more ancestors just inches beneath their heads.

Çatalhöyük invalidated the long-standing assumption that the first cities in history sprang up in Mesopotamia and spread from there. Mellaart proved that Anatolia was at the heart of the Neolithic revolution, a fact that rendered every history textbook in the world instantly obsolete. It also vaulted Mellaart into a rare pantheon of world-famous archaeologists, alongside Schliemann of Troy and Howard Carter of King Tut's tomb. In the judgment of one colleague, Mellaart "changed history"—and not just in the sense of doing something historic. He changed how we view and even understand history.

Mellaart worked fast, and as his team churned through the mound of Çatalhöyük, they unearthed scads of buildings and bones (480 skeletons spread across 160 homes), as well as the occasional artistic treasure. The most magnificent piece was a statuette of an obese "fertility goddess" sitting on a throne, with leopards flanking her. Before long, he had experts from Paris, London, Vienna, and Harvard begging to collaborate. By this point, he'd all but abandoned his quest for the Sea Peoples. To hardcore archaeologists, this was far more exciting. Some called him a "prophet" of the Neolithic.

But as the saying goes, prophets are never honored in their own land. The investigation into the Dorak treasures had petered out after officials failed to find Anna Papastrati's home in İzmir. But Turkish archaeologists still mistrusted Mellaart because he'd never adequately explained what happened there. Even his coup at Çatalhöyük couldn't erase their concerns. To be clear, the Dorak and Çatalhöyük work had no connection archaeologically or logistically: The sites were separated by hundreds of miles and thousands of years. But the Dorak controversy nagged the Turkish government. Where had the treasures gone? And where was Anna?

The tensions finally came to a head when tabloids got ahold of the story. In May 1962, Turkey's second-largest newspaper opened a three-day fusillade against Mellaart with a headline that stretched across eight columns. The tenor of the stories was simple: *Fat, greedy foreigner steals Turkey's heritage.* One story even claimed (falsely) that eyewitnesses had seen Mellaart poking around the Dorak gravesites himself. A furious Mellaart denounced the "gutter press," but the mud stuck.*

After this, Turkish officials could no longer let the Dorak affair slide. They reopened their investigation and soon made a shocking accusation: that Mellaart was working with a smuggling ring. According to this theory, he'd written the magazine article to hype the goods and drive up their prices on the international market. Then, after the goods sold, he'd pocket a cut of the proceeds. The government opened an official criminal inquiry into Mellaart's conduct.

Oddly enough, Mellaart was also beginning to suspect that something criminal was afoot—only in his version of the story, *he* was the victim. To his mind, Anna was a classic honey trap, a seductress working on behalf of someone sinister. She hadn't just "run into" him on the train; she'd tailed him and deliberately worn the bracelet to lure his attention. Then she'd used him to authenticate the goods before disappearing.

Unfortunately for Mellaart, Turkish authorities didn't buy this, partly because they caught him out in a few lies. Under Turkish law, archaeologists had to report all artifacts they found to the government, and Mellaart claimed to have reported the Dorak treasures right away in 1958, shortly after seeing them. In reality, he'd merely slipped a mention into a long report on Çatalhöyük the next year. So while he technically did disclose the goods, he did so in a slippery way.

* Stories about Mellaart in Turkey did not exactly hew to Pulitzer levels of accuracy. One later article reported that the Dorak goods included a tombstone inscribed "3000 B.C." It seems the people of Dorak were curiously well informed about the coming of Christ.

Another lie involved Mellaart's wife. Behind the scenes, he'd been telling colleagues that he'd met Anna in 1952, years before marrying Arlette, because he still feared her wrath for staying at a young woman's home. This fib was understandable, but telling different stories to different people made Mellaart look shifty and undermined his credibility.

Given the ongoing controversy, the Turkish government denied Mellaart's permit to dig at Çatalhöyük in 1964. Mellaart threw a shit fit in response. He was visiting the U.K. when he found out, and he protested to the Turkish ambassador in London. Arlette's father, the descendant of the grand viziers, also worked his contacts in Turkey.

Eventually, the two sides reached a compromise for 1965. Mellaart could continue digging at Çatalhöyük, but another archaeologist would serve as administrative head. Moreover, the government was sending two minders to monitor work there—as well as, Mellaart claimed, three unofficial spies: two servants and a guard. Mellaart especially hated the guard, denouncing him as a "Gestapo" agent and fuming over the man's habit of hovering over Mellaart's shoulder whenever the archaeologist had a spade in hand. "If I'd stepped back suddenly at any time, I would have knocked him over," Mellaart recalled. "And my God, I felt like doing it sometimes."

Sadly, Çatalhöyük had suffered in Mellaart's absence. In 1963, he'd come close to reaching the bottom occupational layer of the mound. Doing so would help answer questions about the city's earliest inhabitants and why they'd built this enigmatic city. But the permit fiasco in 1964 had left Çatalhöyük exposed to the weather for two winters, and the hole that Mellaart's team had excavated was now filled with water—a malarial, mosquito-ridden pond. Mellaart had no choice but to fill it with soil and start over elsewhere.

Mellaart's motto in 1965 was, essentially, *Let's move dirt.* He was determined to reach the lowest layer of Çatalhöyük—to "hit natural," as archaeologists say. To this end, he hired three dozen burly diggers, veterans from previous years who all hailed from the same village and worked well as a team. It was bottom or bust.

It turned out to be bust. One day that summer, one of Mellaart's government minders wandered into an antique shop 20 miles from the site. On the shelves, she was shocked to see three figurines from Çatalhöyük for sale. Illegally.

The shopkeeper was one Aydın Dikmen, who moonlighted as a drummer in a jazz band at an amusement park. The minder seized the figurines and demanded that Dikmen tell her where he'd gotten them. Dikmen sputtered that four diggers from the site had wandered in one day and sold them. The minder grabbed Dikmen by the ear and drove him to Çatalhöyük to confront Mellaart.

The sight of the figurines stunned Mellaart: He recognized them as authentic but swore he had no idea how they'd reached the shop. Dikmen then spotted the crooked diggers and pointed them out. They denied everything. A heated argument ensued, and the workers got so incensed that they quit—and convinced every one of their fellow villagers to quit alongside them.

The incident left Mellaart in despair. The last thing he needed was another black mark with Turkish officials. He'd also lost most of his manpower, and now had just two weeks to reach the bottom of Çatalhöyük. He managed to scrape together a crew of six diggers from two other villages for some final, hurried excavating, but the permit expired and the dig closed before they hit natural.

Meanwhile, there was a twist in the Dorak tale. A husband-and-wife team of British journalists caught wind of the Mellaart scandal and visited Turkey to dig up some dirt of their own. It was not easy reporting there. Among other frustrations, they had their mail opened, got endless runarounds from Turkish bureaucrats, received threatening messages ("Interpol says do not investigate"), found themselves tailed by (rather inept) government spies, and even got arrested once. They persisted anyway, and discovered an important fact. Turkish officials had tried locating Anna Papastrati at 217 Kazim Dirik Street in İzmir. But Anna actually lived in the suburb of Karşıyaka across the bay—and Karşıyaka had its own Kazim Dirik Street. The journalists raced over. Had they found Anna at last?

In Karşıyaka, things got even more tangled. A taxi driver informed them that the city had changed the name of Kazim Dirik Street to 1777 Street. The duo finally located the latter—a twisting, tree-lined, cobblestone road with a slapdash mix of small homes, open lots, and cafés with men smoking hookahs. After going back and forth, the reporters located 217 and knocked. The women inside had lived there for 30 years and had never heard of Anna Papastrati. However, they added, in addition to changing the street names, the government had also recently renumbered every home in town. In fact, the women's address had changed four times in a dozen years.

However discouraged, the reporters kept doggedly knocking at any home along the street that resembled Anna's villa. Finally, a creaky old woman at one place confirmed that she had heard of Anna before. People had knocked on her door a few years earlier and asked for her. The reporters jumped. Who were these people—government officials, friends of hers, someone more menacing? The woman shrugged. She had no idea. When asked if she might know where the original 217 was, the woman couldn't say. Her own address had changed six times in 19 years. The reporters then visited the local registrar's office and learned that even it hadn't bothered keeping track of all the address changes. Between all the renamings and renumberings, no one knew where the old 217 Kazim Dirik Street was. The journalists never found a trace of Anna.

Mellaart could only groan. He now had proof that Turkish officials had botched their original investigation; they hadn't even visited the right city. But even a blunder of that magnitude fell far short of exonerating him, and without that exoneration, Mellaart's worst fears came to pass: The Turkish government denied his permit to dig at Çatalhöyük in 1966. Worse, his employers in Ankara, embarrassed at Mellaart's conduct and perhaps fearful that the Turks would shut down other digs if they didn't act, condemned Mellaart and withdrew their sponsorship of his work—an effective ban. Over the next few years, Mellaart would receive invitations to dig in other places: Cyprus, Israel, Jordan. He refused every offer. His heart and home were in Turkey. But the Turkish government had had enough of James Mellaart. He never excavated again.

The real tragedy, however, is what happened to Çatalhöyük. To protect against looting, the Turkish government erected a fence around the site. Unfortunately, they also left it exposed to the elements. Before long, rain and wind and glaring sunshine destroyed several priceless murals, and mudbrick walls that had stood for 9,000 years began to crumble. Three long decades passed like this. Only in the 1990s did archaeologists resume digging and shore up what they could. But for 30 years, one of the most important archaeological sites in history fell into ruin because James Mellaart and the Turkish government got into a pissing match over Dorak.

Since the 1960s, rumors have occasionally swirled about glimpses of the Dorak treasures. A statue here, a sword fragment there, in

Boston—or no, wait, Texas. But people always heard the rumors thirdhand, and no one ever managed to photograph or document anything. And despite the massive influx of archaeologists into Anatolia since the 1960s—thanks in no small part to James Mellaart's prophetic work there—nothing resembling the Yortan-Dorak treasures has ever turned up again.* They remain strangely, suspiciously sui generis.

So what happened at Dorak? Where did Anna and her treasures disappear to?

Some people swear that the Turkish government set Mellaart up, perhaps resentful of his fame or in revenge for Schliemann at Troy. But this seems doubtful. Mellaart met Anna in 1958, years before his Çatalhöyük digs. Why would the government frame a no-name junior archaeologist?

A more popular theory holds that Anna was the front for a gang of smugglers who used Mellaart to authenticate the treasures and boost their value. The gang presumably either sold the goods to someone who's kept remarkably quiet, or ditched them and ran when the Mellaart scandal blew up in the press and the items got too hot. Or perhaps the smugglers forged the treasures entirely to unload on some rube, and media coverage blew the plan up.

If Anna was indeed working with smugglers, the real question becomes whether Mellaart was in on it. Perhaps "Anna" was really someone else, and Mellaart changed key details to protect them. For

* Indeed, scholars today don't think that a distinct "Yortan people" ever existed, just a distinct style of pottery that misled scholars when their knowledge of ancient Anatolia was weaker.

what it's worth, Mellaart went to his death in 2012 insisting he'd been duped. He swore he'd told the truth and nothing but, and many archaeologists believed him.

But other clues cast doubt on his innocence. Recall Aydın Dikmen, the jazz-drumming antiques dealer who got caught with artifacts from Çatalhöyük. Dikmen and Mellaart knew each other in Turkey in the 1960s. Dikmen later moved to Munich, where Interpol raided his apartment in 1998 and found 350 pieces of art looted from Cyprus, most of it plastered inside false walls. The $60 million bust proved the largest recovery of stolen art since Nazi caches were seized at the end of World War II. During the investigation, Interpol also found that Dikmen was forging artifacts, shaping them with lathes and dentistry tools, then artificially aging them by roasting them over electric grills, dousing them in acid, and burying them in dirt. Of particular interest, Dikmen admitted he'd been forging pots from a site in Anatolia—a site Mellaart had worked on before Çatalhöyük. Dikmen was also caught with fake items from Troy, including idols that looked an awful lot like an idol Anna had shown Mellaart. In fact, some reports have speculated that Dikmen was the real-life Anna.

Or perhaps there's a simpler explanation. As of now, the only tangible evidence that Anna existed is the letter she sent to Mellaart saying she loved him. But there are some fishy details there. In the letter's address line, Anna misspelled her own street name: Kazim Dirik became Kazim Dir*e*k. Perhaps that's just a typo, but sharp-eyed reporter Suzan Mazur noticed another anomaly. Anna wrote the date of the letter, October 18, in the international style, 18-10. But instead of the numeral 1, she typed a capital *I* in the numbers: I8-I0. It's a strange choice. Who would do that?

Mellaart's wife, for one. After having her son in 1955, Arlette worked as a secretary at the British archaeological institute in Ankara that sponsored her husband. And for whatever reason, in correspondence, she often typed a capital *I* instead of a 1. Is it really a coincidence that Anna did the same? How ironic if, after all Mellaart's smoke about worrying what his wife would think, she was maybe helping him perpetrate a fraud the whole time.

As bad as that looked, worse was coming. After Mellaart died, his son Alan began going through his papers. It was not a quick task. Mellaart had kept seemingly every envelope and scrap of paper he'd ever jotted down a thought on—even penning notes on the cardboard inserts in cigar boxes—and had crammed it all into hundreds of crates and storage envelopes spread across two studies and two garages. Alan also allowed an archaeologist named Eberhard Zangger to comb through the mess, since Zangger and Mellaart had collaborated a bit before. Zangger soon found signs that Mellaart had been forging scholarly evidence for decades.

As one example, late in life Mellaart returned to his first archaeological love and put together a manuscript about the Sea Peoples—in particular, about some ancient inscriptions that supposedly proved that they really did hail from Anatolia, as he'd always maintained. He never published the work, but did allude to the inscriptions—written in an obscure hieroglyphic language, Luwian—in three articles. He also wrote letters to Zangger teasing the work.

How Mellaart first got involved with the inscriptions is quite the shaggy-dog tale. According to his hoarded documents, a French archaeologist first spotted the inscriptions on some limestone ruins in a Turkish village in 1862. They stretched an incredible 95 feet long. Alas, after he made careful notes on them, local villagers pillaged the stones to build a mosque. In retaliation, a local government flunky ordered the villagers' homes searched for other looted artifacts, and several bronze tablets emerged with more precious writing. All were shipped off to a museum, which promptly lost one of them. It turned up later, but the Ottoman sultan seized the tablets for safekeeping and locked them in his palace. Scholars clamored to get a peek for decades; but only after several wars, the crumbling of the Ottoman Empire, and other upheaval did a group finally convene to translate everything. Mellaart was roped into the project late and, unluckily, all the other scholars died one by one. (Shades of Agatha Christie.) Before his own death, Mellaart tapped Zangger to complete the project, since Zangger shared his conviction that the Sea Peoples came from Anatolia.

In going through Mellaart's mess of documents, Zangger found sequential drafts of Mellaart's never-published manuscript on the inscriptions. To his horror, as he read, Zangger saw the number of "lost bronze tablets" multiply in each version, from one to two to three to 25. At one point, as if struggling to keep his own story straight, Mellaart jotted a note to himself: "How many were there?" Zangger found other passages where Mellaart blatantly contradicted himself or made obvious blunders, as well as evidence of forgery from other sites, including fake murals.* Overall, Zangger described the office as a "forger's workshop."

* For what it's worth, Zangger believes that the limestone inscriptions in Luwian could be genuine—he's "agnostic" on the matter. And his academic partner Fred Woudhuizen, a Luwian scholar, was convinced that an original existed, from which Mellaart copied the inscription. (Among other things, the sketches of Luwian hieroglyphs in Mellaart's papers show passages that are coherent and grammatical. Given how few people can read Luwian, he didn't see how anyone could produce a forgery so intelligible.) Still, neither think the copper plates ever existed—that's bunk. And they acknowledge that Mellaart's misdeeds may have damaged the credibility of the sketches beyond repair. Meanwhile, most other scholars reject the whole story as fake.

And if he committed forgery in these cases, why not with Dorak? Confronted with such evidence, former colleagues of Mellaart's have twisted themselves inside out trying to exonerate him. One called his work "a tour de force of imagination founded on scholarship." Another said that Mellaart had merely inserted a "'corrective' body of evidence" into archaeology, to ensure that the historical record reflected his obviously correct theories. A third argued that Mellaart had simply exercised some creativity, since "the things that he wanted to find did not always coincide with the facts." (So awkward, that.) Put less euphemistically, Mellaart committed systematic fraud to support his conviction that Anatolia had a past every bit as grand as Greece and Rome.

In retrospect, it sure seems convenient that an ambitious scholar hoping to link the mysterious Sea Peoples with Troy and Egypt just happened to stumble into goods from a tomb near Troy with Egyptian gifts inside and a sword depicting oceangoing vessels. To be sure, some people who've seen the 60,000-word treatise he wrote on the Dorak treasures insist it would be impossible to fake such detailed scholarship. I'm not so sure. It simply looks like the world-building of J. R. R. Tolkien or George R. R. Martin with a dash of Jorge Luis Borges.

Zangger echoes this sentiment. After Mellaart was banned from digging in Turkey, he lived on for a long, empty half century. Zangger suspects that, decade by decade, he withdrew into his imagination and began faking evidence to make his Anatolian fantasyland come true. As noted before, an admirer once gushed that Mellaart "changed history." He was righter than he realized.

And the saddest part is, it was so unnecessary. The incident with Anna supposedly took place in 1958. Later that same year, Mellaart discovered Çatalhöyük—a real, genuine archaeological marvel whose artifacts provide real, genuine insight into humankind's greatest transition, and prove beyond all doubt that Anatolia has a past as glorious as anywhere on earth. But because of Dorak, Mellaart was banned from exploring that past. His invented treasures cost him the real ones.

CHAPTER FOUR

LOST RELICS

In May 1945, a security guard in Egypt beheaded a man. Ali Khalifah was guarding some irrigation equipment at a site north of Luxor when a thief, he claimed, approached in the night. So Khalifah killed him. But not everyone in the nearby village of Nag Hammadi believed this story—in part because Khalifah also lopped off the thief's head, an act of desecration. The next morning, presumably in retaliation, Khalifah was shot in the head, and his corpse was dumped next to the decapitated body.

Umm Ahamd, Khalifah's now widow and the mother of his children, felt certain she knew who'd killed her husband: the adult son of the village's hated sheriff. She told her sons to sharpen their mattocks—digging tools with pointed picks—and prepare for revenge. Around six months later, the sheriff's son fell asleep one day while selling molasses by the roadside. Umm rallied her boys, who snuck up with their mattocks and had at him. One, Muhammad Ali, later proudly declared that he'd hacked the man's heart out and devoured it.*

Those mattocks would soon become legendary in Nag Hammadi, although not for their role in the murder. Within days of the incident, a few of the brothers, including Muhammad, traveled to some cliffs seven miles northeast of Nag Hammadi to dig up fertilizer for the family fields. Given the tension over the killings, they brought four heavies along on camels to watch their backs as they worked.

The cliffs were an ancient Egyptian necropolis, a burial ground; bodies were slotted into hundreds of small crevices that pockmarked the bluffs. Locals considered the place haunted, but its topsoil made dandy fertilizer. On this day, the brothers found a cache at the foot of a slope, beneath a giant boulder that had tumbled off the nearby heights long ago.

Before long, one of the brothers, Abu, struck something with his mattock—a red jar buried in the soil. He set about unearthing it. It stood two feet tall, with a twelve-inch waist and seven-inch mouth. A bowl, glued in place with bitumen, sealed off the top.

The discovery caused a dilemma for the brothers. Should they open the jar? On the one hand, they feared they might unleash a jinni, an evil spirit. On the other hand, the jar might contain gold. After a tense debate, hope conquered fear. Using the same mattock he'd brained the sheriff's son with, Muhammad cracked open the jar.

He later claimed, truthfully or not, that particles like sand whooshed out of the hole and lifted magically into the air, before

* Accounts differ on certain details after this point. Because of the blood feud, scholars could not interview the brothers until years later, by which time memories had faded.

suddenly vanishing. When that died down, the brothers peeked inside the jar and groaned. All they could see were some lousy old books.

Still, they knew that old books—or codices, as scholars call them—often fetched good money. So the brothers removed them from the jar, careful not to damage the brittle papyrus pages. There were a dozen codices total, one of which had a cover made of gazelle hide; another had a serpent tooled onto the spine. Ali offered the camel guards a share of them, but they refused to touch the contraband. So Ali unwound his turban, wrapped the codices up, and slung them over his shoulder for the ride back.

Along the way, he apparently had second thoughts about their value, because when he arrived home, he tossed them into a heap of straw and other oven fuel in the courtyard. During the next few days, the police jailed him for the murder of the molasses vendor, although he never faced formal charges.

After his release, Ali went home and discovered that his mother had burned some pages of the books to warm tea and bake bread. Ali rescued the remaining texts and tried peddling them to people in town who had connections with antiquities dealers. These middlemen recognized the writing as Coptic, which likely made them Christian documents. But Ali couldn't drum up much interest in them; even when he offered a simple swap for cigarettes, the middlemen refused. Later, he managed to barter a few for sugar and tea, and one sucker paid 40 oranges and 12 Egyptian pounds (over $800 today) for four others. Ali counted himself lucky there.

The Nag Hammadi middlemen sold the codices to other middlemen, and this motley lot—a grocer, a lawyer, a cinema owner, a hoodlum with one eye—began shuttling the manuscripts to dealers in Cairo. There, in March 1946, a French scholar wandered into one dealer's shop and perused seven of them. After skimming a few pages, he noticed the name Seth, the younger brother of Cain and Abel. Another section was titled the Apocalypse of Peter, a seeming companion to the Apocalypse of John, better known as the Book of Revelation.

After leaving the shop, the scholar alerted a colleague who specialized in Coptic documents, and they returned the next morning at 10 a.m.—hours before any self-respecting antiquities dealer would open. Eventually the dealer wandered by, surprised to see people waiting for him. Inside, he spread the manuscripts out for the specialist.

After one glance, the scholar's mouth went dry, and he feared that his pounding heart would betray his excitement. He instantly recognized these as early versions of Bible books—perhaps the earliest Bible books ever uncovered. Trying to play it cool, he dismissed the manuscripts to the dealer as some ratty old spells. Then he made a mistake. He offered 700 Egyptian pounds for them—vastly more than any "spells" were worth. The dealer no doubt realized something was amiss. First, the scholars were waiting for him to arrive, and now they were offering an absurd amount of money. The dealer quickly explained that he was selling the manuscripts on consignment, and would have to consult with the actual owners before making any deals. The French scholar spent the next two weeks staring at his phone, fighting the urge to call the shop and ask more questions. He finally dropped by again, and was crushed to learn that he'd lost out. Another dealer had snapped them up for 7,000 Egyptian pounds.

When word trickled back to Nag Hammadi about the incredible price the manuscripts had fetched, the brothers who'd discovered them were livid; they assumed their middlemen had ripped them off. True to form, they stormed into the home of one, a teacher, seized him by the collar, and threatened to murder his daughters if he didn't get the books back. They later opened fire on his house to prove they weren't messing around. But the mayor of the town got word of the threats and told the brothers to cool it. They ended up settling with the teacher for 20 Egyptian pounds.

Meanwhile, rumors were swirling of offers of 5,000 Egyptian pounds for a single codex. But nowadays, even those prices look like a steal. The Nag Hammadi manuscripts have since rewritten the entire history of Christianity, and revealed it to be far stranger, and far more lurid, than anyone dared imagine.

Perhaps most importantly, the Nag Hammadi manuscripts contained forgotten gospels and lost books of Revelation. Some of these accounts hardly seem Christian. Among other things, the Gospel of Thomas fails to mention the virgin birth, the Last Supper, and Jesus's resurrection. A few texts even mock the canonical gospels, with passages that are frankly blasphemous. One criticizes God as an "arrogant beast" for surrounding Himself with sycophantic angels who worship Him for eternity. Another derides God as an asshole for booting Adam and Eve out of the Garden of Eden after they ate from the Tree of Knowledge. (Who, after all, could object to a little learning?) Similarly, some accounts praise the serpent in the Garden who tempted Eve as the best friend humankind ever had, the source of our most miraculous gifts. As one scholar said, this is Christianity through the looking glass—an unsettling, bizarro version of a religion we thought we knew.

The Nag Hammadi books date from the 300s A.D., although they're probably copies of texts originally written a century or more earlier. We know nothing about the authors except the most important thing: that they were heretics. Many Church fathers wrote about heretics in scathing terms, denouncing them as apes and swine, and the early centuries of Christianity were marred with campaigns to suppress and murder these supposed heathens. As a result, few heretical writings have survived into modern times. The Nag Hammadi texts allowed these men and women to speak for themselves, without the distortions and biases that their enemies' accounts introduced.

Scholars now classify these codices as part of a larger group of apocryphal books of the Bible that the early Church couldn't quite stamp out. In some cases, as with their reevaluation of the serpent in the Garden, what the heretics say makes sense—arguably more sense than the standard version. In other cases, it's easy to see why Church leaders got so incensed. In the Infancy Gospel of Thomas, the five-year-old Jesus gets into a spat with a playmate and curses the lad, leaving him withered and deformed. Jesus also kills a second boy merely for bumping into him. In the Acts of Thomas, Jesus sells one disciple into slavery. Later in Acts, a bridegroom enters his bedchamber on his wedding night and finds, to his understandable surprise, Jesus lying next to his new wife. JC then lectures them on the evils of "filthy intercourse" and the "ghastliness of children."

Other apocrypha are even wilder. In one, Mary breathes fire. In another, dragons bow down and worship Jesus, Daenerys-style. In the most mind-bending account, Jesus appears to Mary as an angel before his own birth and then somehow impregnates her *with himself.* Perhaps strangest of all, the Infancy Gospel of James includes an account of a woman who refuses to believe that Mary was really a virgin, and goes so far as to jam her fingers inside the Mother of God to probe her hymen. Offended, Mary turns her vagina into a flamethrower and sears the woman's hand into a blackened stump.*

Despite being apocryphal, these books still influence Christianity. The classic Nativity scene with the oxen and donkeys doesn't appear

* However macabre, the Infancy Gospel of James was popular in ancient times: 140 copies survive today. Compare that with the many, many books we've lost throughout history—including the entire Library of Alexandria—and you can see how remarkable that is.

in Matthew, Mark, Luke, or John, but right alongside the story of Mary's fire-breathing vagina. More profoundly, several of the books all but deify Mary, which helps explain the cult of the Virgin that still flourishes around the world today.

These competing narratives also help make sense of a few unsettling moments in the canonical gospels. For the most part, Jesus is a pretty chill dude in the Bible. But what about the time he curses a fig tree and causes it to wither and die? Or the time he expels a host of demons from a man and transfers them into a herd of swine, then sends the swine tumbling off a cliff? Was that necessary? Such stories seem out of character with the standard Jesus—but fit right in with the Jesus who smites playmates. To extend the looking-glass metaphor, these heretical accounts hold a mirror up to mainstream Christianity and reveal blemishes that the beholder never expected.

Beyond banning heretical stories about Jesus, the early Catholic Church also tried to eliminate Jesus's rivals—other would-be messiahs.

According to Greek and Roman sources, Palestine in the early first century A.D. was overrun with shaggy-haired preachers wandering around calling themselves Son of the Most High. (One actually trained a parrot to flutter around him squawking "Apsethus is a god.") Most of these preachers buttressed their claims by performing "miracles" such as restoring sight to the blind, making the lame walk, and walking on water. Sound familiar? Another stock trick involved multiplying food, and not just bread and fish but crisp veggies and even olive oil and vinegar for dipping. "This wasn't just loaves and fishes," one scholar noted, "but side orders."

Jesus wasn't even the most popular savior. There were maybe 7,000 Christians on earth circa A.D. 100, but tens of thousands of people seemingly venerated Asclepius, a demigod renowned for raising the dead. Jesus's biggest competition was Apollonius of Tyana, a man whose first biographies might have predated the gospels and therefore inspired tales about Jesus. During the pregnancy of Apollonius's mother, an angel appeared unto her and announced that she carried a god inside her. His birth was also heralded with a sign in the heavens, a bolt of lightning. He then spent his adulthood roaming around in robes and preaching. The Romans arrested and condemned him, and while Apollonius took an easier way out than Jesus—vanishing from court in a poof, rather than suffer crucifixion—he did make a cameo afterward to his disciples, and even confronted a doubting Thomas type. The reason no one has heard of Apollonius today, despite his widespread fame once, is that adherents of Jesus stamped his cult out, decrying him as the Antichrist.

They did the same to oddball offshoots of Christianity. One of these condemned groups worshipped Jesus alongside Homer and Pythagoras. Another venerated him among a panoply of 365 divine beings; initiates had to have sex 365 times as an offering to each. Especially pious folks went through the cycle twice.

As rival sects were stamped out, the ranks of orthodox Christians swelled to roughly six million people by the 300s. Then the Roman emperor Constantine converted and began using his governmental power to battle heresies. Several strident Christian emperors succeeded him, until one outlawed all heresies in 379.

After that, adherents of weird Christianities were exiled, stripped of possessions, and even flogged or executed in extreme cases. (Just like Jesus would have wanted, I'm sure.) Even death was no escape. Back around the year 300, a priest named Arius had pointed out that fathers always exist before their children in nature—how could it be otherwise? He added that God the Father must therefore have preceded Jesus the Son in heaven. Perfectly defensible deduction.

Well, a century later the Church decided that God and Jesus were both coeval and eternal, and Arius's views were denounced as an abomination. To drive this home, the emperor Theodosius II erected a statue of Arius for passersby to spit, urinate, and poop on.

Unsurprisingly, Christianity became stricter and more homogenous during this period, as well as more boring. This era also saw the heretical Christians near Nag Hammadi bury their sacred texts beneath a boulder. What other choice did they have?

Naturally, after the codices emerged in 1945, scholars wondered whether other, similar caches existed. Alas, the blood feud in the nearby villages bollixed any search attempts.

Three months after the murder of the molasses vendor, the man's brother took revenge and killed two men from Muhammad Ali's clan. Miraculously, several years passed before the next bout of violence. But just when the hatred had seemingly thawed, the molasses vendor's son and six other gunmen crept up to a funeral procession along the Nile in canoes and opened fire, killing 10 people and wounding 27. The vendor's family lived near the cliffs where the codices had turned up, and given the ongoing hostility, Ali and his brothers refused to visit the area, no matter how much archaeologists begged them to point out the spot.

Finally, three decades after the codices appeared, one archaeologist bribed Ali to visit the area while disguised as an "American"—presumably trading his robe and turban for blue jeans and a Stetson. Even then, Ali consented to go only during Ramadan and only at dusk, a time when Muslims are usually indoors gobbling down food after a day of fasting. On a quick drive-by, with Muhammad slunk down in the back seat, he pointed to a spot on the cliffs and they sped off. The archaeologist eagerly returned to dig, but found nothing.

Annoyed, the archaeologist then challenged Muhammad's manhood and dared him to go back on foot and lead him to the spot. An incensed Muhammad agreed. This time, he walked straight to the place of discovery—which differed from the place he'd pointed out before. To be sure, this site resembled his description of a spot in the shadow of a boulder. But digging there again revealed nothing, not even the shards of the red jar.

It seems likely, then, that Muhammad's memory was off. Even today, it's unclear exactly where the codices first emerged—and whether any more heretical messiahs remain to be discovered in the cliffs near Nag Hammadi.

Probably the most coveted lost treasures from the Bible are the relics of the Jewish Temple in Jerusalem.

The first Temple, built by King Solomon to house the Ark of the Covenant, was burned down by Nebuchadnezzar's army in 586 B.C. King Herod finally built a second Temple around 20 B.C., and the structure truly should have been counted among the Seven Wonders of the Ancient World. Its highest point soared perhaps 180 feet; the temple gates alone stood 50 feet tall.

The Temple served as both the Vatican and Fort Knox of the Jewish people: a religious citadel that housed the vast wealth of Israel. The edifice was white limestone and marble, with a gold eagle standing watch above the entrance and entire walls inside plated with gold. One sculpture of a golden vine had clusters of grapes as tall as human beings. Whenever Temple custodians needed to sweep beneath it, 300 priests had to grunt and strain to lift it off the ground.

Within a century, it was all gone.

Palestine belonged to the Roman Empire in the first century A.D., and the Jewish people there never quite accepted Roman dominion.

Caligula outraged them by proposing to erect a statue of himself as a "living god" inside the Temple; only his assassination avoided a war over the matter. Equally chafing, greedy Roman governors in Palestine regularly skimmed money from Temple coffers for aqueducts and other projects. The Jews grew tired of these mandatory "loans," which the Romans never paid back, and a revolt broke out in A.D. 66. Rome used the unrest as an excuse to send in troops and assert tighter control.

A general named Vespasian—banished to Palestine after falling asleep during one of Nero's interminable poetry readings—directed the invasion initially. But in A.D. 69, after the violent deaths of several emperors in a row, Vespasian was bullied into accepting the crown himself: His soldiers declared him their emperor and actually drew their swords and said they'd run him through if he refused to challenge another claimant to the throne. Vespasian feigned reluctance (the stunt with his soldiers was possibly staged), but marched off to fight in a civil war, where he soon triumphed.

Meanwhile, Vespasian's son Titus took over the army in Jerusalem and laid siege. To hasten victory, his army also pounded the city walls with battering rams and tortured any captives they could round up; so many people were crucified that the area ran out of wood. After nearly five months without food, the citizens of Jerusalem were rooting through dunghills for scraps and eating leather shoes. One mother killed and ate her infant son. According to some sources, up to 1.1 million Jews perished during the four-year war, while a further 114,000 were either chained together and marched south to slave away in Egyptian mines or dragged off as fodder for gladiator matches.

Most bitterly of all, the Romans burned down the Temple, albeit probably accidentally. Rather than assault the 50-foot gates, Titus's troops tried to smoke out the resident priests by tossing firebrands inside. The resulting blaze was apocalyptic. The Temple's jars of holy oil burned with thick, acrid smoke, and actual streams of gold ran out of the flaming ruins.

No one knows how many gold and silver relics the Romans melted down and hauled away (we'll circle back to this in a moment), but Titus had strong incentives to grab as much as he could. His father Vespasian came from country-bumpkin stock, and as a new emperor, Vespasian needed quick cash for several reasons: to boost his prestige, to replenish the imperial treasury after the reckless spending of Nero, and to restore several gutted neighborhoods in Rome after a huge fire a few years earlier. In fact, Vespasian and Titus financed the construction of Rome's most famous building, the Colosseum, from the sack of the Jewish Temple.

Still, even if most of the Temple's holy objects were melted down, Titus took care to preserve a few things. Early in the Bible, God appeared unto Moses and instructed him to craft several items: a two-foot-tall menorah, a pair of silver trumpets to summon the faithful and commemorate sacrificial offerings and feasts, and a special golden table to hold offerings of bread. Jews had passed these objects down for untold generations ever since, making them the most sacred relics in Judaism: the holiest of holies.

Titus stole them—both to humiliate Israel and assert Roman dominance. After the objects reached Rome, they formed the centerpiece attraction in perhaps the grandest triumphal parade in Roman history. Tens of thousands of people turned out to gawk at them, alongside captured Jewish leaders in chains.* Afterward, Vespasian lodged the treasures at one of the loveliest buildings in Rome, the

* This parade to humiliate the Jews was commemorated on the Arch of Titus, which still stands in Rome today. For ages, Italian Jews refused to cross beneath it. Meanwhile, Hitler and Mussolini strolled through practically arm in arm in 1938. Today a fence blocks passage beneath, although local guides reportedly give Jewish tourists permission to spit on it.

Temple of Peace, which featured columns of pink granite nearly 60 feet tall. They remained on display for almost four centuries.

After this point, the fate of the Temple treasures grows shadowy, but the best evidence indicates that they disappeared from Rome in the mid-400s. One night during that era, the emperor Valentinian was gambling with a senator named Maximus; they played Roman checkers. Maximus lost, and handed over his signet ring as payment. Valentinian turned around and sent the ring to the senator's wife—along with a deceitful message, supposedly from Maximus, asking her to hurry to the palace. When she arrived, Valentinian raped her.

Upon learning of this outrage, Maximus began plotting against Valentinian, and arranged for his assassination in 455. Afterward, he seized the throne for himself. Since his own wife had died in the meantime, Maximus consolidated his power by marrying the late emperor's wife. She, however, despised Maximus, and treacherously sent word to a tribe of barbarians called the Vandals, encouraging them to invade. They did so happily, and spent 14 days pillaging Rome. Among the boatloads of treasure they dragged home to Carthage were, reportedly, the menorah, the silver trumpets, and the offering table from the Jewish Temple.

Assuming the relics did reach Carthage, they stayed there less than a century. In the late 300s, the increasingly unwieldy Roman Empire had split into eastern and western realms. The sack of the Vandals left the western empire teetering; it fell in 476. But the eastern half, ruled from Constantinople, continued to quarrel with the Vandals. In particular, the Vandals took perverse delight in torturing Christians, and in 533, the pious emperor of the eastern empire, Justinian, finally had enough. He declared a holy war on Carthage and invaded.

However formidable in their prime, the Vandals had grown soft and decadent after destroying Rome, and Justinian's troops walloped them. The Vandal king did manage to pack his most prized treasures into a boat, which slipped out of the city's harbor and fled—only to get driven back by a storm. Justinian's men captured it and rerouted it to Constantinople. According to one of Justinian's advisers, Procopius, the cargo included "the treasures of the Jews, which Titus ... brought to Rome." Procopius doesn't specify the trumpets, menorah, or offering table, but many historians assume that's what he meant.

If so, the treasures spent even less time in Constantinople than in Carthage. According to Procopius, a savvy Jewish man in Constantinople approached someone who had the ear of Justinian and pointed something out. The Romans had stolen Israel's treasures once and were subsequently destroyed by invaders. Then the Vandals stole the treasures and were themselves destroyed by invaders. Now Justinian's regime had stolen the treasures and, well ... it didn't take much imagination to fill in the rest. Word of this "curse" quickly reached Justinian. But if that unknown man hoped to spur the return of the treasures to the Jews of Jerusalem, he didn't quite succeed. The panicked emperor did return the relics to the city, but according to Procopius, he entrusted them to the "sanctuaries of the Christians" there.

Unfortunately, Procopius didn't specify which sanctuaries. Perhaps the stout Church of the Holy Sepulcher. Perhaps a monastery-fortress on some forbidding cliff outside the city. Perhaps somewhere now forgotten. To make matters worse, Jerusalem suffered through several crises over the next century, including outbreaks of plague and two brutal invasions. Amid all the breathless accounts of atrocities, with nuns raped in the streets and corpses piled up "like the carcasses in a butcher's shop," no one bothered recording the fate of a few relics. Maybe some priest concealed them underground, Nag Hammadi–style.

Or maybe the invading forces seized them and melted them down. Regardless, they vanished from history.

There is one common rumor about their fate: that the Christian community in Jerusalem somehow spirited the treasures to the Vatican in Rome, where they remain today in an underground lair. In fact, an Israeli government official once publicly accused the Vatican of hoarding them. To be clear, there's zero evidence for this beyond some 900-year-old rumors from the Middle Ages. But unless the Vatican throws open its holdings for inspection (unlikely), conspiracy theories to this effect will continue to swirl.

If the menorah, trumpets, and offering table seem lost, other Temple treasures might be recoverable—in particular, the gold and silver in the Temple treasury. Vespasian and Titus certainly made off with plenty of lucre in A.D. 70. But perhaps not all of it, according to none other than the Dead Sea Scrolls.

One day in the winter of 1946–47, three Bedouin goatherds, all cousins, were tending their flocks near the beige hills of Qumran, a tiny oasis close to the Dead Sea. One unruly billy scrambled up a bluff and wandered off, so Juma Khalil sighed and set out to retrieve it. Halfway up the slope, he spotted a modest-size hole, something a cat might dart into. Like bored young men everywhere, Juma loved throwing rocks, so he grabbed a stone and took aim. It zipped right into the hole. However satisfying that felt, he never would have given the moment a second thought, if not for the noise he heard a moment later—a pot shattering.

Juma picked his way over to inspect the hole. He was tempted to explore it, but like the Nag Hammadi brothers before him, he felt torn. Had he lucked into some gold? Or had he unleashed an evil spirit? He decided to return to camp and seek his cousins' advice. The trio debated the matter without reaching any conclusion. But a few days later, just after dawn, 15-year-old Muhammad snuck off to investigate. He cleared away some rubble around the hole and squeezed inside. In the dim light, he found a handful of jars, which contained three leather scrolls. As scholars now know, the texts were the Book of Isaiah, a commentary on the biblical Book of Habakkuk, and a list of regulations for a religious community.

When Muhammad returned to tell his cousins, they beat him up—convinced he'd hidden the cave's real treasures for himself. Muhammad eventually persuaded them he was telling the truth, so Juma schlepped the scrolls to an antiquities dealer in Bethlehem a few months later, hoping for a nice payday. A bit nonsensically, the dealer saw that they were made of leather and alerted the town cobbler to get his opinion. Eventually, someone reached out to the archbishop of the local Syrian Orthodox Church, who eagerly acquired the scrolls, hoping to cash in himself. Meanwhile, the Bedouin around Qumran had unearthed four more scrolls in other caves: a second Isaiah, a collection of hymns, a book describing an apocalyptic battle between good and evil, and a paraphrase of Genesis. The archbishop acquired the Genesis, and an antiquities dealer scooped up the other three.

The antiquities dealer wanted to sell his scrolls to a professor of archaeology at Hebrew University named Eliezer Sukenik, but this proved tricky. The United Nations had recently carved out the nation of Israel, which led to widespread unrest among the locals. Fortifications and roadblocks were thrown up, and the dealer and Sukenik found themselves on opposite sides. A clandestine meeting was finally arranged, and the dealer showed one scroll to Sukenik through a barbed-wire fence. Eventually, Sukenik got a pass to view the scrolls in person, and purchased them for his university.

Sukenik coveted the other scrolls as well. But given the tension in the region, the Syrian archbishop refused to deal with any Jews. Instead, he smuggled his scrolls to the United States, where, incredibly, he placed a classified ad in the *Wall Street Journal* to sell them. (The scrolls "would be an ideal gift," he suggested.) A banker stepped forward and purchased them for a quarter-million dollars, which left the archbishop feeling mighty satisfied: He had not only cashed in but kept the precious relics out of Israeli hands. Or so he assumed. The banker was actually a front for Sukenik's son. The man did indeed gift them to the younger Sukenik, who smuggled them back to Hebrew University.

Meanwhile, a war had broken out over the partition of Israel, and outside archaeologists couldn't risk visiting the Dead Sea region. This gave the Bedouin free rein to scour every hillside nook for miles, searching for more scrolls to sell. As a result, manuscripts began trickling into shops in Jerusalem—or at least scraps of manuscripts. While the first seven scrolls were relatively whole, later ones were mere shreds and tatters, often arriving in pieces no bigger than postage stamps. Scholars purchased whatever they could, piecing them together by matching the handwriting on different fragments, as well as the animal skin or papyrus used. In a few cases, they matched scraps by lining up the wormholes in them—places where some hungry critter had gnawed its way through consecutive layers of a scroll.

Overall, parts of roughly 850 scrolls turned up at 11 caves over a one-and-a-half-mile stretch. One-sixth were written in Aramaic, with a handful in Greek; the rest were in Hebrew. (A few dozen were actually written in code, although scholars easily cracked it.)* The

* The code was a simple substitution pattern, the kind you'd get from making $a = 1$, $b = 2$, $c = 3$, etc. Given modern analytical and statistical techniques, these are trivial to decipher.

bulk of the scrolls date from the first century B.C., and most of the rest from the first century A.D.

These scrolls are often deemed the greatest archaeological discovery of the 20th century, based on what they reveal about both Christianity and Judaism at a pivotal moment in history. Passages from every book of the Old Testament save Esther are represented, and many are the oldest extant versions of the books, providing a glimpse of how they evolved over time. Moreover, multiple copies emerged of noncanonical books like Enoch and Jubilees, which proves these books circulated widely and were likely cherished back then, even if Jews and Christians today look askance at them. Beyond biblical texts, the scrolls contained poetry chapbooks, collections of aphorisms, lists of laws, compilations of exorcisms and spells, and a few texts allegedly written by angels. Perhaps most importantly, while mainstream Judaism at the time was fixated on rituals and interpretative debates, these scrolls betray a preoccupation with end-times and an imminent apocalypse. In fact, while the scrolls never mention Jesus, they do obsess over a coming messiah—which surprised scholars, who'd long assumed that early Christianity represented a clean break with Judaism. Not so.

By the time archaeologists could return to the Dead Sea, the Bedouin had picked the hillsides pretty clean. But not entirely. In March 1952, while poking around a spot a mile north of Qumran, a few archaeologists noticed some potsherds at the foot of a cliff. Scaling the rock face, they found a concealed cave whose roof had collapsed. Amid the debris lay the single oddest discovery of the entire Dead Sea cache: two "scrolls" made of long, thin sheets of copper wound into cylinders. (Or at least they used to be copper; the metal had long since rusted into brittle copper oxide.) A little writing in Hebrew was visible, but the cylinders were far too fragile to unwrap.

So the archaeologists coated them in celluloid and gently extracted them for study.

They noticed that the edge of one cylinder had rivet heads that lined up with a series of holes on the edge of the other; clearly, the two scrolls had been joined in antiquity. This single scroll—now called the Copper Scroll—would have been a foot wide and eight feet long. Beyond that, archaeologists had no idea what to make of the thing. A few eager beavers suggested ways to unravel it, but the methods seemed more likely to do harm than good. So it just went on display in a museum in Jerusalem, resting on a bed of cotton in a glass case.

In an unwelcome twist, a German scholar named Karl Georg Kuhn visited the museum and made a wild claim. Peering into the case, Kuhn noticed a few letters etched into the copper. Because he was looking at the back of the scroll, the writing was backwards, and he could barely make out the letters anyway. But he convinced himself that he could read a few words—including "buried" and "gold." From there, he leaped to the most dramatic conclusion possible, declaring that the Copper Scroll was a list of buried treasure. His colleagues groaned. Even back then, the idea of finding buried treasure was trite, a cliché, and they didn't need anyone spouting off nonsense. "Few took the learned professor seriously," one colleague recalled. "Some blamed the heat of the Jerusalem summer, others the strength of the local *arak*" liquor.

By 1955, an archaeologist in England had devised a workable plan to open the brittle scrolls. He coated them in airplane glue to provide a flexible, protective skin. Then he jerry-built a cutting machine from surplus military parts and a neurosurgical saw. Starting on the outside, he sliced each cylinder into thick horizontal strips, steering as best as he could around any text. Twenty-three pieces resulted.

The writing proved to be clumsy Hebrew, rife with misspellings and oddly shaped letters. (Perhaps the artisan who inscribed the scroll couldn't read and was simply copying another document.) As for the content, to the dumbfoundment of nearly everyone, the German scholar Kuhn turned out to be right. Unlike every other Dead Sea Scroll, the Copper one contains no religious material. Without any preamble or introduction, it just starts listing buried treasure. It references 64 caches total—mostly gold or silver ingots, although a few entries mention incense and other valuables. The range of hidey-holes was impressive: salt pits, gulches, dovecotes, wells, beneath corpses in a cemetery. While some of the places referred to are obscure ("in the cave of the old washer's chamber"), most of the caches seem to be concentrated in three areas: near Jericho, near Qumran, and near the grounds of the fallen Temple in Jerusalem, the so-called Temple Mount.*

As for how much loot we're talking, the scroll uses a unit of weight called a talent: There might be 100 talents of gold secreted inside a dam, or 50 talents of silver beneath a wine press. Frustratingly, the weight of a talent has varied over time, so it's hard to give precise figures. But it's a staggering amount by any measure. Two deposits contain 900 talents of silver and/or gold, up to 68,000 pounds each, depending on the measuring standard. All the hoards combined contain some 4,600 talents, up to 175 tons, plus hundreds of gold and silver bars, vessels, and other objects.

Scholars have a theory about where this gold came from. They've found other copper scrolls from antiquity inside Greek temples, mostly lists of votive offerings and catalogues of temple archives.

* In fact, the selection of an illiterate person might have been a security measure: If the scribe couldn't read the treasures' locations, he couldn't go out and dig anything up.

(Copper was preferred for important records like these because it's more durable than papyrus or parchment.) Assuming that Jewish scribes were following this same practice, the Copper Scroll's caches of gold and silver were probably related to the Temple in Jerusalem. In fact, one entry references a tax collected on crops to support Temple priests, while another mentions certain priestly garments.

Unfortunately, beyond a vague connection to the Temple, it's hard to get more specific. Scholars have dated the Copper Scroll to between A.D. 30 and A.D. 130—an unhelpfully broad range. The middle years cover the Jewish Revolt of the late 60s, which could mean that the Copper Scroll documents Temple treasures squirreled away during the war with Rome, or even smuggled out during the doomed final days of the siege. On the other hand, if the scroll dates to the 70s or later, the riches might represent taxes collected to build a third Temple and then hidden to forestall more obligatory Roman "loans." Or perhaps the list is a copy of an earlier record, in which case the scroll itself (i.e., the physical object) could still date to the 100s, while the buried treasures themselves date back to the Temple after all.

As far as anyone knows, not a single gold flake from the Copper Scroll has ever turned up. Given that goose egg, some scholars have proposed that the document is merely a collection of fables about buried treasure, similar to lore about El Dorado or the pot o' gold at the end of a rainbow.

But most scholars don't buy that. Inscribing text on copper is a pain, so why go through all that labor for some fairy tales? The dry language of the scroll—nothing but locations, weights, and depths to dig—also lacks the embellishments you'd expect from any folklore worth the name. Rather, it seems likely that either the Romans tortured Jewish priests into betraying the location of the caches (we know this happened sometimes), or that Bedouin chasing goats in later centuries stumbled across the treasures and helped themselves. If the latter is true, then the cave where the Copper Scroll was found turned out to be, ironically enough, a much better hiding spot than any of the locations it listed.*

The low odds of finding any Temple treasures nowadays has not deterred people from searching for them, often on the flimsiest of evidence. Most of these expeditions involve the Copper Scroll riches, since their locations are at least theoretically known, but other Temple goods have fired the imaginations of archaeologist-looters as well.

In 1908, a Finnish biblical scholar supposedly detected a secret code in the Book of Ezekiel that revealed the location of Solomon's treasures from the first Jewish Temple. He convinced a brash young English earl named Montagu Brownlow Parker to finance an expedition to find them, and the two set off to Jerusalem. Apparently the directions in Ezekiel were a bit vague, however, because upon arriving, they thought it best to hire a clairvoyant to determine the exact spot to dig. Even then, several years of empty excavations followed.

A desperate Parker finally bribed the governor of Jerusalem with $25,000 (around $900,000 today) to let him dig under the Dome

* In 2016, the Museum of the Bible in Washington, D.C., acquired 16 fragments of the Dead Sea Scrolls, only to realize later that they're all fake. And not even good fakes, considering they were inked onto the wrong material—leather, instead of parchment. Sadly, the museum's troubles did not stop there. In 2021, it had to return more than 8,000 items plundered in the aftermath of the war in Iraq in the early 2000s.

of the Rock, a site on the Temple Mount that's sacred to Muslims. The earl's team snuck in disguised as Arabs and began hacking away. A security guard caught them and alerted authorities, at which point news of the illicit dig rocketed around town. Some said Parker had stolen Solomon's crown. Others said he swiped a sacred sword belonging to Muhammad the Prophet, or even the Ark of the Covenant. However bogus, this scuttlebutt outraged every soul in Jerusalem—a rare moment of religious solidarity in the city. Days of riots followed, and the earl was run out of town empty-handed.

Something equally daft happened in France. As background, a few scholars—and a load of conspiracy theorists—believe that the Vandals never got their hands on the Temple's riches when they sacked Rome in 455. Rather, they believe the Visigoths snatched them during an earlier sack in 410, then hauled everything back to their capital in France. A few centuries later, during a time when the Visigoths faced military threats on several sides, they supposedly buried the loot at a secret location.

Nothing much happened for the next 12 centuries, until a priest named Bérenger Saunière took over a small parish in southwest France named Rennes-le-Château. Rennes-le-Château was possibly an old Visigoth village, and one day Saunière was poking around the altar in his church. The stones supporting the altar were segments from Visigoth pillars, and Saunière realized they were hollow. Inside one, he reportedly found a piece of ancient parchment. It was a treasure map, and after recovering the booty, he became rich beyond the dreams of avarice. One account estimated his wealth at a fantastical four trillion francs.

In support of this story, local people cited the fact that Saunière's tiny parish (fewer than 300 people) suddenly had funds to rebuild half the town, as well as construct a new municipal water supply and pave the local highway. Saunière also decorated his church with sparkling new statues and erected a grand villa for himself with gardens, an orange grove, and a strange tower he kept locked at all times. Moreover, on his deathbed, he allegedly confessed the source of his riches to another priest who (legend has it) never smiled again after that day.

In reality, a later investigation found that Saunière was simply running a scam. Priests back then could make extra cash by saying Masses for the dead for a fee. The Vatican limited priests to three such Masses per day, but the enterprising Saunière was doing nearly five dozen. It's not clear whether he was zipping through them at hyperspeed or simply lying about how many he performed. Either way, he probably never saw a shekel of the Temple treasures.

Nor has anyone else, in well over a millennium. Shockingly, that's a relief to some scholars. To be sure, they acknowledge that if we did somehow recover any Temple relics—especially the menorah, trumpets, and gold offering table—they would instantly become some of the most prized artifacts in the world, right up there with the Rosetta Stone and King Tut's golden mask. But the political situation in Israel is complicated right now, to say the least. In particular, a few millenarian groups there are determined to build a third Temple someday, and do so right where the first two stood. This isn't just talk, either. They've hewn and blessed the cornerstones already, and some of them argue that the reappearance of the Temple relics would constitute a sign from God that it's time to start building in earnest.

The problem with this plan is that constructing a new Temple would likely require tearing down the Dome of the Rock, one of the holiest sites in Islam. Gulp. To be clear, these groups occupy the fringe in Israel: Their views in no way represent mainstream attitudes, and the Israeli government has blocked previous attempts to drag the cornerstones to the Temple Mount. But given Palestine's intense history, even the actions of a few fringe players could easily start a holy war that engulfs the entire Middle East. Perhaps with the missing Temple treasures, then, it's safer to leave well enough alone.

CHAPTER FIVE

LOST BONES

At first, the postcard must have delighted Franz Weidenreich. As a paleoanthropologist who studied human evolution, he had spent the past year agonizing over the fate of some fossilized human ancestors that he'd left behind in China during World War II—the famed Peking Man bones. Given Japan's choke hold on China at the time, he'd been unable to reach anyone there to determine their whereabouts. But his Chinese colleagues had somehow managed to slip a note to him in New York. Weidenreich eagerly scanned the message.

One line jumped out: "Where is Nellie?" Weidenreich frowned. At the time, the Peking Man bones were the oldest prehuman ancestors ever discovered. To capitalize on the intense public interest in them, Weidenreich had invited an artist to his lab back in Beijing. Under his direction, she'd fleshed out a replica of Peking Man's skull with clay, adding lips, eyes, hair, even an enigmatic Mona Lisa smile—transforming a dusty old cranium into something uncannily humanlike.

The sculpture had moved Weidenreich. He was a Jewish refugee from Nazi Germany, with family members dying in concentration camps, and his faith in humankind had been sinking. But the portrait in clay must have soothed him, made him appreciate the deep kinship that all humans share. He'd named the sculpture Nellie.

But why were his Chinese colleagues asking about its location? The message baffled him.

Until, horribly, he understood. Before being run out of China, Weidenreich had tried to smuggle the Peking Man bones to New York to save them from destruction. He'd failed, and he assumed his colleagues back in China had taken measures to protect them. But apparently not. In asking where "Nellie" was, they were really asking where the bones were. Weidenreich sank down in his chair. If they didn't have the bones in China, and he didn't have them in New York, where on earth were they?

It's a question the world is still asking. The Peking Man bones were arguably the greatest cache of prehuman fossils ever discovered—as close as we've ever come to finding the fabled "missing link." Then they vanished. Scientists have spent eight decades scouring the globe for them, watching in despair as lead after lead evaporated. And only recently has the first legitimate clue turned up, a hint that could maybe—maybe—resolve one of the greatest mysteries in the annals of science. Where is Nellie?

There's an old joke about the Holy Roman Empire: that it was neither holy nor Roman nor an empire. Peking Man's name is a bit like that.

Peking is an outdated name for Beijing. And Peking *Man* was actually a collection of bones from at least 40 different men, women, and children. For historical continuity, I'll refer to them as "Peking Man" here, but the fossils represented a lot more than one adult male.

Peking Man belonged to a species called *Homo erectus,** the first hominins ever who were basically our size and our shape—the first ones you could squint at in the distance and wonder, Is that one of us? *Erectus* represents an inflection point in our lineage—a period of transition from shaggy ape-man to proto-human—and Peking Man in particular sheds light on several facets of that transformation. As anthropologists Noel Boaz and Russell Ciochon put it, Peking Man was "the starting point for many of the major paleoanthropological debates over the past 75 years ... [on] the use of fire, the beginnings of human language, the evolution of the brain, hunting, cannibalism, stone and bone tool use, and ancient human diet." All in all, they were strikingly modern.

At least we think so. More than any other field, the study of human ancestry depends on comparing old specimens with newly discovered ones. If only we had Peking Man's bones, we could analyze them in vastly more detail, using technologies not even dreamed of during their discovery. But about all that remains of Peking Man today are some plaster casts and a few molars. Boaz and Ciochon call this disappearance "the single greatest loss of original data in the history of paleoanthropology."

The story of this loss begins the winter after World War I. A young engineering student named Otto Zdansky—a balding, bespectacled fellow with a full brown beard—was shivering in his apartment in

---

* Specifically, Peking Man belonged to the subspecies *Homo erectus pekinensis.* The relationship between *pekinensis* and modern humans isn't clear, but *Homo erectus* generally was our ancestor.

Vienna, unable to heat it due to lingering wartime fuel shortages. Thievery was rampant in town as well. One day on campus, he heard about a program to study paleontology at a university in Sweden. Anything seemed better than staying in Vienna, so Zdansky signed up and shipped out. He was bombing his engineering tests anyway.

Zdansky thrived in his new field and published a thesis on fossil turtles. His adviser then encouraged him to join an expedition to hunt for fossils in China, including ancient humans. At the time, there was a roaring debate about where human beings had originated: Africa or Asia? Charles Darwin favored Africa, but most paleontologists politely ignored him and focused on Asia as the cradle of humankind—the "paleontological garden of Eden." The Asia theory had gained significant support a few decades earlier when a scientist on an island in Southeast Asia uncovered a few scattered hominin bones, the famous Java Man. The hunt was on for more.

Zdansky's job offer was not exactly generous. He would receive train fare and room and board, along with a salary of zero dollars and zero cents. But, lacking other options, Zdansky agreed, and boarded a ship that spent six weeks chugging to Asia. He arrived in Beijing in 1921.

Beijing back then was not the busy metropolis of today. Buildings were low and squat, and caravans of two-humped camels sometimes wandered the streets. Upon arriving, Zdansky sought out the fossil expedition's leader, geologist Johan Gunnar Andersson. Andersson showed Zdansky the site they planned to excavate: a lumpy outcrop 30 miles southeast of Beijing named Chicken Bone Hill, after some fossils there.

The site seemed promising. Rudely, however, the team set up their tents and cots in a nearby temple, preventing the locals from worshipping. Eventually, a local farmer schemed up a way to root the "foreign devils" out. He approached them and said, "There's no use staying here.

I know a place you can collect much bigger and larger dragon bones."

In saying this, the farmer wasn't pulling anyone's leg. In the West, dragons have a reputation as sinister fire-breathers who hoard gold. But in Chinese lore, dragons are guardians of humankind, benefactors who bestow blessings: Their dried blood formed rubies, and their saliva made rich perfume. Chinese peasants also believed that fossils were ancient dragon bones, and often ground them into powders for medicinal teas and elixirs; they allegedly cured everything from paralysis and liver disease to insomnia and impotence. So in promising the scientists a site rich with "dragon bones," the farmer was being generous. The site was in fact called Longhushan—Dragon Bone Hill—and the farmer personally escorted Zdansky and Andersson there.

As soon as they laid eyes on Longhushan, the scientists were smitten. The site was an old limestone quarry, and as they gazed down into a fissure, they saw fossils sticking right out of the walls. It was a bonanza. Andersson and Zdansky quickly transferred all their gear to the site and, to the farmer's satisfaction, left the temple alone.

Longhushan abounded with fossils for a few reasons. In ancient times, the hill offered caves for shelter and was close to clean streams, making it an attractive home. The occupants of those caves seemingly included packs of hyenas the size of modern lions, who often dragged back game to gnaw on—including hominins. Finally, the cool temperatures of caves help preserve bones, and cave-ins bury the material, a necessary step for fossilization.

Andersson left most of the grunt work to Zdansky that summer. The site's bare cliffs often grew scorching hot in the sun, but Zdansky patiently endured the sweat-drenched afternoons and frequent sunburns as he chipped away at the limestone, gluing together bone fragments and packing the delicate pieces in plaster to ship to Sweden. He unearthed bits of rhinoceros, giraffe, bear, beaver, buffalo, and saber-toothed tiger. He also found a hominin tooth, an upper right molar that looked like a shriveled date with an ivory cap on top. It was the first hint of Peking Man, the first glimpse of a potential progenitor of humankind in Asia.

By all rights, Zdansky should have run to Andersson and alerted him. But he and Andersson had been quarreling lately, and he feared that Andersson would commandeer the tooth and publish something on it himself, instead of allowing Zdansky to. So Zdansky slipped the tooth into his pocket and told no one.

Two summers later, Zdansky uncovered a second tooth, which he also kept to himself. But any plans to quickly write something up were derailed on his way back to Sweden in 1923 when, mysteriously, someone crept into his car on the Trans-Siberian Railway and stole all his field notes.

Zdansky finally wrote up his analysis of the teeth in 1926. The results were announced at an academic conference on Dragon Bone Hill at the lush, marble-fronted Swedish Embassy in Beijing. The news blindsided Andersson and electrified the other attendees. Had they found the missing link at last?*

Sitting in the audience that day, completely smitten, was a 42-year-old Canadian anatomist named Davidson Black. With Zdansky and Andersson on the outs—Zdansky would move to Cairo to pursue other work—Black eagerly assumed responsibility for examining fossils from Longhushan.

Black was a tall man with owlish glasses who sometimes worked in a formal white lab coat—a stiff affectation that belied his warmth

* At the time, scientists had uncovered Neanderthal fossils in Europe, but those bones seemed too humanlike to be a true missing link. Java Man seemed closer, but there were too few bones to be sure; the Java site also lacked evidence of tools and fire.

and boyish enthusiasm. He taught anatomy at Peking Union Medical College in Beijing, an institute funded by the Rockefeller Foundation. The school trained Chinese doctors in Western medicine, although Black had to learn to adjust to local ways of doing things. Upon arriving in 1919, Black asked city officials to find cadavers for his anatomy labs. Eager to help, the police chief had several criminals beheaded and trundled the bodies over. As diplomatically as possible, Black explained that decapitated corpses were less than ideal for medical studies, and that he hoped that different arrangements could be made in the future. The police chief said he understood completely. Days later, a group of shackled men showed up at Black's office. One carried a note from the police chief: "Kill them any way you'd like." After that, Black reached out to the local morgue.

Although he proved a dedicated teacher, anatomy was merely a fig leaf for Black's all-consuming obsession with ancient humans. Unfortunately, his boss at Peking Union, physician Henry Houghton, thought that digging bones out of caves was indulgent nonsense; they were in China to teach medicine and save lives, not dig in the dirt for long-dead half-humans.

This hostility forced Black to limit his paleontology to nights and holidays; he often stayed up all night working, despite the toll on his health. Even then, historians speculate that Houghton was scheming to fire Black for his extracurricular paleontology. Eventually, Black ran a bureaucratic end around, convincing the Rockefeller Foundation to fund a separate paleontology lab within the medical college, with Black as its head. This bought him some security, but didn't ease the demands on his time. Worse, Houghton seemingly took the lab's presence as an insult and never forgave it.

Given the delicate situation at Peking Union, Black couldn't dig full-time at Dragon Bone Hill. Instead, Chinese scientists began to play prominent roles, especially Wenzhong Pei, an archaeologist with bushy hair, a Clark Gable mustache, and a bucktooth grin. Over the next few years, Pei and his crew unearthed scads of animal fossils, as well as crafted stone flakes and burned bones—exciting signs of tool and fire use. They sensed they were close to something big, especially after parts of two hominin jawbones turned up.

The breakthrough came in December 1929, during a cold snap that froze the water in the camp's washing pails and made working outside almost intolerable. Diggers had recently unearthed two new caves. Pei's crew lowered him into one on a rope, but he found little inside except hyena vertebrae. He crawled into the other on his hands and knees. It looked more promising, so he asked for a candle and began nibbling away at a rock wall inside with a pick. Around 4 p.m. on December 2, a bit of sandstone crumbled off, and his heart began pounding. Staring back at him was the unmistakably smooth dome of a skull.

But a skull of what? Despite his excitement, Pei made himself work slowly to avoid damaging anything, removing just pebbles with each pick stroke. He could scarcely breathe. But as the skull emerged, he saw no antlers, no snout, no strange crests or ridges. At last, he let himself smile. He'd found it: the first nearly complete skull of a human ancestor.

It differed from a modern human cranium in some ways. We *Homo sapiens* have thin-crust skulls, while Peking Man's species—*Homo erectus*—has a deep-dish noggin, thick and durable. (Scientists have occasionally mistaken bits of erectus skulls for turtle shells during digs.)

We don't know why Peking Man had such chunky skulls—perhaps to defend against violent blows during prehistoric melees. Human craniums might also have thinned over time to help radiate heat from our hot-rodding brains. Regardless, the similarities between our skulls and Pei's skull far outweighed the differences. This was, recognizably, a near-human. In an instant, the oldest-known branch of our ancestral line had jumped back half a million years.

Despite his exhaustion from a long, cold day of digging, Pei lit more candles and worked through the night to extract the skull from the rock matrix. He then coated it in protective layers of plaster, cotton, and burlap soaked in flour paste. As a final touch, he wrapped everything in an old blanket and bound it with rope to resemble the bindles that peasants in the region often carried: an effort to camouflage the fossil. There were police checkpoints on the road to Beijing, and he feared that some nosy cop would seize the skull. Even to reach his bus north, Pei had to strip off his clothes and ford a river with the bundle, holding it over his head to keep it dry.

On the bus, Pei vowed he'd be arrested before he let anyone crack the plaster open and risk damaging the skull. As it was, the lazy checkpoint patrols barely glanced at him, and he bounded up the steps to Black's office a few hours later. Black all but hyperventilated with joy, then stayed up all night himself removing the plaster and cleaning the skull with a dental pick until it grinned back at him.

The next season, Pei rigged up a digging machine with cables and pulleys to excavate faster. Over the next few years, dozens more hominin bones emerged, including 13 skulls. Meanwhile, Black put together a speaking tour to promote Peking Man. It was characteristically grueling, dragging him to the Middle East, India, Europe, and North America. For a little flair, he wore a Peking Man tooth in a brass capsule around his neck and showed it off.

The tour proved wildly successful, earning Black standing ovations at nearly every venue and stirring intense interest among the public. Most people were awed to think we'd perhaps unearthed our biological Adams and Eves. But the news alarmed others, especially in the United

States. The Scopes Monkey Trial of 1925—when a biology teacher in Tennessee was hauled into court for defying a ban on teaching evolution—had roiled the American public, provoking nasty debates over the "dangerous" idea that human beings evolved from an apelike ancestor. Many people at the time had longed for science to resolve the dispute with fossil evidence—and now, Peking Man seemingly had. Over the next few years, people for and against evolution followed the news about Peking Man as avidly as others followed *Tarzan* serials at the cinema.

In late 1933, Davidson Black returned to China, exhausted from his tour. His colleagues at the medical school warned him to slow down, but he paid them no mind. He should have. One night in March 1934, he collapsed near his desk—dead at age 49 of a heart attack. He was wearing his white lab coat when they found him.

After Black's death, Franz Weidenreich, the refugee from Nazi Germany who would commission the "Nellie" sculpture, took over the Dragon Bone Hill site. Although people remember him brooding constantly over his daughters and mother-in-law in the concentration camps back home, Weidenreich proved a capable administrator, and new fossils kept turning up. By 1937, Pei's crews had excavated a volume of dirt equivalent to a building 12 stories tall, and a comprehensive picture of the Peking Men, Women, and Children was taking shape.

The average Peking male stood five foot one, the average female four foot nine. All had thick necks, broad shoulders, and arms that dangled to nearly their knees, a relic of their tree-swinging past. Facially, the Pekings lacked chins and had flat noses, high cheekbones, and low, brooding brows. Their brains were almost double the size of the brains of the preceding genus in the fossil record, and roughly three-quarters the size of ours today. Most scientists believe they lacked the anatomy to speak, although some hold that rudimentary speech emerged during puberty. They made stone chisels and hammers and seemingly wielded fire—to keep warm, drive off hyenas, or cook meat. They lived in the Dragon Bone Hill caves off and on between roughly 780,000 and 410,000 years ago.

Perhaps the most important aspect of the Peking bones was the sheer number of them. Many big discoveries in paleoanthropology consist of a single, incomplete skeleton: an iffy basis for drawing conclusions. To see why, imagine that some archaeologist a million years from now finds a single *Homo sapiens*. Now imagine it's Shaquille O'Neal or Tom Thumb. Either one would give archaeologists a skewed view of humankind and bias their results. (In fact, if they found both men, they'd likely classify them as different species.)

In contrast, the Peking fossils consist of some 40 men, women, and children. We can therefore be confident we have a representative sample—and a sample from a crucial era in hominin history, when modern behaviors were emerging. All in all, the Peking Humans rank right up there with Lucy and Ardi as the most important fossils ever discovered. Which makes their disappearance all the more crushing.

Understanding why the Peking fossils vanished requires a bit of background about the power struggles in China at the time. The regime of the feckless Puyi—the "last emperor" of Hollywood fame—was crumbling, and in 1927, a civil war broke out between communists led by Mao Zedong and nationalists led by Chiang Kai-shek. Given Dragon Bone Hill's proximity to Beijing, diggers there regularly heard gunfire and booming artillery, and winced to see soldiers trudging past. Boxes of fossils were regularly seized and searched for smuggled weapons.

To add to the chaos, imperial Japan invaded China in 1937, conquering the nation and committing some of the ghastliest atrocities of the 20th century. Ten million Chinese citizens would eventually die under Japanese rule, on par with the number of lives the Holocaust claimed. That summer, Wenzhong Pei's crews finally abandoned work at Dragon Bone Hill; it was simply too dangerous there. Sadly, three workers who stayed behind to protect the site were seized, tortured, and bayoneted.

As it happened, the ruling Japanese army in China did not interfere with foreign institutions, including Peking Union Medical College. But the paleontologists there hardly felt secure. Peking Man had achieved worldwide fame, and word got around that Japanese officials had seized several Chinese diggers to interrogate them about the fossils. Franz Weidenreich suspected that the Japanese had plans to confiscate the bones—partly for their scientific value, but mostly to humiliate the Chinese people by seizing a cultural treasure. According to some sources, Emperor Hirohito himself encouraged the theft.

Weidenreich took to storing the Peking bones inside a safe; he also made plaster casts of them and took detailed notes. By January 1941, he'd done all he could, and with violence in China on the upswing, he decided to flee to New York—his second international hegira in seven years. He felt confident he could smuggle some casts out. But what about the actual bones?

Weidenreich considered hiding them in his luggage. Ultimately, though, he feared that customs officials would confiscate them. So he rang up the American embassy in Beijing and asked the ambassador to smuggle them out in his diplomatic baggage, which could not be searched. The ambassador refused. He feared the bones would be damaged, and perhaps felt queasy about commandeering Chinese artifacts; it would reek of colonialism.

That left Weidenreich with one option: transferring the bones to a U.S. Marine base along the coast for military transport. This wasn't Weidenreich's top choice. American marines in China had a bad reputation as drug-addled knuckleheads who were shockingly easy to bribe and had the highest rates of venereal disease in the entire U.S. military. But better to gamble with them than let Hirohito's minions seize the fossils. Weidenreich had to leave for New York in August before he could resolve the matter, but begged Peking Union Medical College to reach out to the marines and safeguard the bones as the common heritage of humankind.

Unfortunately, the responsibility to arrange all this fell to the head of Peking Union, Dr. Henry Houghton. Houghton still considered the bones worthless, and as some historians have noted, he should have been overjoyed to rid himself of them. But he apparently still resented the presence of a dirty fossil lab in his pristine medical school. So, pettily, he did nothing, echoing the U.S. ambassador's fears about the bones being confiscated at customs, and adding that he couldn't possibly appropriate Chinese cultural treasures. Even when one of Wenzhong Pei's colleagues begged Houghton to help—personally assuring him that the Chinese government would allow the bones' removal as an emergency measure, to keep them from the Japanese—Houghton refused to help. In private, he considered the bones useless, if not contemptible, and couldn't fathom why anyone would steal them.

By this point, Japanese anthropologists were poking around the Peking Union lab, and the Japanese army had stationed guards outside the college to keep an eye on workers. Pei and the remaining staff endured several tense months on the job, during which one enterprising technician named Lanpo Jia meticulously copied all his field notes onto toilet paper, page after page, and snuck the sheets past the guards each night. Pei's crew finally wrapped the bones in gauze, cotton, and tissue paper, and packed them inside two wooden crates or footlockers, labeled only "A" and "B," just in case a chance to move them arose.

It finally did. Facing pressure from both the U.S. ambassador and the president of the Rockefeller Foundation, Houghton sighed and finally reached out to the U.S. Marines in fall 1941. Even then, he acted with no haste; arrangements took weeks. But at last, in November, he secured permission to ship the bones out.

At this point, the story gets murky, even contradictory. After late November 1941, there are no firm, unambiguous accounts of the Peking bones' whereabouts.

The most common report holds that the paleontology staff loaded the footlockers into wheelbarrows one night and dashed them out to a waiting car. After a long, rattling train ride, they arrived at a marine base called Camp Holcomb near the Manchurian border in early December. The plan was to evacuate them the following Monday on the S.S. *President Harrison,* a ship chugging up from Manila to grab some U.S. troops.

Unfortunately, that Monday happened to be December 8—the day after Pearl Harbor. As the *President Harrison* approached China, Japanese ships attacked it, so the captain purposely ran aground to prevent its seizure. That left the troops at Camp Holcomb stranded—along with the Peking Men, Women, and Children.

With the United States and Japan now at war, the Japanese army had no more reason to respect the rights of American institutions in China. Within hours, several Japanese scientists, flanked by armed guards, stormed into the lab at Peking Union and arrested several officials, including Houghton. Pei was also arrested and locked up for 50 days, during which time he was grilled about the fossils' location and accused of being an American spy. Accounts differ on the timing, but at some point the Japanese learned about the safe and broke it open. They were enraged to find only plaster casts inside. But their interrogations and raids profited them nothing. No one had any idea—or at least wouldn't admit to knowing—where the fossils were.

Given that dearth of knowledge, rumors multiplied like mad. One held that Japanese troops had intercepted the train en route to Camp Holcomb, searched the baggage onboard, and dumped the fossils as junk. Other people speculated that the troops had confiscated the remains and sold them on the black market, perhaps as "dragon bones" for locals to grind down into medicine—in which case the Peking Man fossils would have ended their time on earth in some poor old man or woman's teapot, an elixir to ease their own aching bones. Other rumors held that the footlockers reached the marine base safely and were buried, or else fell into enemy hands after Japanese soldiers ransacked the base. Still other people swore the marine story was a diversionary tactic, a ruse, and that the bones were buried behind the U.S. embassy in Beijing. Or secreted away in a Swiss warehouse or French medical institute. Or smuggled out on a Russian ship to Yalta. Or rescued by Chinese nationalist forces and taken to Taiwan. Everyone had a theory.

Amid all this, Chinese anthropologists from Peking Union managed to get a postcard to Franz Weidenreich in New York, hoping against hope that the fossils had somehow reached him. He read their message—"Where is Nellie?"—with alarm. He'd assumed, naively, that Pei and others had safely secured the bones *somewhere.* He scrambled to find out what he could, but came up empty: China was a black hole of information during World War II, with virtually no messages going in or out.

At last, the war ended, and some communication with China resumed. But to Weidenreich's dismay, the window soon slammed shut again. The Japanese invasion in 1937 hadn't resolved the civil war between the nationalists and communists there. It simply interrupted it, and fighting resumed in 1945, even more ferocious than before. Amid the turmoil, the fate of some old bones was a low priority.

By the time the communists won the civil war in 1949, memories of what might have happened to Peking Man were growing dim. Over the following years, scientists concerned about the fate of the fossils dutifully followed up on every lead, but nothing ever came of them. A decade of futility slipped past, then another.

As the search grew more desperate, weirdos and grifters popped up to exploit the situation. Ransom demands arrived: one for $500,000 from a woman who claimed her husband had smuggled the bones out of Asia, and a second for a cool million from an expat Chinese businessman. A Chicago financier was indicted on 37 counts of fraud for raising $640,000 to search for Peking Man, then paying off personal debts and traveling instead. One scientist fielded a call from a woman who used dowsing rods to hunt for Sasquatch in Maine; she apparently figured some caveman bones couldn't be much different. Eventually both the FBI and CIA got involved, and Henry Kissinger's entourage asked about Peking Man during his diplomatic trip to China in 1972. All to no avail. Poignantly, some of those involved wondered whether it would have been best to let the Japanese seize the bones in 1941. At least they would have been well cared for, instead of missing for good.

True, a few teeth from Peking Man survived in Sweden. And in 1951, two splinters of hominin leg bones, originally misclassified, turned up in Peking Union's general fossil collection. We also have the plaster casts of the skulls and other bones. But studying those is like studying the xerox of a painting; however faithful, plaster can't capture all the details. And not to get too metaphysical, but those plaster dummies never appeared inside our ancestors. They aren't the *Ding an sich,* the thing in itself.

Scientists can only fantasize about what we might learn from the originals. Microscopic analysis of some of the plaster skulls has revealed subtle cut marks from tools, and part of a fossil skullcap that turned up at Longhushan in 1966 shows similar marks.* A few researchers interpret those cuts as signs of cannibalism among Peking Man: people hacking at the faces of dead compatriots to strip the jowl muscles, and possibly get at their brains. But it seems risky to make such dramatic accusations based largely on plaster copies; we'd need the originals to be sure.

More speculatively, Peking Man might reshuffle the family tree of humankind. Contrary to what most scientists believed in the early 1900s, we now know that modern human beings evolved in Africa. But there is an important caveat. As we radiated outward from Africa long ago, DNA evidence indicates that we met and mated with at least two other prehistoric species, the Neanderthals in the Middle East and Europe and a group called the Denisovans in greater Asia.

But did this happen only twice? Exciting new skull fossils have turned up in China over the past few decades, fossils that date from the era after Peking Man. They seem to blend Peking features with modern human features—a clue that perhaps we interbred with the descendants of Peking Man, too. Or perhaps the elusive Denisovans—today known almost exclusively through DNA sequencing—are somehow related to the Peking People. If so, we might need to update the standard out-of-Africa narrative, since at least some human ancestors would have come from Asia, just as many anthropologists once believed. Plaster casts can certainly help explore this idea, but

* Digging at Dragon Bone Hill resumed after the Chinese Civil War. You might be wondering whether other Peking Man fossils remain buried, awaiting discovery. Probably not. While six teeth were excavated in the 1950s, plus a jawbone and that bit of skullcap, nothing close to the original bounty emerged. The site has likely been tapped dry.

it sure would be nice to have the original Longhushan fossils to confirm. Remember, too, that wonderful new analytical tools are being invented all the time, which could reveal even more of our story.

But unless we find Peking Man, we'll never know what we don't know—which, in many ways, is the most painful loss of all.

Back in the 1930s, given a lack of other known hominins for comparison, paleoanthropologists tended to emphasize how different Peking Man was from modern humans. Not anymore. In light of other ancient skeletons (Lucy, Ardi), what strikes us most about the Dragon Bone Hill fossils today is how familiar they seem, how much like us. This makes their disappearance even more poignant. For the Chinese people especially, their loss has meant decades of bitterness and pain.

Still, a few scientists—some of whom weren't even born when the bones vanished—never gave up. And in 2010, one of them fielded the first legitimate lead since World War II, when a message popped up in his email.

The message recounted the story of Richard Bowen, a U.S. Marine corporal once stationed at Camp Holcomb in China. Bowen hadn't been there when the Peking fossils potentially first arrived in 1941; he'd served there during the Chinese Civil War, when American GIs were still occupying patches of former Japanese territory. As the last 125 marines left in the area, Bowen's company at Camp Holcomb was fighting rearguard action, and in 1947, they found themselves in a dicey spot.

Their camp sat on the beach; the terrain reminded Bowen of Cape Cod. Nationalist ships occupied a nearby harbor, while communist troops dominated the surrounding hillsides. This left the marines stranded in the middle, with the two sides shooting at each other over the top. Not safe. Before long, the communists began targeting the marines themselves. Camp Holcomb had a canteen that served peanuts and room-temperature beer. The warm brewskis disgusted the marines, so one night a few of the more knuckleheaded ones snuck out to score some ice. The communists seized them and took them prisoner.

Emboldened, a few ragtag communist soldiers marched into Camp Holcomb one afternoon not long after. They announced that a quarter million troops had the area surrounded and that the Americans had best surrender.

Bowen and his marine buddies smirked. A quarter million troops? Sure. They took one look at the messengers' threadbare uniforms and rusty rifles and told them to scram.

The communists withdrew, saving their reply for that night. After dusk, they started lighting campfires as a show of force. Just a few at first. Then more, and more, and more. Soon the entire hillside was ablaze with thousands upon thousands of fires. Richard Bowen said it looked like the world's biggest Christmas tree. It terrified him.

Fearing annihilation, the marines worked like crazy to fortify the camp, digging trenches and pits for machine guns. To guard against a surprise attack, they often dug all night, then collapsed asleep at dawn.

One night, while excavating a foxhole, Bowen's shovel hit something solid. He brushed aside the dirt and, to his bafflement, found a footlocker. After clearing off the lid, he opened it up. Inside were a bunch of bones.

Given that it was the middle of the night, in a hostile land, with a quarter million troops ready to pour down the hillsides into his camp, the last thing Bowen wanted was a blunt memento mori. He had a job to finish anyway, so he reburied the footlocker and shifted over a few feet to dig anew. But the moment always stuck with him. A few days later, a ship arrived to evacuate the marines. Back in

America, Bowen would wonder about the bones every so often. Where had they come from? Why were they there?

Decades later, while watching a television documentary, Bowen heard a passing reference to the lost fossils of Dragon Bone Hill and how they'd allegedly reached Camp Holcomb before his arrival. He'd never heard of Peking Man, and recalled thinking, "Gee whiz." Sometime afterward, he read a book on Peking Man's disappearance, and grew convinced that he really had seen the fossils.

Bowen mentioned all this to his son Paul. The whole thing probably seemed like just another rambling tale from his old man, but just in case there was something in it, Paul emailed a few scientists in China. None responded, so he reached out to a South African archaeologist who worked with human remains.

The South African was staggered. Still, given all the bogus leads over the years, he remained wary, and began investigating Richard Bowen to confirm where he'd been stationed and when he'd served. Surprisingly, everything checked out. Although still perhaps leery of getting his hopes too high, the archaeologist got in touch with two Chinese colleagues and arranged to visit the old Camp Holcomb grounds to see if anything remained to salvage.

A few months later, they arrived at a city near the camp. They hunted up an elderly local man to serve as a guide. He actually remembered the marines from his youth; he said they treated him well. And yes, he knew right where the spot was. He could take the archaeologists there.

You can imagine the tension as the trio approached the site, their faces pressed against the windows of the car. Had the 70-year-old mystery of Peking Man finally been solved?

Alas. The three scientists arrived at the old Camp Holcomb—and found a bunch of warehouses. The area had been industrialized in the

1970s and paved over. There was nothing they could do but stare, and try to fend off dark thoughts about the fossils being pulverized by a bulldozer and scattered amid the soil. If so, as one historian noted, Peking Man had been "reclaimed by the dragon, the traditional protector of the Chinese earth and its treasures."

But there is a glimmer of hope here. The industrial park on the old Camp Holcomb grounds is slated for updating soon, and the Chinese government is keenly aware of the possibility of recovering the fossils. The moment they break ground, every worker on site will have their eyes peeled for shards of an old footlocker and bits of jawbone and skull. Perhaps we can snatch the Peking Men, Women, and Children back from the clutches of the dragon yet.

That said, recovering anything remains a long shot. Richard Bowen was not a scientist, and might have mistaken animal bones for hominin ones in the dark. Or maybe it was just a hasty grave for soldiers from World War II. Regardless, the fossils could easily have been crushed during the warehouse excavation. In which case, from dust they came, and unto dust they have returned.

But maybe Bowen was right. And maybe the world got lucky and the bones ended up beneath a parking lot or road that covered and sheltered them, keeping them intact. If so, these invaluable fossils—and the solution to one of the greatest mysteries in science—may lie no deeper down than a Chicago pothole.

In reflecting on this story, I can't help but think of Philippa Langley, and how she discovered the bones of Richard III beneath another parking lot. I have no idea what the Chinese equivalent of the *R* for Richard would be. But if anyone in China ever sees a portentous glyph scrawled on some asphalt near the old Camp Holcomb and feels a shiver run down their spine, I pray they prove as dogged as Langley, and bring those long-lost men, women, and children to light.

CHAPTER SIX

LOST CIVILIZATIONS

Rakhaldas Banerji surveyed the archaeological ruins before him with glee. He was already imagining how to announce this discovery to the world—and how best to humiliate his rival in the process.

It was a rare moment of joy for Banerji that season, the winter of 1922–23. He was excavating in what's now rural Pakistan (then part of British India), and his diabetes had been flaring up painfully for weeks, including eruptions of pus-filled sores. And while he was managing a productive dig, he was being transferred away from the region soon in disgrace.

At age 37, Banerji bore an uncanny resemblance to Hercule Poirot: plump and mustached, dandyish in dress and haughty in manner. Even admiring biographers admit he was pouty and spoiled, and spent ruinous amounts of money on art, high teas, and lavish meals. That pampered lifestyle proved a poor preparation for the rugged life of an archaeological dig—in this case, at a lumpy hill called Mohenjo-daro, "mound of the dead." Instead of sumptuous dinners, Banerji gnawed on roasted camel meat, and his feeble tent couldn't block the whipping wind. But even after shivering nights of no sleep, even after pustules broke out all over his body, he refused to abandon the work.

He'd come to the region seeking one of the great lost treasures of antiquity. In 326 B.C., Alexander the Great crossed the Indus River northeast of Mohenjo-daro. Despite having established the greatest empire in history to date, Alexander was still gobbling up new land. But on the march eastward, his weary soldiers mutinied and forced him to turn for home. Still, to commemorate their adventures, his men reportedly erected several 75-foot-tall altars, one for each of the dozen gods in the Greek pantheon. After making the proper sacrifices and holding some horse races, the soldiers withdrew. Banerji wanted to find the ruins of the altars—a discovery he hoped would make him famous.

Frustratingly, he wasted several years in a fruitless search. But in the course of his travels, something else turned up. He got disoriented one day while riding through a dense forest along an old riverbed. Thickets and thorny bushes confronted him on all sides, and it took hours to extricate himself. When at last he did, he entered a clearing at the foot of a high, overgrown mound. Banerji hopped off his horse to rest. And upon landing, he stepped on something odd—a flint blade, clearly ancient. Had it been randomly discarded here? Or was it somehow connected with the mound?

He filed the incident away in his mind until late 1922, when he happened to pass near Mohenjo-daro and decided to take a closer look. The mound was surrounded by a thousand acres of rolling hills, sand dunes, and prickly scrub brush. A decade earlier, a short excavation had taken place there under the supervision of a nepotism brat named D. R. Bhandarkar (his father was a powerful Indian archaeologist). Bhandarkar had snatched up a coveted professorship that Banerji thought he deserved more, and Banerji had loathed Bhandarkar ever since.

During his excavation, Bhandarkar had poked around and declared that Mohenjo-daro was of no interest—perhaps 200 years old. But Banerji recalled that flint blade near the other mound and suspected otherwise. So he pitched some tents and hired local diggers to investigate.

Sure enough, a few feet down, his crew uncovered an old stupa (a Buddhist meditation chapel), along with a grand pillared hall, a courtyard 70 feet long, and fresco paintings. Crucially, he found no Muslim coins there, meaning the site had to predate the Islamic takeover of the area circa A.D. 700. Even more encouraging, they found a layer of ash beneath the stupa—and beneath that, an entire buried city. There were pavements, walls, shrines, and artifacts, including gambling dice, burial urns with cremated remains, and flint scrapers.

Far from being 200 years old, the site was ancient—perhaps dating to the days of Alexander. Banerji was thrilled. He couldn't wait to humiliate Bhandarkar for missing all this. It made his aching joints and weeping sores worth it.

Then, one cold afternoon, Banerji's team found something

even more wondrous. We don't know the circumstances of the discovery—whether a digger rushed up to Banerji in excitement, clutching the tiny treasures, or whether he merely hollered and forced the ailing archaeologist to hobble down into the pit himself, step by aching step.

But at some point during the excavation of a staircase and nearby drain, a digger found two soapstone seals: small, carved stamps. To prevent tampering, merchants and tax officials in ancient times used such stamps to "sign" clay tablets and to mark the dabs of clay that sealed up jars of trade goods. That fateful day at Mohenjo-daro, Banerji's crew found two seals, one broken, one whole. Both portrayed an animal that Banerji called a bull, but that's now known as a "unicorn"—a hoofed, four-legged beast with a graceful scimitar horn.

But it wasn't the mythological creature that stunned Banerji. It was the writing on the seals—a half dozen letters. He had no idea what language this was. Yet it tickled a memory in his mind. Years earlier, during the excavation of another site in British India called Harappa, eerily similar seals had turned up—seals also adorned with animals and mysterious writing. Which didn't make sense to Banerji. Harappa lay 400 miles away, a journey of a month or more in ancient times. The seals and the writing nevertheless implied that the two sites shared a common language and customs—perhaps even belonged to the same empire.

But which empire? Oddly, for a country as culturally rich as India, its history before about 300 B.C. was a blank. Only a few rude artifacts and graves had turned up, and as far as anyone knew, the subcontinent had no empires in ancient times, no unifying culture.

Here, however, was proof otherwise. Tracing the tiny unicorn with his fingers, Banerji must have felt his heartbeat quicken. Forget

Alexander's altars. Banerji had no idea how old Mohenjo-daro or Harappa were. But he was certain of one thing: that he was standing amid the ruins of a lost civilization.

Archaeology under British rule in India was a disgrace—little better than organized looting. In 1900, the governor-general of India decried this archaeological banditry, ruing that "a century of British vandalism and crime" was destroying India's heritage.

Things started to change in 1902, when a new director of Indian archaeology arrived, 26-year-old John Marshall. Unpromisingly, Marshall had never set foot in Asia (he cut his teeth excavating in Crete), and the man was almost pathologically meticulous. His housekeepers in India learned to dread his intricate instructions whenever he traveled—on how to tend his vegetables, how to store his curtains properly with mothballs, how to place the legs of his furniture in pots of kerosene to keep ants from devouring the wood, and more. But attention to detail makes for a good archaeologist, and he instilled a sorely needed professionalism among his subordinates in India.

Marshall also won support for archaeology among everyday Indians by shoring up dilapidated shrines and driving out pests such as bats, insects, and British colonial officials, who often commandeered local monuments for office buildings or barracks. Equally important, Marshall insisted on hiring Indians for excavations, including as lead archaeologists. One hire, in 1911, was an ambitious dandy with a background in coins and inscriptions: Rakhaldas Banerji, who became one of Marshall's assistants.

They did not get along. Marshall recognized Banerji's talent, but Banerji's reckless conduct in the field would soon fray Marshall's patience.

This behavior was a by-product of Banerji's childhood. He was born in 1885 to a wealthy father whose Brahmin ancestors had owned estates on a feudal scale. Banerji's seven brothers and sisters all died in childhood, and as the sole survivor of well-to-do parents, Banerji was spoiled to no end—especially since he seemed unlikely to live long himself, due to his chronic diabetes. He developed a taste for luxury while young, and would throw temper tantrums in which he tore paper money to shreds, heedless of its value. He married at 15 and had two sons, adding to his already substantial expenses. But even after his parents died in 1903 and the family fortune began draining away (possibly due to lawsuits against their estate), he refused to curb his spending even slightly. In an era when a single rupee could buy 80 pounds of rice and feed a family for weeks, Banerji would tip porters at railways stations 10 rupees just for carrying his bags. (One biographer called him "a man of corpulent figure with a matching heart.") Out at remote dig sites, most archaeologists had mail delivered by messengers on foot or bicycles. Not Banerji. He insisted that a horse-drawn carriage bring his letters. Less charmingly, during visits to temples and small museums, he would snatch whatever statues and relics caught his eye and ship them to a museum he had ties with in Calcutta (modern Kolkata).

In all, gobs of government money disappeared from Banerji's department with no record of how he'd spent it (sometimes on office furniture). It's a testimony to his genius, and Marshall's patience, that Banerji nevertheless earned steady promotions and rose to become head of archaeology in India's western district in 1917.

At the time, Marshall's top priority was excavating the ruined city of Harappa, where a handful of soapstone seals from ancient merchants had turned up. Most were squares one to two inches long, and they featured pictures of animals along with enigmatic writing. Marshall wanted to hunt for more, but funding shortfalls and labor shortages due to World War I delayed things. Finally, in 1921, Marshall sent a top assistant to Harappa to dig, archaeologist Daya Ram Sahni.

In contrast to his grumbling complaints about Banerji, Marshall praised Sahni to the skies for his intelligence and professionalism. (Perhaps with Banerji in mind, Marshall once noted that Sahni's "modesty is a particularly pleasing feature.") Sahni had a soldier's upright bearing, with thick eyebrows and a mole on his right cheek. He arrived at Harappa to find several rolling mounds on a bleak, treeless plain. Over 35 days, Sahni's crew excavated three trenches on two of the mounds, the largest of which was 12 feet deep, 16 feet wide, and 500 feet long. In it, they uncovered loads of artifacts—pottery, figurines, stone bangles, and a host of toys, including rattles, miniature carts with wheels, and clay dolls of birds, lions, dogs, and bulls. They also found two soapstone seals.

All of which left Sahni yawning. He yearned to find buildings and metal tools, coins and brilliant art—not toy birds. The Harappa site seemed boring, provincial, and he refused to return in 1922, preferring to switch locations. Marshall gave his blessing.

Meanwhile, Marshall continued to clash with Banerji, who'd finally worn out his welcome with one too many tantrums and financial lapses. Realizing he'd disgraced himself, Banerji requested a transfer from India's western district to Calcutta in 1922—an effective self-banishment. Marshall approved the measure.

But the transfer would take time to go through, and after striking out on his search for Alexander the Great's altars, Banerji decided to dig at Mohenjo-daro that winter—a last hurrah out west. And to his credit, despite his lordly appetites and creaky health, Banerji sucked it up, bolting down camel meat in the cold and watching sores erupt all over his body but refusing to interrupt his work.

All of which paid off when the unicorn seals turned up. Based on the presence of stone scrapers at Mohenjo-daro, Banerji suspected that the buried city was quite ancient—perhaps the oldest ruins in India. The discovery of Harappan-style seals then clued him in to something bigger still: that despite the hundreds of miles separating the cities, they shared a common culture, a culture that had vanished from history.

It's interesting to ponder why Banerji grasped this truth so quickly at Mohenjo-daro, while Sahni abandoned Harappa as worthless after five weeks. To be sure, having dug a year earlier, Sahni couldn't have known about the spatial reach of the lost civilization. But he saw scores of similar artifacts, including the seals with the proto-writing, and he had seen them first. So why didn't they register as significant?

Possibly because, for all his excellent qualities, Sahni lacked Banerji's imagination. Between archaeological digs, Banerji penned novels about ancient India, historical romances in the vein of Sir Walter Scott that brimmed with sorcery, prophecy, and chivalrous deeds. In short, Banerji spent his free time inventing new worlds, and upon seeing the Mohenjo-daro artifacts, his fertile mind conjured a whole civilization. A lively imagination isn't always an asset in historical scholarship: 99 times out of 100, it's best to hew to facts. But every so often, you need to take a leap. While Sahni shrugged at the trinkets in Harappa, Banerji's heart soared with the hope that he'd found something magical. And he had. We now call Banerji's lost society the Indus Valley (or Harappan) Civilization.

For his part, Marshall laid aside his vexation with Banerji and threw his support behind his assistant's discovery—especially after another archaeologist, Madho Sarup Vats, carefully compared artifacts from Harappa and Mohenjo-daro and highlighted the similarities between the pots, tools, bangles, and clay figurines at the two sites. Vats clinched the case by pointing out that both cities built walls from sun-dried mud bricks of the exact same dimensions: 11 inches by 5½ inches by 2¾ inches, a perfect 4:2:1 ratio.

Excited by these revelations, Sahni retracted his disdain and returned to Harappa to dig in late 1923. Marshall also expanded the excavation at Mohenjo-daro—the largest Indus city at one square mile—by hiring more than a thousand diggers and approving plans to build dormitories for them, so they wouldn't have to huddle in tents all winter. Over the next few years, as they churned through mountains of dirt, a comprehensive picture of the Indus Valley Civilization emerged.

As archaeologists now know, the IVC stirred to life 8,000 years ago, and culminated in a glorious "mature period" between 2600 and 1900 B.C. It was the largest urban civilization of its day, with a million people living in 1,500 settlements spread over a region double the size of Montana. The world's first-known plowed fields appeared there, and the people ate marvelously well: wheat, oats, beans, lentils, barley, and millet, flavored with basil, turmeric, cinnamon, cumin, garlic, ginger, and coriander. Unlike contemporary societies in ancient Egypt and Mesopotamia (modern Iraq), there are no signs of pharaohs or emperors in the IVC. That's not to say they definitively didn't exist. But if they did, they were uncharacteristically modest for tyrants: There are no obscene palaces or braggadocious monuments, and the graves contain no hoards of gold or sumptuous treasures. Perhaps not coincidentally, everyday men and women lived better lives in the Indus Valley than in Egypt or Mesopotamia, with one-sixth surviving beyond age 55, quite old for the time.

So how did this thriving civilization vanish from India's memory? For one thing, it seemingly went into sharp decline after 1900 B.C., as many cities were abandoned. And without gaudy palaces or monuments to mark them, the sites were forgotten, since little remained for people to gape at. (As long as the pyramids stand, no one will forget ancient Egypt.) In a related matter, the IVC lacked forts and defensive works—a fact that, along with the absence of armor and art glorifying battle, hints that Indus cities rarely waged war.* For better or worse, invading armies give a civilization a reputation abroad and leave scars that don't fade.

Instead of war and monuments, the Indus people poured their energy into public works, especially hydrological projects like wells, dams, and reservoirs. Mohenjo-daro boasted of a stately pool 40 feet long, perhaps for religious rites, and many Indus buildings sat atop brick platforms to raise them above floods. (One archaeologist estimated that the largest such platform took 1,000 laborers 4,000 days to build—an astounding achievement given the lack of emperor-strongmen to organize the effort.) The Indus civilization also built the world's first toilets. And before you start snickering, consider that sanitation systems probably improved the health and happiness of your average person far more than any ancient Wonder of the World. Even small villages had bathrooms connected to underground sewers whose terra-cotta pipes flushed effluvia out of

---

* Some scholars refuse to believe that the Indus people never fought wars; humans being humans, wars are perhaps inevitable. If nothing else, the Indus almost certainly had thugs among them. Still, evidence for widespread warfare simply doesn't exist.

the city; these sewers even had brick "manhole covers" to facilitate cleaning.*

Another peculiarity of the Indus civilization is the lack of public art, be it murals, reliefs, or statues. Instead, people focused on miniatures. The largest known figurines are maybe 18 inches tall. The best-known, a bearded "priest-king," stands just seven inches tall; there's also an alluring "dancing girl," whose left arm is adorned with bangles. And Indus jewelry rivaled anything in the ancient world, with beads of gold, silver, shell, agate, and jasper. Artisans drilled holes into the beads using a bow and an ingenious bit that required heating metamorphic rock until it was almost diamond-hard.

Above all, the Indus people crafted seals, which one archaeologist lauded as "masterpieces of controlled realism, with a monumental strength ... out of all proportion to their size." Again, merchants and customs officials likely used the seals to secure merchandise, although the stellar craftsmanship—and the rings on back, to attach leather cords—suggest that people likely wore them around their necks for show and maybe even used them as ID badges. The different animals displayed—rhinos, tigers, water buffalo, goats, rabbits, elephants, and the cryptic "unicorns"—might correspond to different clans, hometowns, or worker guilds. A few seals show human beings, including a man on a throne in a yoga pose *(mulabandhasana).* One seemingly portrays a human sacrifice.

Beyond their artistic value, the seals reveal how adventurous Indus traders were. A few seals have turned up at ancient Mesopotamian sites, presumably dropped there long ago by Indus merchants

* IVC citizens seemingly had better bathrooms than the average person in modern India until recently. The 2011 Indian census revealed that half the population—over 600 million people—lacked access to toilets or latrines. Recent government campaigns have improved that figure but have not eliminated the problem.

who'd navigated 1,300 miles of open sea to the Persian Gulf. Meanwhile, there's zero evidence of Mesopotamian traders reaching India.

In summarizing the Indus civilization, one historian marveled at its "success in combining artistic excellence, technological sophistication, and economic vigor with social egalitarianism, political freedom, and religious moderation over more than half a millennium." Banerji and company didn't know all this in the 1920s; the full picture emerged only gradually. But they did know they'd uncovered something epochal—something that would resonate far beyond the world of archaeology. India at the time felt beaten-down and humiliated, trapped beneath the bootheel of the British Raj. The discovery of the IVC changed everything. It instantly elevated India to the realm of Egypt and other legendary kingdoms. This instilled pride and respect in people who desperately needed it, and helped unify the population.

Unfortunately, for all the good it did initially, the discovery of the IVC had sinister effects as well. Because after India achieved independence, this millennia-old civilization became a coveted political prize—and far from uniting the subcontinent, helped tear people apart.

The historian Eric Hobsbawm once said that "historians are to nationalism what poppy-growers ... are to heroin-addicts." They "supply the essential raw material." The same holds true for archaeology. The heritage that archaeology reveals forms a huge part of our collective identities, helping us anchor our fleeting lives in something enduring. The most spectacular discoveries also become national symbols and rallying points—King Tut's mask, the bronzes of Benin, Irish harps, and more.

Regrettably, people with political agendas know all this, and all too often treat the past as a bin to root through for heroes or events that they can hold up to justify their goals—ready-made propaganda. And if they can't find exactly what they need, they have no compunctions about twisting archaeology to suit their purposes.

This happened in China with Peking Man. Again, while *Homo sapiens* evolved in Africa, hominins in Europe and Asia did breed with us and contribute some genetic material to modern humans. Perhaps the descendants of Peking Man did as well. However, many nationalists within China take the idea of non-African contributions way too far, arguing that Dragon Bone Hill was the very wellspring of humanity.

Sometimes this belief manifests itself in harmless ways. Wenzhong Pei, who discovered the first Peking Man skull, was buried near Dragon Bone Hill so that his body could return "home" to the supposed cradle of humankind. And before the 2008 Olympics in Beijing, Chinese officials lit the ceremonial torch at Dragon Bone Hill in front of a replica of the Nellie sculpture.

Other beliefs about Peking Man and human evolution in Asia have a sinister edge. In 2012, the head of propaganda for the Chinese government published a paper noting that certain physical traits separate human beings from apes—a lack of body hair, an upright gait, long legs relative to our arms. He then asserted, with zero evidence, that everyone "knows" Chinese people have the least body hair, the flattest butts when standing, and the shortest arms of any race on earth. The Chinese must "therefore" have evolved into humans before other groups, and are farthest along the evolutionary road to perfection. His arguments echo the ludicrous phrenology of 19th-century Europeans, who ranked different races by skull volume.

Sadly, Chinese scientists who challenge such claims have been smeared as traitors and subversive "scum." Worse, opposition to African evolution often deteriorates into mockery and abuse of African people. As one critic commented, in China nowadays, "the most fundamental of scientific questions—where we come from—has been subordinated to the demands of nation, pride, and self-image."

Even uglier things happened in Nazi Germany, which used archaeology to justify war crimes. Adolf Hitler certainly had nutty ideas about ancient history (for example, that classical Greeks were actually ethnic Germans who'd wandered down south, perhaps for the sun, surf, and wine). But the biggest loon was SS chief Heinrich Himmler, who founded a vanity archaeology bureau called the Ahnenerbe (Ancestor Legacy) to conduct what he called "politically correct" research into Germany's past.*

Under Himmler's direction, the Ahnenerbe tried to establish links between Scandinavian runes and Japanese scripts, to demonstrate that the Japanese were really Aryan and therefore acceptable to align with. An ally of Himmler's wrote a 700-page book claiming that the lost continent of Atlantis existed, and that Jesus of Nazareth was not even remotely Jewish. Less comically, the Ahnenerbe harvested skulls from graves and from executed prisoners to study the supposed defects of other ethnic groups. Indeed, the Ahnenerbe supported the catastrophic German invasion of Russia in 1941 in part to gain access to the skulls of "Jewish Bolshevik" prisoners out east. To this end,

---

* Hitler once complained: "It's bad enough that the Romans were erecting great buildings when our forefathers were still living in mud huts; now Himmler is starting to dig up these villages ... and enthusing over every potsherd and stone axe he finds. All we prove is that we were still throwing stone hatchets and crouching around open fires when Greece and Rome had already reached the highest stages of civilization." Der Führer nevertheless recognized the propaganda value of Himmler's notions, and kept his grumbling private.

Ahnenerbe officials sent detailed memos to the Eastern Front on how best to decapitate such people without harming the skulls. They also sent metal containers filled with preservatives for transporting the heads to the Reich.

Equally tragic, Nazi archaeologists scoured museums and dig sites for artifacts from ancient Germanic tribes. And if they could trace any item, however tenuously, to foreign lands like Poland or Czechoslovakia, they trumpeted this as "proof" that ancient Germans once owned those lands, and that modern Poles or Czechs were squatting there. The Nazis then felt justified goose-stepping in and seizing more Lebensraum.

Overall, archaeology unites countries every bit as much as flags, battles, and epic poems. And despite Eric Hobsbawm's observation above, it's not always a matter of providing "raw material." Archaeological data often needs interpretation, which leaves it open to manipulation. As another historian, Ernest Renan, has said, "Forgetting history, or even getting history wrong, is an essential factor in the formation of a nation." That certainly was the case in India after the discovery of the Indus Valley Civilization.

In May 1924, Rakhaldas Banerji traveled to northern India to meet with John Marshall and others and examine the latest Indus Valley artifacts. Although Banerji was still ailing from the harsh winter at Mohenjo-daro, he and his colleagues had a productive meeting, and in September, Marshall announced the discovery of the Indus Valley Civilization to the world in an article in the *Illustrated London News*, the same magazine that would later publish the infamous drawings of the Dorak-Yortan treasures.

In it, Marshall marveled at the group's fortune in uncovering an unknown civilization, and noted that the site likely dated to before 300 B.C., the days of Alexander the Great. Only after publication did a scholar at Oxford alert Marshall that his team was underestimating itself: Some Indus-type seals found in Mesopotamia had been dated to the third millennium B.C. In a stroke, then, Banerji and Marshall had extended the history of India by 2,000-plus years.

Indian people greeted the news with ecstasy. Their ancestors now stood tall with Egypt, with Babylon, as builders of great empires. Jawaharlal Nehru, soon to be India's first prime minister, visited Mohenjo-daro twice in the 1930s and felt immensely moved.* One contemporary historian added, "What archaeology has achieved for [India] ... is nothing short of a revolution ... It has enabled her to establish her lost links with a great past whose magnificence was beyond her distant dreams."

But that goodwill and optimism would not last.

There's a fundamental divide in Indian history between Dravidians and Aryas.† Nowadays, Arya people generally predominate in the north, while Dravidians inhabit the south. But that tidy split masks a complicated and fraught history.

---

* Oddly, Nehru's mentor, Gandhi, seemed indifferent to the Indus Valley Civilization, even though the seeming lack of warfare among the Indus people dovetailed perfectly with his advocacy of nonviolence.

† The more common term for the Aryas is *Aryans,* a name that originally described a group of ancient people from western Asia. These people defined themselves as Aryans through religion, culture, and language—but not race. (An analogous term today would be *French.*) Bafflingly, 19th-century European scholars used the term as a synonym for Caucasians, and it became notorious under the Third Reich for its association with white supremacy. To avoid those connotations, I'm using the less common terms *Arya* and *Aryas* here.

To oversimplify somewhat, the standard view holds that Dravidian people once ranged across all India, north and south. Then, around 4,000 years ago, Arya males began migrating into India from the steppes of western Asia. The details are murky, but these men probably arrived in waves over several centuries and imported both their language (which became Sanskrit) and the religious texts that shaped modern Hinduism. During this migration, the Aryas pushed Dravidian culture (and possibly Dravidian people) south. At the same time, the proto-Hindu religious and cultural practices of the incoming Aryas became dominant across the subcontinent.

But one important detail of the Arya migration remained controversial. Did the group push south peacefully and accumulate power gradually, or did they storm in and conquer?

In the early 1900s, the conquest theory reigned supreme, to the delight of many Aryas. They'd long scorned Dravidian people as crude and backwards, and claimed that the arrival of their ancestors brought culture to a savage land.

The discovery of the Indus Valley Civilization flipped that notion on its head. Recall that the IVC went into decline around 1900 B.C., when cities were abandoned and sewer systems fell into disrepair. The Aryas were also streaming south then. So did they destroy the Indus civilization upon arriving?

Dravidian activists insisted yes. Suddenly, they could paint the *Aryas* as barbarians, a Visigoth horde sweeping in and crushing a sophisticated, peace-loving culture. The first claims to this effect appeared just months after Marshall's magazine article and only grew from there. Dravidians had long felt like second-class citizens in India, and they delighted in knocking the Aryas down a few pegs.

Still, careful excavations have upended that theory of a ruthless Arya invasion. Rather than a collapse around 1900 B.C., evidence now suggests that most Indus sites declined gradually. That's hard to square with the notion of hordes sweeping in to burn and pillage. Rather, Indus people apparently migrated from large cities to smaller settlements elsewhere, perhaps due to rivers changing course or natural disasters such as floods and earthquakes. In other words, the Indus culture didn't collapse so much as spread out and transform.

Hindu nationalists of course jumped all over this evidence to absolve themselves of blame for the Indus civilization's decline. Then they took things further. These nationalists trace their descent from proto-Hindu Aryas, and they desperately wanted to find a link between their religion and the IVC. They pointed to the stone seals as "proof" of this. No one had deciphered the writing on them, but if you squinted (or so the nationalists claimed), the strokes and squiggles resembled early Sanskrit. To them, this proved that their ancestors never "invaded" India but had always been there—and had in fact built India's first civilization themselves. The fact that certain seals showed people in Hindu yogic poses bolstered their case, as did the use of Hindu sun symbols in other Indus art.

These aren't just academic arguments, either. Hindu nationalists were essentially using archaeology as a title deed—arguing that Sanskrit-speaking people have dominated India since the 2000s B.C. and therefore deserve to rule in modern times. It's no coincidence that Prime Minister Narendra Modi and his right-wing Bharatiya Janata Party glorify the Indus civilization and use its supposed Hindu roots to justify their policies. It's Make India Great Again.

To be clear, the claim that the Arya people founded the Indus Valley Civilization is false: They arrived in India centuries after its mature period began, as demonstrated by both genetic and archaeological evidence. Furthermore, ancient Sanskrit texts describe a pastoral existence—nothing like the urban life of Harappa or Mohenjo-daro. Sanskrit texts also mention horses, chariots, and armor, none of which appear at Indus sites. The scholarly consensus on all this is strong.*

But Aryas and Dravidians continue to bicker. A 2016 Bollywood epic called *Mohenjo Daro* showed Indus-era people speaking a sanskritized tongue, despite a total lack of evidence for that possibility. Dravidian activists denounced the film as propaganda. The two sides have sparred over textbooks as well, as far afield as California. Such disputes have helped ratchet the tensions over Hindu nationalism to scary heights. Hit lists are reportedly circulating, and mobs have lynched people suspected of eating beef in violation of Hindu law.

Frustratingly for archaeologists, these battles distract people from the larger truth: that both Dravidians and Aryas contributed mightily to Indian culture. Certain aspects of modern Hinduism did migrate south with the Aryas, while others were already present among the Dravidians whose ancestors likely populated the IVC. These two

* Again, most scholars today doubt the Arya invasion theory, with its hordes of violent warriors flooding south. And in the 2010s, genetic evidence cast doubt on the idea of any Arya migration, period. In particular, mitochondrial DNA—which we inherit from our mothers—seemed to rule out the idea of ethnic groups migrating into India a few millennia ago.

However, a later study on Y chromosome DNA—which men inherit from fathers—shows strong evidence of migration. In short, Arya men likely migrated south and married native women.

But instead of acknowledging these nuances, some Hindu nationalists play a rhetorical game. They fulminate against the discredited invasion theory and ignore the possibility of a *peaceful* migration. As Indian historian Romila Thapar says, "[The] range of possibilities between the two extremes of invaders or indigenes does not interest them."

cultures then flowed together like two great rivers, and modern India emerged from their union.

But neither side wants to hear that, and the identity politics continue unabated. For a culture that rose to prominence 4,600 years ago, the Indus Valley Civilization remains a potent political force today. Archaeology has become politics by other means.

Despite his transfer away from the Mohenjo-daro region, Rakhaldas Banerji could have made himself a leading scholar of the Indus Valley Civilization. Unfortunately, his field reports on the site were so sloppy and riddled with mistakes that an exasperated John Marshall could not publish them. However important Banerji's vision was in first recognizing the Indus civilization, he lacked the patience to nail down the details. (Meanwhile, his colleague Daya Ram Sahni produced exemplary reports on Harappa.)

Banerji's transfer landed him in Calcutta, where the warmth must have felt heavenly after the brutal winters out west. But over time, the intense summer heat waves left him sicker than ever. Life finally bottomed out after he visited a temple near the city of Jabalpur in fall 1925. Accounts differ on what happened that morning. Again, Banerji was accustomed to taking any artifact he wanted from such sites, as were the people under him. And after his crew appraised some items in the temple, one of the statues vanished—a two-foot-tall idol made of red stone depicting a Buddhist goddess. For what it's worth, Banerji was not on the premises when it disappeared. Perhaps he'd left instructions with an assistant to remove the idol, then made himself scarce. Perhaps the assistant took it on his own initiative.

Regardless, the assistant enlisted a local laborer to schlep the idol to Banerji's bungalow, which the man did atop his head. Afterward, it was loaded into the trunk of Banerji's car for transport to Calcutta. Given its size, Banerji hardly could have failed to notice the idol, either during the initial loading or when they unloaded upon arrival.

All in all, pilfering like this was so common that few people thought twice about it. Except in this case, the head of the temple discovered the theft a week later and grew furious. He wrote to Banerji, demanding to know what happened. Perhaps being a little too clever, Banerji answered that no one on his staff had removed any idols—which was technically true, since the local laborer had. But the temple panjandrum refused to drop the matter, and eventually reported the theft to the police.

Banerji scrambled to cover his tracks. He instructed his nephew-in-law, who worked for him in the Indian archaeology office, to plant the idol in a temple in northern Calcutta. The nephew would then hire some sham detectives to scour the neighborhood until they "discovered" it. After they took possession, Banerji would return the idol to the temple in Jabalpur and look like a hero.

Everything went according to plan—at least until the police started asking questions. Eighteen separate people who lived near the temple testified that they'd never seen the idol before Banerji's bumbling agents showed up. All in all, the theft was small potatoes, but the clumsy cover-up doomed Banerji. His mischief with government funds had already left him vulnerable professionally, and after the scandal came to light in spring 1926, archaeological officials gave him the option of resigning. His other option was being fired.

Being forced to resign embarrassed Banerji. He already felt

crestfallen for missing out on chances to excavate at Mohenjo-daro, and the latest scandal left his reputation bruised. He managed to land a professorship at Banaras Hindu University in northeastern India, but had to go on sick leave soon afterward, and his health never recovered. He succumbed to complications of diabetes in May 1930, at just 45 years old. Despite his childhood family's feudal wealth, he died more or less destitute.

Although his name has sunk into obscurity, Banerji remains important today as the first person to recognize the glory of the Indus Valley Civilization. And remarkably, a century later, archaeologists are still wrestling with the same questions he and his colleagues did. Who were the Indus people? What united them in the absence of a central ruler or common enemy? How much of modern Indian culture traces back to them?

One reason these questions remain unanswered is the rocky state of archaeology in the Indus region. The empire's former territory was divided between India and Pakistan when those nations gained independence in 1947, as were all the Indus treasures: India kept the dancing girl figurine, while Pakistan got the priest-king. (Incredibly, when the bureaucrats divvying the items up couldn't decide who should get one of the most spectacular items, an elaborate necklace of jade and gold, they hacked it in half rather than let either side get the whole piece. They were the anti-Solomons.)

Border wars between the two nations have made working there dangerous at times, and floods, harsh weather, and salty groundwater have also damaged sites. Moreover, Pakistan is less than enthusiastic about funding digs that highlight the nation's non-Muslim past. Overall, archaeologists have excavated just 10 percent of known IVC sites. And one of the largest Indus cities, Ganweriwala, remains almost completely buried a half century after its discovery.*

Given such obstacles, the best hope for deepening our understanding of the Indus Valley Civilization lies in those "little masterpieces of controlled realism," the exquisite stone seals that first stirred Banerji's imagination. If we could only read the script on them and make those mute stones talk, we could learn so much. Unfortunately, as we'll see next chapter, their decipherment presents a formidable challenge—and might even prove impossible.

* As impossible as it sounds, lost civilizations are still turning up today. In 2015, ecologists began studying the Amazon rainforest with lidar, a technology that involves shooting laser pulses from planes and mapping the ground hidden beneath the canopy. The scientists intended to study the biology of the region. Instead, they found sites with platforms, plazas, artificial ponds, and roads that ran for up to 15 miles. The oldest of these "garden cities" date to 500 B.C., and the largest are as big as the pyramid complexes of Egypt and Mexico.

As of now, we know virtually nothing about the people who built these structures. But given the vastness of the Amazon, and the puny amount that's been mapped, thousands more sites might be lurking out there. Revelations like this could invigorate native Amerindians in the same way that the Indus Valley Civilization stirred people in India: instilling pride and helping them fight for land rights in their ancestral homes. Let's just hope they can harness the positive passions of such discoveries without succumbing to the destructive ones.

CHAPTER SEVEN

LOST LANGUAGES

Michael Ventris was just happy to ditch school. He was visiting an archaeology exhibit in London in 1936, tagging along with upperclassmen from his prep school. Ventris wasn't friends with them—he had few friends—but he found his classes dull and thought an afternoon at a museum sounded more fun. Or at least less tedious.

Their tour guide was a wrinkly, mustached 85-year-old named Arthur Evans—the grand old man of British archaeology, and one of the most famous archaeologists in the world. Evans led them to a glass case with clay tablets inside and began droning. Who knows how closely Ventris was paying attention—whether he was peering politely at the funny writing on the tablets, or perhaps letting his eyes wander to another case. Then Evans said something that seized the 14-year-old's attention. His hand snapped into the air.

"Did you say they haven't been deciphered, sir?"

Evans smiled. He'd discovered the tablets on the island of Crete; specifically, they'd turned up in the ruins of a sprawling palace called Knossos, whose 1,300 rooms likely inspired the legendary labyrinth with the Minotaur inside. The tablets dated to around 1350 B.C., a good century and a half before the Trojan War. The writing on them was called Linear B, which had developed from an earlier, vaguely similar script called Linear A. The writing looked like nothing else from ancient times—a series of lines, crosses, and loops scratched into clay.

The elderly Evans chuckled and confirmed that Ventris had heard right: No one could read Linear B. Evans himself had labored for years to decipher it, to no avail. The group soon moved on to other artifacts. But mentally, Ventris never did move on. That undeciphered script would dominate the remainder of his short, sad life.

Despite his wit and charm—he had an elfin face and easy grin—Ventris made little impression on his classmates. Certainly no one considered him a genius, except in languages. He taught himself his mother's native Polish at six, then added French, German, Russian, Latin, Swedish, Italian, and Greek. Even into adulthood, he could pick up languages as easily as a child does. So the undeciphered Linear B fascinated him. He obtained a book with drawings of the script and began studying it at night with a flashlight under his bedcovers. It provided a welcome distraction when his father died in 1938, and then again when his mother committed suicide in 1940, swallowing a bottle of barbiturates after Nazi Germany ravaged Poland.

Ventris published his first paper on Linear B just months after her death, deliberately concealing his age (18) from the journal editor. He then joined the Royal Air Force as a navigator. But even on the way back from bombing raids, he would spread his Linear B papers on the navigating table in back, scrutinizing the runes while flak burst about them.

After the war, he enrolled in architecture school, where he met his future wife, Lois. Despite his obsession with ancient languages, Ventris decorated their apartment in Highgate with sleek modernist furniture, all glass and metal. Picassos hung on the wall.

Sadly, Ventris's obsession strained his marriage, in part because he quit his job in 1950 to focus on Linear B. Things came to a head in June 1952. He and Lois hosted a dinner party one evening for two friends, a fellow architect and his radio-producer wife. But when the guests arrived, Ventris was nowhere to be found. He'd locked himself in his study, scribbling down new ideas about Linear B. Lois gamely poured some sherry and promised their friends he'd be right out. After maybe an hour, her guests were squirming, despite her apologies. They were soon drunk, and dinner was a cold, soggy mess. Lois was furious.

Suddenly, Ventris flung open his office door. He looked disheveled, his normally tidy hair sticking up in tufts. He muttered an apology, then began babbling, "I know it—I'm certain of it!" His guests asked what on earth he meant. Ventris grinned. After spending half his life on the problem, he'd just cracked Linear B.

You need a rare set of skills to decipher a lost language. Linguistic flair, obviously, but also statistical savvy, an eye for visual patterns, and deep cultural knowledge of the region in question—not to mention superhuman persistence and a high tolerance for drudgery. And even then, you might fail. Plenty of scholars have sacrificed friends, lovers, and stable careers to scripts that never yielded their secrets, toiling their whole lives and dying with nothing to show for it.

But to would-be decipherers, the prize is worth the risk. Imagine picking up a book in a language you can't read. You're squinting at the text, not even sure whether it reads left to right or vice versa. Suddenly, all the squiggles rearrange themselves in a flash. They look coherent now: sights, sounds, *voices* leap off the page. Now imagine that not a single human has read this story in 5,000 years—except you. Forget seances: *This* is talking with the dead. That's the high decipherers seek.

For all its allure, though, there's a dark side to decipherment. A language scholar once called undeciphered scripts "powerful kook attractors," a realm full of cranks, skullduggery, and vicious, backstabbing rivalries. There's a streak of irrationality as well. Every decipherer must believe—despite all evidence to the contrary—that they alone can see things no one else can. They need faith that the patterns they're uncovering aren't just chimeras, that they'll somehow triumph where everyone else has failed. Because every so often, they do.

No undeciphered script has ever fascinated people like Egyptian hieroglyphs.* The oldest date back to 3100 B.C., and their use continued until A.D. 394, when a naughty priest chiseled some graffiti onto a temple wall. But after that priest's generation died, all knowledge of hieroglyphs went extinct; no one on earth could read a word. Gradually, as centuries passed, that mystery gave way to mysticism, and people began infusing hieroglyphs with magical powers, claiming that they encoded prophecies and hidden wisdom about the nature of the universe. Indeed, the Egyptians called their script "the words of the gods," as if dictated by divine beings.

* Although people often call them hieroglyph<u>ic</u>s, that's the adjectival form. They're properly called hieroglyphs.

The hieroglyphic script consists of several hundred pictures and symbols. It's absolutely everywhere in Egypt, covering temples, columns, coffins, ceilings, obelisks, even the bandages of mummies. A medieval pilgrim from Baghdad once marveled, "There is hardly the space of an awl or needle-hole which did not have an image or engraving."

After laborious study, scholars in the 1700s clawed their way to a few insights. The Egyptians used 958 symbols overall, far too many for each one to stand for a letter or syllable. At the same time, that was far too few symbols for each one to stand for a separate word. (Even an average five-year-old knows thousands of words.) Beyond that, scholars could only scratch their heads. Did hieroglyphs read from left to right or right to left? Given the lack of spaces, where did one word stop and another start? And why were certain symbols surrounded by ovals, setting them off from other text? No one had a clue.

The first glimmer of hope arrived on a scorching July day in 1799. French soldiers stationed in the Egyptian town of Rosetta were repairing a fort near the mouth of the Nile, patching holes with stones from a rubble heap. They flipped over a 1,700-pound slab of gray rock and found writing carved into it in three scripts—Greek, hieroglyphs, and something unknown. Three years later, the British defeated the French in a battle in Egypt and received the slab as war booty. The Rosetta Stone has been housed in the British Museum ever since.*

Presumably, all three texts conveyed the same message, and scholars eagerly translated the 53 lines of Greek at the bottom. It was a

* To make the writing on the Rosetta Stone stand out, scholars in the 1800s rubbed chalk into the letters. They also coated it with protective wax. But the wax reacted with London's sooty air—as well as the grime on the fingers of people who couldn't resist touching it when guards weren't looking—to turn the stone black. A later cleaning restored its gray hue, with sparkling flakes of mica and a few streaks of pink.

proclamation from a council of priests in 196 B.C. It voiced support for the 14-year-old king of Egypt, Ptolemy V (or Ptolemaios), the latest in a line of unpopular, ethnically Greek monarchs who'd taken control of Egypt a century earlier after Alexander the Great's conquest. The stone touted Ptolemy's achievements—lowering taxes, subduing foreign lands, impaling enemies on stakes—in the hopes of quelling widespread unrest and rebellion. In a word, it was propaganda. The decree was written in multiple languages so everyone could read it.

Above the Greek text came 32 lines of the unknown language, perhaps archaic Syrian. At the top sat just 14 lines of hieroglyphs, because the stone was partly shattered; half the hieroglyphs were missing. Nevertheless, given that they could read the Greek, scholars assumed they'd decipher the hieroglyphs in a few weeks. It took 20 years.

The first clue came in 1811. A linguist named Antoine Isaac Silvestre de Sacy was pondering the funny ovals that surrounded certain hieroglyphs. (French soldiers thought they resembled ammunition cartridges, or *cartouches.* The name stuck.) One day, a student of de Sacy's mentioned that Chinese writing at the time had a system for spelling non-Chinese names. In Chinese, most symbols represent both a word and a sound. And by stringing together the right sounds, you can construct foreign names. For instance, 安德森 means "safety virtue forest," which is nonsense. But it's pronounced "ān-déh-sēn," or Anderson. To make sure the reader knew you meant "Anderson" and not "safety virtue forest," authors sometimes put a box around the text. De Sacy heard this and thought of the cartouches on the Rosetta Stone. The text mentioned Ptolemy, a Greek name that was foreign to Egyptian tongues. So perhaps the symbols inside the cartouches spelled his name, with the cartouche itself meaning, "read this as sound."

Remarkably, de Sacy did nothing with this insight. But a few years later, a 41-year-old British polymath named Thomas Young picked up the baton. Although obscure today, Young had a truly incandescent mind, and did fundamental work in everything from human vision to cartography to life insurance. Most famously, he produced a theory of how waves spread by studying the ripples that swans made while sculling around a pond—work that, incidentally, proved Isaac Newton wrong (not easy). Young was once crowned "the last man who knew everything." So naturally, he took up the puzzle of hieroglyphs. He figured he'd crack them in a few days.

He started with de Sacy's suggestion that the symbols inside the cartouches on the Rosetta Stone might stand for *Ptolemy* (spelled *Ptolemaios* in Greek):*

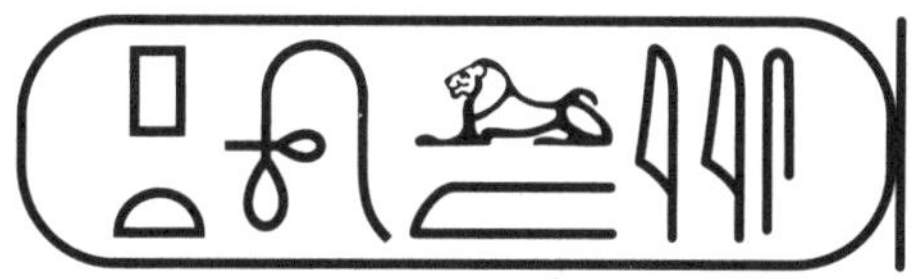

To cheat a bit, here's how Egyptologists now read those characters:

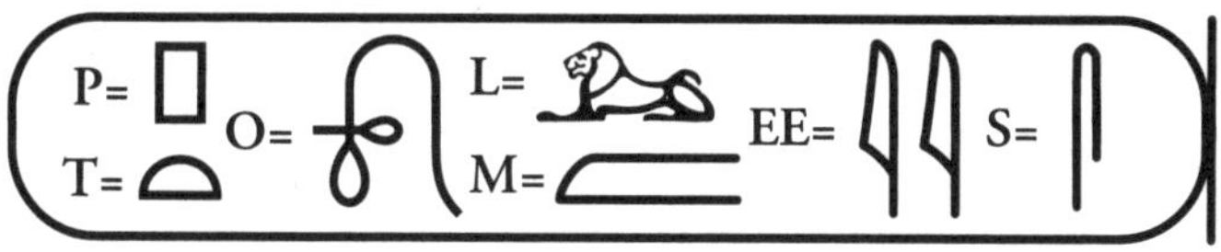

In the transition from Greek to Egyptian, *Ptolemaios* got mushed into something like *Ptolmis,* but it's clearly the same name, and Young managed to assign characters to the *P, T, M,* and *EE* sounds correctly. Beyond that, he struggled. He called the sweeping "ribbon" character *(O)* superfluous and skipped past it. He assigned

* Hieroglyphs read right to left, but I've reversed the direction here for convenience. Note that animals and humans in hieroglyphs always point toward the beginning of a word.

the sound *lo* to the lion and *os* or *osh* to the "shepherd crook" at the end. Not bad, but not stunning—solid C work.

Young also looked beyond the Rosetta Stone, to a temple inscription with another foreign name: Berenika, the wife of Ptolemy's great-great-grandfather. Scholars now read that cartouche as *Brneeka*:

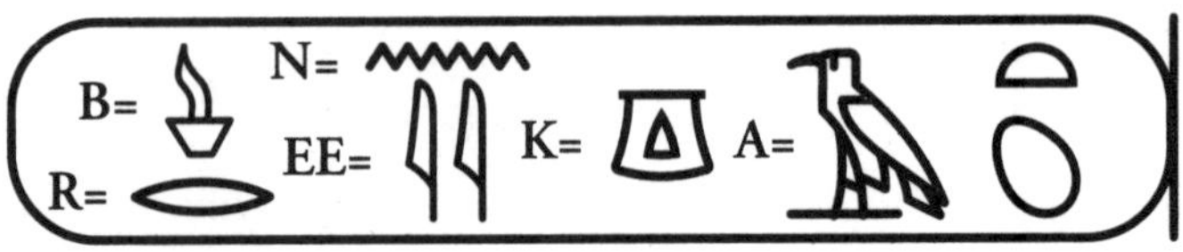

Here, Young did even worse. He got the squiggly line *(N)* and double feathers *(EE)* correct, but assigned *bir* to the *B* character, *e* to the *R* one, skipped over the *K* as superfluous, and decided the falcon read *ke* or *ken.* He guessed that the last two symbols meant "queen," whereas they really mean "this name is a woman."

Young had better luck with the third, unknown script on the Rosetta Stone, the "Syrian." In comparing this writing to the hieroglyphs above it, he noticed a vague resemblance, similar to the resemblance between printed letters and cursive. He therefore guessed that the unknown script wasn't Syrian at all, but derived from hieroglyphs. He was right. Scholars now call that script demotic, a shorthand form of hieroglyphs developed around 650 B.C. with pared-down symbols for quicker writing.

Overall, Young's mistakes outweighed his successes. In 1819, he published translations of 200 hieroglyphic words, only around 80 of which were correct. And even some of those were merely half right. For instance, he correctly interpreted one symbol as *pharaoh* because it appeared next to royal names, but he didn't grasp its literal meaning of "great house."

One stumbling block was Young's belief that hieroglyphs stood for sounds *only* inside cartouches and only with foreign names. For other words, and for Egyptian names, he decided that hieroglyphs never stood for sounds. This was a holdover of the medieval belief that hieroglyphs were divinely inspired and normally encoded lofty philosophical wisdom, not "mere" utterances. Given this myopia, Young fell well short of deciphering the language of the gods.

That honor would fall to a scholar 17 years Young's junior, the Frenchman Jean-François Champollion. Champollion grew up poor, with a volatile, alcoholic father whose shenanigans and reckless spending sometimes left the family on the verge of eviction. But the man did bestow one gift to his son: As a bookseller, he had ready access to thousands of texts, and his boy proved a prodigy with languages, mastering enough Greek and Latin by age nine to read Homer and Virgil. At age 10, Champollion began reading obsessively about ancient Egypt, and presented his first scholarly paper on Egypt at 16. Afterward, he told the audience that he would someday decipher hieroglyphs. You can imagine them chuckling at his youthful folly. But he did exactly what he vowed.

Champollion began his quest by studying Coptic, an Egyptian language that arose in the 200s A.D. Although its use declined sharply after the Muslim conquest of Egypt, it persisted within the Coptic Church, a sect of Christianity that kept the language alive in the same way the Catholic Church did Latin. Given its Egyptian roots, Champollion was gambling that Coptic shared some vocabulary with hieroglyphs and would help him understand the writing.

It did, although not without serious delays. Champollion had a fiery temperament, and his uncompromising politics—he despised the French monarchy—cost him his university job in 1816 and got him banished to the boondocks for several years. He subsequently fell victim to a chronic illness, suffering from a hacking cough, dizziness, and fainting spells. But he kept plugging away at Coptic, even befriending a Coptic priest in France and attending Masses. Before long, he was dreaming in the language. "I speak Coptic alone to myself," he confessed to his brother, "since no one can understand me." The Travis Bickle of linguistics.

Meanwhile, hieroglyphs themselves had stumped him. At the time, scholars assumed that every hieroglyphic symbol outside cartouches stood for an object or idea. A lion, for instance, might mean the animal itself, but might also mean "dignity" or "strength." Similarly, a snake might mean either a serpent or "wickedness." But something about that notion seemed off to Champollion. "The most contradictory objects are put right next to each other," he complained, "producing monstrous alliances." A snake might sit next to a sun, which sat next to a jar or some feathers. What the devil could that mean?

Around this time, Champollion wrote to England with a request. He owned two engraved drawings of the Rosetta Stone, but some discrepancies between them made him fearful that they contained mistakes. So he wrote to authorities in England for a plaster cast of the stone, an exact copy. He meant to contact the Society of Antiquaries but accidentally wrote to the Royal Society—whose foreign secretary then was Thomas Young.

The letter spooked Young. His own attempts to decipher hieroglyphs had stalled, and he feared the Frenchman would surpass him. He began making discreet inquiries about Champollion's progress.

Meanwhile, Champollion never got his cast. So, at wit's end, he put the Rosetta Stone aside and began studying some cartouches on an obelisk stolen from southern Egypt a few years prior. Like the Rosetta Stone, it had inscriptions in both hieroglyphs and Greek. It also had two names in cartouches: Ptolemy and Cleopatra. Those names share several letters, and in comparing the hieroglyphs for each, he noticed something: that the *T* in Ptolemy was rendered 𓏏, while in Cleopatra it was 𓂧 (an open hand). He realized that these were homophones: different symbols with identical sounds, like *C* and *K* in English. It was his first real progress.

From there, he examined another cartouche, one that had no parallel Greek inscription to guide him:

He knew some of these sounds from other names. Leaving blanks for the unknown hieroglyphs, he got the string AL_SE_TR_. He guessed it read *Alksentrs,* how a foreigner might pronounce the Greek name Alexandros. More progress. Plus, he now had another pair of homophones: The shepherd crook in the middle and dotted line at the end both read *S.* Similar work led to the decipherment of the names Caesar, Tiberius, Nero, Claudius, and Trajan.

So far, Champollion was simply aping Young's strategy, albeit with better results. But he soon sprinted past his rival. He began studying cartouches in truly ancient inscriptions, long before Greek influence in Egypt. One from Egypt's New Kingdom (1500s–1000s B.C.) looked especially interesting:

The double shepherd crook at the end meant S-S. He didn't recognize the "chandelier" in the middle (really, fox skins), but for the dotted circle, he drew on his Coptic. It looked like a sun. The Coptic word for "sun" was *ra,* so he plugged that in, just to see what happened. Did any pharaohs have names like RA_SS? Of course—Ramses! Not only had he secured a new sound-symbol, *M,** he'd also demonstrated a link between hieroglyphs and Coptic. Equally important, he'd shown that the sounds of *Egyptian* names were encoded in hieroglyphs.

At least he hoped so. To make sure he wasn't fooling himself, he hunted down another cartouche:

Given the *M*-chandelier and *S*-crook, it read _M-S. But what about that bird? As an Egypt obsessive, he immediately thought of an ibis, a symbol for the god Thoth. So was there a pharaoh named something like Thoth-M-S? Indeed: four pharaohs named Thutmose in the 1400s B.C.

Now Champollion was ready to take a leap. What if hieroglyphs could stand for sounds not only inside cartouches but outside them, too? He had a hunch how to test this. The ibis in the Thutmose cartouche stood for a god. Similarly, the Egyptians had a sun god; and based on the Coptic, perhaps its name was Ra. Moreover, both the Thutmose and Ramses cartouches contained the chandelier-crook combination. Perhaps that pair meant "born of": Ramses would mean "born of [the god] Ra," while Thutmose would mean "born of Thoth." Assuming that was true, the Egyptian word for "birth" might sound like "*M-S.*"

* He was close: The chandelier–fox skin actually stands for the sound *M-S.*

Crossing his fingers, Champollion consulted his facsimile drawings of the Rosetta Stone and scoured the hieroglyphs for any chandelier-crook pairing outside the cartouches. He found one instance, eight lines from the bottom. His heart pounding, his eyes leaped down to the Greek passages, at roughly the same distance from the bottom of that section. Did they say anything about birth?

Holy shit. The Greek lines mentioned honoring Ptolemy V—on his birthday.

Champollion discovered this just before noon on September 14, 1822. He jumped up from his desk and took off sprinting for his brother's office. He arrived five minutes later, flung open the door, and cried, "I've got it!" Then he swooned and collapsed.

Hieroglyphs were far from deciphered at that point—millions of hours of work lay ahead. But make no mistake, Champollion had just kicked the door open, and transformed an impossible task into a merely laborious one.

A century later, archaeologist Howard Carter would chisel the first hole into the wall of King Tut's burial chamber in Egypt, then peer inside with a candle. An impatient companion would ask, "Can you see anything?" Breathless, Carter answered, "Yes—wonderful things!" As the first person to glimpse the deep structure of hieroglyphs, Champollion could say the same.

The decipherment of hieroglyphs proceeded apace over the next century, opening up the whole magnificent history of Egypt. The work also provided surprising, and unwelcome, insight into the history of writing. Because however disappointing it might sound to lovers of literature, writing as we know it almost certainly derived from the silliest, most lowbrow language around: puns and rebuses.

Initially, the first "writing" was pictures: You'd scratch an ox or chariot onto a clay tablet. But you can't say much that way. What if you wanted to talk about death or yesterday, or some abstract concept like truth? Writing needs verbs, too, which are harder to capture with pictures. (*Run* or *jump* might be easy, but what about *anticipated* or *insulted*?)

One solution was puns. In English, you could talk about your son by drawing a circle with rays. In Egyptian, the sound *MWT* meant both "vulture" and "mother," so mothers became vultures in inscriptions. For similar reasons, a lotus stood for 1,000 and a finger for 10,000.

Rebuses are extended puns. What does this say?

If you know your *Hamlet,* we've now added a preposition *(to),* verb *(be),* conjunction *(or),* and negation *(not).*

Egyptian hieroglyphs contained loads of rebuses. Scribes also used so-called logographs for certain concepts (logographs in English include $ and %) as well as onomatopoeia. Charmingly, the hieroglyphs for cat read "meow," while the string for donkey was "heehaw."

However clever this was, scribes eventually (thankfully) ran out of puns, at which point they resorted to other strategies. The Egyptian word for "mouth" began with *R.* So for an *R* sound, they drew a mouth () and told people to ignore everything except the first letter, similar to the military's Alpha-Bravo-Charlie alphabet.*

You might also have noticed another issue above. In many cases

* The idea of hieroglyphic characters is regaining popularity in our globalized world—at airports, on maps and menus, in emoji.

(Brneeka, Alksentrs), Egyptian texts skipped over vowels. That can introduce ambiguities. In English, how would you know whether *fr* means fear, fair, four, fur, or fire?

To resolve this problem, Egyptian scribes added extra signs called determinatives. Sans vowels, the Egyptian hieroglyphs for *old* and *praise* looked the same, so a scribe chiseled a geezer with a cane after the former and a man with hands raised in worship after the latter. No more ambiguity. Determinatives distinguished between *stairs* and *foot, winter* and *fruit, beautiful woman* and *cow,* and scores of other combinations. And because determinatives always appeared at the end of words, modern scholars got a bonus insight into where words stopped and started, despite the absence of spaces.

Overall, Egyptian hieroglyphs consisted of three kinds of symbols: 26 that stood for single sounds; around 80 that stood for two or three consonants *(MS, NB);* and several hundred that either represented a thing or idea, appeared in puns and rebuses, or acted as determinatives.

If you're thinking, *God, what a mess,* you're right. It was messy. But that's easy to say in our age of streamlined alphabets. (We don't usually think about the ABCs as technology, but they are; alphabets had to be invented.) Plus, it's possible that clear, simple communication wasn't the point of hieroglyphs. To the contrary, perhaps scribes reveled in the complexities, because they didn't want riffraff reading the inscriptions.

The wide array of symbols also looked beautiful. Champollion may have complained about "monstrous alliances"—random objects appearing side by side—but illiterates running their fingers along those birds and beasts and strange mystical symbols were suitably awed. If any script looked like something the gods would write, hieroglyphs was it.

After recovering from his swoon, Champollion prepared a lecture and announced plans to reveal his decipherment to the world on September 27, 1822. Coincidently, the polymath Thomas Young was visiting Paris then and attended the talk. Before long, Young was squirming in his seat. How had this sniveling 31-year-old bested *him,* the most incandescent mind in the world?

Young was not a confrontational man, but in the months after the lecture he began picking Champollion apart in print, implying that the young scholar was derivative and had merely "extended" Young's own work. Champollion, meanwhile, lacked all such decorum, and blasted his older rival's "ridiculous boasting." Things deteriorated into a feud. Pettily, neither man would fully acknowledge the other's contributions, and historians are still apportioning credit today—though the lion's share clearly falls to Champollion. As one historian noted, "Young discovered parts of an alphabet ... Champollion unlocked an entire language."

Thomas Young died in May 1829, at age 55, still grumbling about Champollion on his deathbed. Champollion survived him by just three years, collapsing from a stroke after an impassioned lecture and dying of complications a few months later. He never saw the Rosetta Stone in person. But the once poverty-addled youth did scrimp and save enough money to visit Egypt before his death. He grew his beard out on the journey and dressed in robes to pass as a local. He then trawled up and down the Nile, slipping into dusty temples incognito and reading the hieroglyphs from ceiling to floor—the only person alive who could do so. It was the most glorious few months of his life. As he joyfully wrote to a friend from Egypt, "Notre alphabet est bon." Our alphabet works.

The decipherment of hieroglyphs provided scholars with strategies for attacking other lost languages, as well as the hope—no small thing—that such scripts could even be deciphered.

The next script to fall was the world's oldest writing, Mesopotamian cuneiform, which dates back to perhaps 3500 B.C. It proved knotty to decipher because the letters are abstract shapes; unlike hieroglyphs, it lacks the lions and suns and birds that can sometimes provide clues about the meaning. But after decades of steady progress, the work reached its apex in 1872. A 32-year-old currency engraver and cuneiform obsessive named George Smith was battling through some lines on a six-inch clay tablet at the British Museum over his lunch break when the meaning suddenly clicked. He cried out, "I am the first man to read this after two thousand years of oblivion!" Then he began running about the room and tearing his clothes off. You can imagine other patrons gaping.

But his excitement was warranted. Smith was reading the famed *Epic of Gilgamesh,* possibly the first story ever recorded. It includes an episode where a man receives a warning from a god about a flood, then builds an ark and places his family and several pairs of animals inside. The man eventually gets stuck on a mountain and releases a bird to scout for dry land. Only this man wasn't Noah: *Gilgamesh* far predates Genesis, and Smith's work showed that the biblical story was likely a remix of older heathen legends.

Such dramatic fare proved rare, however. Most ancient tablets, cuneiform and otherwise, contain no fables or epic poems. They're mostly receipts or inventories—records of how Gorg owes Grug two pieces of silver for some grain. That was certainly the case with the next script that scholars deciphered: Linear B from the eastern Mediterranean.

Most Linear B tablets that survived until modern times came from palace archives in the Mediterranean—lists of local officials, military goods, and ritual offerings. They were originally inscribed on soft clay, then baked hard when the palaces burned down (a rare time when fire actually preserved historical documents). Some tablets contained pictograms for goods like pigs, cups, and spears, followed by obvious numbers, like 𐄉 or 𐄋. Often, the far right column of the tablet contained more numbers—presumably a sum. By counting up the tick-marks and comparing different entries, Arthur Evans—the doyen of British archaeology, who sometimes led schoolboys on tours—deduced the signs for ten (𐄐), a hundred (𐄙), and a thousand (𐄢). Next to those large numbers, he also sometimes noticed the related symbols 𐀵𐀰 and 𐀵𐀯, which he took to mean "total"—the first deciphered words in Linear B.

Other clues were subtler. Early on, scholars guessed that the pictograms 𐂀 and 𐂁 meant "man" and "woman." Then, in 1927, an archaeologist noticed one line that read:

𐂁 𐄍 𐀒𐀺 𐄇 𐀒𐀷 𐄇 𐄏

His Spidey sense began tingling. There were seven ticks for women, then one tick for the next two items. Nine total. There were also nine ticks in the sum column. That meant that 𐀒𐀺 and 𐀒𐀷 must belong to the same general category as *woman,* or else you wouldn't add them together. He deduced that 𐀒𐀺 and 𐀒𐀷 must be human beings, probably *boys* and *girls.* He was close: He got the sex backwards. But his reasoning was spot-on.

Beyond that, scholars counted up all the symbols on different tablets and found 89 unique, non-pictographic characters—too many for an alphabet and too few for a hieroglyphic system. Linear B was therefore a syllabary, where each character encodes one syllable.

Finally, based on various clues, they determined that Linear B was written left to right. For example, if inscriptions didn't fill an entire line, they always started at the left and ended before they reached the right edge, never the reverse. In addition, scribes sometimes ran out of room on the right and had to cram several characters in: something they would logically do only at the end of a line.

In the 1940s, scholar Alice Kober produced a massive analog database of information about Linear B symbols. It eventually swelled to 180,000 slips of paper, which she filed into cigarette boxes in her home in Brooklyn, New York. Unfortunately, Kober died of cancer at 43 (all those cigarette boxes were hers) and lost the chance to pursue her work further.*

The stage was thus set for Michael Ventris. Ventris had pursued his architectural degree with the goal of designing dashing modern buildings, but by the late 1940s he was stuck sketching blueprints for schools. As someone who'd never liked school (or children), he found the work soul-deadening. Deciphering Linear B was his creative outlet. He spent every lunch hour and evening toiling away, and despite the anger it caused his wife, he eventually quit his job to pursue deciphering full-time. In addition to studying the tablets, Ventris circulated a questionnaire about Linear B to other scholars, which included the most pressing question of all: What was the underlying language?

There were a few theories. Archaeologists at the time knew that Greeks from the mainland had colonized Crete in the mid-second

* Dramatically, archaeologists in Greece unearthed a cache of 600 Linear B tablets in 1939, which significantly boosted the number of known texts. They remained locked in a vault in Athens during the war, but photographs of them slipped out on the last Allied ship to escape the Mediterranean in 1940 before World War II closed the sea to travelers.

millennium B.C. The bulk of Linear B tablets came from Crete, so perhaps the script represented Greek in some form. But Ventris didn't buy that idea, thanks to work by Arthur Evans. Evans had excavated the palace at Knossos on Crete beginning in 1900, blowing much of his family's fortune to dig out the ruins and restore them. This was the sprawling, 1,300-room palace linked to King Minos and his Labyrinth with the Minotaur—an estate full of dazzling frescoes, multistory towers, and a 400-person theater. Evans more or less fell in love with Knossos, and understandably so: The art and architecture were far grander than anything unearthed from sites in mainland Greece from that era. Moreover, no writing ever turned up at those sites, which hinted that the mainlanders were illiterate. In all, Evans dismissed continental Greece as a mere "branch," even a "plantation," of the dynamic Knossos culture. The idea that Linear B could represent Greek was inconceivable.

Evans favored the idea that Linear B represented an indigenous Cretan language. But after the old man's decades of toil came to naught, Ventris proposed the radical notion that Linear B represented a mysterious language called Etruscan, spoken in certain regions of Italy before the Roman Empire swallowed them. (It was an Etruscan soothsayer who warned Caesar about the Ides of March.)

Linguistically, the vast majority of European languages derive from an ancient mother tongue called Proto-Indo-European. But Etruscan sits outside this language family, which seemed appropriate for the sui generis Linear B script. According to lore, the Etruscans had also migrated to Italy from the region near the Aegean Sea, where many Linear B tablets originated.

Still, by 1952, the prospects for deciphering Linear B looked bleak. Scholars had exhausted every clue, and had only a handful of words to show for it. So a desperate Ventris began making guesses.

He noted that one common symbol in Linear B, the so-called double axe, 𐀀, nearly always appeared at the beginning of words. This suggested that the axe was a vowel,* and Ventris randomly assigned it the sound *ah.*

Another guess involved Cyprus. Cyprus had its own ancient script, albeit one that arose a thousand years after Linear B. Scholars had deciphered the sounds of the Cyprus script thanks to some Rosetta Stone–like inscriptions with multiple languages on them. A few Cypriot symbols looked kinda sorta like Linear B letters, and Ventris gambled that perhaps the sounds were similar, too.

These were shaky suppositions: Languages can change dramatically over a millennium, and the resemblance between the letters might be mere coincidence anyway. But Ventris plowed ahead, and in May 1952 he equated the Linear B symbol 𐀙 with the Cypriot symbol 𐠙, or *na,* and the Linear B 𐀴 with the Cypriot 𐠯, or *ti.* Ventris then examined some tablets from Crete. He made yet another assumption that the names of Cretan towns must appear somewhere on them, possibly near the top. So he began scanning the headings for symbols to plug in.

---

* Here's the reasoning behind this guess: In syllabic languages like Linear B, most symbols stand for a consonant-vowel combination, while a few stand for pure vowels. As an example, pretend that φ stands for "ma" and γ for "pa." *Mama* and *papa* would be written φφ and γγ. Note that you don't need a separate vowel symbol for *a* because the vowels are already built in.

Consonant-vowel combination signs can appear anywhere within a word. Pure vowel signs are different. They rarely appear in the middle or at the end of words, because unless you were saying something odd like "ma-a-ma" or "pa-pa-a," a pure vowel sign would be redundant. The only place you'd need a pure vowel sound is the beginning of a word, like a-gen-da. That's why Ventris guessed that the axe symbol—which appeared almost exclusively at the beginning of Linear B words—must represent a pure vowel. As for why he picked *a* instead of another vowel, that was dumb luck.

To understand his method, consider this invented example. Let's say Ventris found a potential place-name, . Based on the Cyprus script, he might guess that =*oak* and =*ma*. The word would read "oak-__-__-ma." Maybe *Oklahoma.* If so, he now had two more syllables, =*la* and =*ho*. Then he'd hunt around for another place-name on a different tablet with one of those new syllables. Say he finds . That reads __-la-__-ma. How about *Alabama*? This in turn produces two more syllables, =*aa* and =*ba*, at which point he can hunt for a third place-name. And of course, once he'd derived a stable of syllables from the place-names, he could try out those syllables in other, unknown words.

However simple this sounds—like a Sunday-afternoon crossword—things were far murkier for Ventris. Indeed, when he began plugging his newly won syllables into non-place-names on the tablets, the results confounded him.

One word that emerged was *coriander,* a Greek spice. But Ventris knew that Greek had no connection to Linear B; the archaeological evidence from Knossos and elsewhere said so. Still, perhaps this was an anomaly, a word that the Linear B people borrowed from Greek. Languages do that.

He turned next to the words for *boy* and *girl,*  and . Plugging in the proper symbol-sounds produced *ko-wo* and *ko-wa*—which, to his horror, echoed the classical Greek terms for *boy* and *girl, kouros* and *korē.* Worse, plugging sounds into the words for *total,* 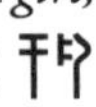 and , produced *to-so* and *to-sa,* similar to the masculine and feminine forms of *so much* in classic Greek. Ventris groaned. Not only was this more Greek, but the grammar showed gender inflection—a feature common in Indo-European languages but less common outside them. In particular, several Indo-European languages inflect gender through *-o* and *-a* endings. In contrast, Ventris's darling

Etruscan language was not Indo-European, and therefore stood little chance of using *-o/-a* inflection.

Ventris no doubt had a good sulk about his spoiled Etruscan hypothesis—a beautiful theory slain by some ugly facts. But his annoyance soon gave way to a liberating thought: Who cares? Maybe Linear B was Greek after all. If so, he might have to eat crow for disparaging the connection for so long. But if the script really was Greek, he now had a major head start on decipherment.

He began scouring other Linear B tablets, and more classical Greek terms popped out: *kerameu* for "potter" (cf., ceramics), *tekotone* for "carpenter" (cf., tectonics, things joined together). After this, the normally aloof Ventris lost his cool. He shook his wife Lois awake at two o'clock one morning, jabbing his notes with his finger and babbling about chariots. Then came the dinner party, when he locked himself in his study with some texts. Before long, several new words tumbled out. More and more followed, the momentum building. Suddenly, it was like he'd donned glasses for the first time—whole lines suddenly blinked into focus. To be sure, he found no psalms or lyrical odes that day; the texts were more like personnel files and bills of lading. But he could read them! He finally flung open his study door, his hair affright, to find a scowling wife and two drunk guests. He hurried through an apology, then declared, "I know it—I'm certain of it!" Linear B was Greek.

It was an odd Greek, an archaic Greek, several centuries older than Homer; it would have sounded as alien to him as Chaucer does to us today. But it was Greek nonetheless. More specifically, Linear B recorded the language of the so-called Mycenaean Greeks, famed as the heroes of *The Iliad* and *The Odyssey*; as such, it was perhaps the language that the real-life counterparts of Achilles and Odysseus spoke.

As for all the evidence Arthur Evans had marshaled to disprove the Greek–Linear B connection—well, he was wrong. Not about everything. The palace at Knossos did predate sites on mainland Greece, and Cretan civilization was every bit as grand as Evans imagined. But the story of Linear B is more complex than he realized. As far as scholars can tell, the predecessor script Linear A arose centuries earlier and probably recorded a native Cretan language. Scholars also know that most palaces on the island were destroyed around 1450 B.C., with evidence of looting and burning. Probably not coincidentally, there's a surge of Mycenaean influence on Crete after this point, as reflected in pots and the style of graves. But the reason behind that surge isn't clear. Perhaps mainland Mycenaean Greeks invaded and conquered Crete, which would explain the destruction of so many palaces. Mysteriously, however, the main palace at Knossos—which you'd think would be a top target—survived the wider collapse and thrived for another century. So perhaps the incoming Greeks simply filled a power vacuum after a civil war or social unrest on Crete destroyed the other palaces. Or perhaps the Knossos kings and the mainland Greeks formed an alliance to attack other sites. Regardless, illiterate Greeks moved to Crete and encountered Linear A writing, which they no doubt thought was pretty nifty. They then adapted that writing system to record the Greek language. In the end, then, maybe Evans was half right: His beloved Cretan civilization had indeed developed an ingenious native script. But that script was Linear A. Linear B, as the boy he'd led on that tour showed, was Greek.

It just so happened that Ventris's female guest at dinner that night, Prudence Smith, produced radio shows for the BBC, and she begged Ventris to record a segment for broadcast. Ventris hesitated; he felt shy. Smith's bosses at the Beeb also frowned when she approached them the next day. The story seemed too fantastical. Had some unemployed architect really decoded the greatest linguistic mystery in the world?

But Smith insisted, and she finally convinced Ventris to visit the studio. On July 1, 1952, he announced his discovery to the world. It was the happiest moment of his all-too-short life.

Linear B had comforted Ventris after his parents died and then again when his marriage began crumbling. (Lois would invite friends on vacations with them, because otherwise she and Michael just stared at each other over meals, lacking anything to say.) But with Linear B deciphered, he could no longer take refuge there. He also had no more excuses to avoid work. But, having quit his previous job, he could reenter architecture only sideways, through a fellowship that involved building a database of blueprints. It proved excruciatingly dull. Ventris wanted to *design* things, not tabulate data. He eventually quit the fellowship in a rambling letter to the sponsor, declaring that he "deeply doubt[ed] the value of both my vaunted intelligence and ... of life itself." He added, poignantly, "All I can ask you is to temper your justifiable anger with a little compassion."

Two weeks after quitting, on the night of September 5, 1956, Ventris realized he'd left his wallet at his in-laws' home. He insisted on retrieving it. Returning at 1 a.m., he spotted a so-called lay-by north of London, a rest stop along the road's shoulder for sleepy drivers. While pulling in, he smashed into a parked lorry and died instantly. He was 34 years old—even younger than Rakhaldas Banerji and Jean-François Champollion had been. The inquest ruled the death an accident, but friends and colleagues always wondered. Some would later note that Ventris's son died of a heart attack in his 40s, so maybe Ventris suffered one, too. Others had darker thoughts: that perhaps he'd done something desperate and deliberate. Regardless, he was gone. As one historian noted, aptly citing a Greek poet, "Those whom the gods love die young."

In the decades after Linear B, scholars deciphered several more lost scripts, including one (Linear Elamite)* in 2022. The most spectacular crack involved ancient Mayan, an icon-based script whose glyphs have a psychedelic, pop art feel—polka-dot mollusks, bucktoothed jaguars, zonked-out ducks, and more:

As with Egyptian hieroglyphs, the beauty and mystery of the glyphs seduced scholars into believing all sorts of nonsense. Some predicted

* Elam was an ancient kingdom in Iran. The decipherment of Linear Elamite was a bizarre tale, full of burglary, buried treasure, and international smuggling rings. For the full story, see the bonus notes on my website, *samkean.com/books/the-museum-of-lost-things/extras/notes*. Excitingly, reading Linear Elamite could now help decode the oldest known undeciphered script, the 3,000-year-old proto-Elamite.

that the script encoded the "cabalistic rites" of an "esoteric cult." Others predicted that the script would reveal the Maya to be serene spiritualists whose pacifism and adoration of nature could provide a strong moral counterpoint to the crassness and violence of the modern age. They could not have been more wrong.

The Maya had books—bark-paper volumes bound in jaguar skin that folded out like road maps—but the Spanish destroyed most of them in the 1500s. So the bulk of Maya writing today comes from pots, temples, tombs, and monuments. Beginning in the late 1800s, scholars worked out the calendar and counting system (base-20, with dots and bars). Unfortunately, they didn't know the names of any rulers or cities, so they couldn't apply the strategies that proved so fruitful with hieroglyphs and Linear B.

The one thing decipherers had going for them was the survival of 30 Maya languages into modern times. They could therefore use words in those languages as a decipherment aid. In addition, in a grim irony, a Spanish priest who burned many Maya books inadvertently helped resurrect the language four centuries later. No one knows why he bothered, but the priest interrogated one scribe and jotted down an "alphabet" of symbols and sounds. He made several mistakes, but recorded enough correct information to get scholars going.

For instance, a few sharp-eyed researchers noticed that certain glyphs always appeared above carvings of dogs, parrots, turkeys, and jaguars. Using the priest's alphabet and knowledge of modern Maya languages, they pieced together a few animal names, such as *tzul,* "dog." In the mid-1900s, a grocer who'd been exiled from Nazi Germany became obsessed with Maya culture while living in Mexico and teased out several city names in a similar way. Then a Russian American archaeologist noticed that carvings of humans often contained two distinctive glyphs …

... followed by dates from the Maya calendar separated by 12 to 31 years. She reasoned that the carvings depicted kings, and the dates recorded when they were born and when they ascended to the throne.

Unfortunately, Maya glyphs are so complicated that this simple pattern-matching didn't get very far. The real breakthrough sprang from an incident right out of Indiana Jones.

In 1949, an archaeologist was exploring a vine-choked, guano-slicked temple in eastern Mexico with elaborate inscriptions on the walls inside. But one day, something on the floor snatched his attention: a stone slab with a hole in it. Getting down on his knees, he peered inside—and saw steps leading downward. A hidden chamber.

His hopes sank upon prying loose the six-inch-thick slab. After a few feet, the staircase down was filled with rubble, which was cemented together with mortar. He ordered his workers to start chipping away. Given that only one person could fit into the narrow passage down, clearing it out took the rest of that digging season, as well as three more. (At one point, they thought they'd reached the bottom, only to find that the stairway made a U-turn and kept descending. That was a low day on-site.)

Finally, in June 1952—the same month Michael Ventris decrypted Linear B—the team broke through a granite wall 80 feet down. Behind it lay more mortared rubble, and behind *that* sat the toughest, most stubborn wall yet, a full 12 feet thick. It took a week to batter through. At last, they found a corridor with two steps at the far end, leading up to a cramped space with a half dozen human skeletons inside, presumably sacrificed in some dark rite.

More exciting still, they noticed a triangular wall slab in the corridor with a missing chink. One digger slid a crowbar in—and encountered no resistance. There was a hollow space behind: a hidden chamber within the hidden chamber! Wrenching open the triangular slab took two more days of grueling work with ropes and crowbars. Then, at last, they entered. The lead archaeologist later recalled his first moments inside: "The spacious crypt seemed to be carved in ice, since its walls were covered with a shiny calcareous layer ... numerous stalactites hung from the vault like curtains, and thick stalagmites gave the impression of huge candles."

They had found a vaulted burial chamber, untouched for 1,300 years. It contained a 13-foot sarcophagus with an ornately carved lid showing someone descending into the underworld. Inside the sarcophagus, they found a hoard of necklaces, beads, and rings, plus a spectacular jade mask covering a skull.

But whose skull? Inscriptions on the sarcophagus listed several dates—presumably its occupant's birth date, date of accession to the throne, and death date. There was also a glyph on the lid that seemingly named the king inside, a promising start. In addition, the archaeologist reasoned that the temple above the hidden chamber had been built to honor the deceased, and that the decorations up there would commemorate his life and achievements. Sure enough, when linguists scoured the temple walls, they found multiple inscriptions listing the same three dates. Everything was falling into place.

At least initially. Because unlike on the sarcophagus—which had a single name-glyph associated with the dates—things were not so simple on the temple walls. Some of the name-glyphs there looked identical to the glyph on the sarcophagus, which made sense. But others contained additional elements, or looked completely different. Indeed, the amount of variety was baffling. What did all those variations mean?

It took two decades to answer that question. At a conference in 1973, several frustrated Maya scholars finally pooled their thoughts and worked out both who the ruler was and—the real prize—how Maya writing worked.

The ruler's name was K'inich Janaab' Pakal. He's more commonly known as just Pakal, which means "shield," and there were indeed multiple ways to write his name:

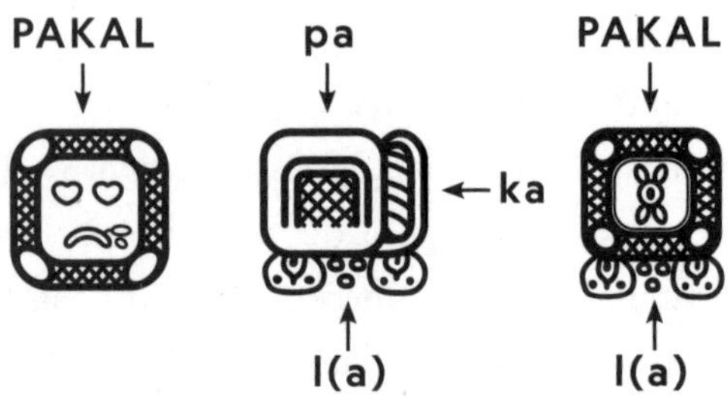

One way (left) involved a picture of a shield. That's the basic glyph that appeared on the sarcophagus and in a few places in the temple above. But temple scribes also sometimes rendered Pakal's name using syllabic symbols (center): pa-ka-l(a). (The final *a* is silent.) A third way to write his name in the temple (right) combined pictures and symbols. But notice that the scribes didn't include all three syllables in the rightmost picture, just one.

Why? They apparently just liked the way it looked. As we now know, Maya writers had immense flexibility. They could combine pictures and syllables in whatever way looked most beautiful to them, and they loved playing around with different styles, reminiscent of the elaborate calligraphic arts of the Golden Age of Islam. That explains all the variety among the name-glyphs in the temple: There were multiple "correct" ways to write *Pakal.*

The same held true for other words, too. Consider these depictions of *balam* (jaguar) and *chum tuun* (stone seat):

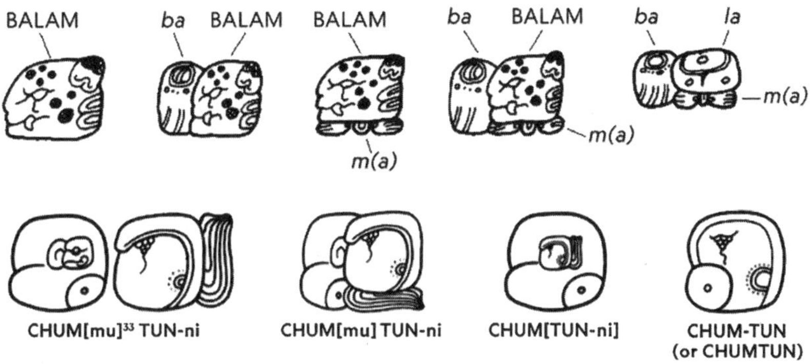

Scribes could place the glyphs side by side, flip them 90 degrees, have one peeking out from behind another, make little bow ties of them, shrink and superimpose them, or create a mishmash of multiple effects. They had total artistic freedom.*

However refreshingly different, this writing system proved a gigantic headache for scholars. But dozens of them kept plugging away after 1973, piecing together word after word until they could read nearly every tomb and temple wall. And what did the texts reveal?

* In 1984, archaeologists in Guatemala found a royal tomb stuffed with treasure, including a pot decorated with leopard spots. One glyph on it caught their eye, and as soon as they got back to civilization, they bought a Hershey bar, dialed the number on the back packaging, and begged chemists at the company to analyze the residue inside the pot. Can you guess why?

After the archaeologists shipped the pot off, the Hershey lab confirmed that the residue was indeed cocoa, a cherished drink in Mesoamerica.

That the Maya were hardly peaceful saints. They boasted about their military prowess, injected hallucinogenic drugs with enemas, and reveled in the suffering and torture of their enemies. In other words, the Maya were just as vainglorious and flawed as people everywhere. But at last, they could tell us so in their own voice.

One often overlooked point about decipherment is that it exists along a continuum. On one end sit scripts like Egyptian hieroglyphs that are almost completely decoded. Then comes ancient Mayan, which scholars can read around 85 percent of. (For one thing, they still don't know what *Janaab'* means in K'inich Janaab' Pakal's name.) Moving farther along, there's the Chinese bone writing of circa 1200 B.C.—messages carved onto ox or turtle bones and used to cast fortunes—where scholars can decipher roughly a third of it. With other scripts, we might understand the numbers or the calendar and little more. Finally, at the far end of the continuum, sit a few scripts where we can't read a single syllable.

One especially frustrating case is Etruscan, the pre-Roman script that Michael Ventris adored. The Etruscans used Greek letters to record their language, so scholars today can pronounce all the words. We also know that Latin borrowed certain terms, including *atrium* and *stilus* (pen). Best of all, there's a huge corpus of texts to work with: around 13,000 inscriptions on everything from mummy wrappings to gambling dice. Unfortunately, most Etruscan texts are short, which makes decipherment difficult because there are fewer symbols to scrutinize for patterns. Worse, roughly 9,000 of those inscriptions appear on grave markers, which use stylized, truncated language. (Imagine trying to reconstruct English from nothing but tombstones.)

Overall, scholars have clawed their way to around 250 words. But unless we discover an Etruscan Rosetta Stone, the language will likely remain mute.

If scholars can pronounce Etruscan words but know little of the underlying language, the *rongorongo* script from Rapa Nui (Easter Island) presents the opposite case: We know it must encode a Polynesian language, but have no idea how to map the symbols onto sounds.

Delightfully, many characters in rongorongo—which means "chanting" or "recitation"—resemble Keith Haring doodles:

Scribes chiseled them onto stone tablets and wooden "talking boards" with obsidian blades or shark teeth, and 19th-century missionaries report they were read in an unusual manner.

Imagine a board with two dozen lines of text. You started with the bottom line and read left to right. Then you flipped the board 180 degrees and started reading what's now the second line from the top. When you finished that, you flipped the board again and read the third line from the bottom, and kept flipping back and forth until you finished.

Sadly, most talking boards were burned in the mid-1800s, though we don't know why. Some sources claim that, after the arrival of missionaries, a zealous group of newly converted Christians set them afire as sinful heathen relics. Other sources claim that the natives burned the boards in raids during a civil war. Still others argue that slave raiders from Peru so devastated the island's population that rongorongo fell into disuse; the remaining population, cold and impoverished, burned them as firewood. Regardless, only a few examples of the script remain today, including a drawing of a tattoo and a handful of symbols carved into a skull.

More than most scripts, rongorongo has attracted its share of kooks. One "translation" claimed to reveal the inner workings of a Kamasutra sex-cult that deflowered virgins. Another provided eyewitness "testimony" of encounters with aliens.

You might be wondering whether artificial intelligence could crack undeciphered scripts. Linguists are pessimistic. In the past, computer "intelligence" has struggled with even basic decipherment skills, such as spotting allographs (different forms of the same letter, like a and ɑ) and ligatures (joined letters, like æ and œ). Advanced AIs could probably handle such tasks, but computers in general don't excel at the sort of hunch-based, trial-and-error work that Champollion and Ventris employed.

In particular, computers would likely struggle to determine the underlying language—a key step in every successful decipherment so far. You also need to convert scripts into numerical data for computers to parse, and languages don't always reduce so easily. Think of the trippy jaguar and bird mashups in ancient Mayan. How would you numberize that?

The most intractable computing problem is tiny sample sizes. Fancy AIs require gobs of data to train on, and most undeciphered scripts simply don't have enough. As a rough estimate, one scholar suggested that a script of N letters requires a corpus of at least N^2 characters for any hope of decipherment.

That scales up fast. For Hebrew and its 22 letters, you'd need $N^2 = 484$ characters overall. Russian's 36 letters would require 1,296. Syllabic scripts run up to 90 characters (8,100). Classical Egyptian used 700 hieroglyphs (490,000), while modern Chinese has 5,000 symbols (25 million). Now consider the so-called Phaistos disc from Crete, which dates to around 1700 B.C. It's the only known example of its script, and there are 45 different symbols present. By the N^2 formula, scholars would need more than 2,000 characters. The disc contains 242—a tweet's worth of language. Not even a supercomputer could do much with that.*

In sum, to decipher an unknown script, you need a large body of text (ideally with lengthy inscriptions), at least some clue about the underlying language, and scores of analysts willing to dedicate their whole careers to research that might not pan out. It's a wonder it ever happens. And with all that in mind, we can finally circle back to the ultimate unclaimed prize among undeciphered scripts: the enigmatic writing on the tiny stone seals of the Indus Valley.

To adapt the old Mark Twain joke about quitting smoking, deciphering the Indus Valley script is easy. More than a hundred people have done it. Just not correctly.

Archaeologists know of roughly 5,500 Indus texts—mostly on stone seals, but also on pottery, ivory rods, copper plates, and a town "signboard." The most authoritative count lists around 400 different symbols, with the most common being a U with epaulets: ; other signs look like trees and fish. The total corpus contains around 19,600 characters, which exceeds the N^2 benchmark. Unfortunately, 40 percent

* In 2009, computer scientists added Egyptian hieroglyphs to Unicode, the computer language that renders digital characters. So with the right keyboard, you can now text in hieroglyphs. Maya glyphs are coming, too, although that script will be harder to render with its stacked and/or shrunken characters. Besides being cool, these additions aid scholars by providing universal identification numbers for symbols and by speeding up the ability to share information digitally and populate databases. Unicode already encompasses 155,000 characters in nearly a thousand languages.

of those texts are duplicates. Equally bad, most are short, an average of four symbols. Some are a single symbol, and even the longest-winded runs just 26 letters—the length of the English alphabet.

We can determine some things about the writing. Four hundred symbols are too many for an alphabet or syllabary, so the script probably combines syllables, puns, pictographs, and logographs ($, %), similar to Egyptian hieroglyphs. We know the writing proceeds right to left in most cases (93 percent)* because inscriptions generally start on the right edge and sometimes get crowded on the left. Vertical strokes (||||) probably represent small numbers, and scholars think they've identified the symbol for 10 (one semicircle, ∩), 20 (two semicircles, ∩∩), and 30 (guess how many semicircles). Such numbers precede what appear to be nouns, so perhaps adjectives preceded nouns generally. Statistical analysis can even help divide strings of symbols into words. Consider this invented example, where the numbers indicate how often two symbols appear consecutively in the overall corpus:

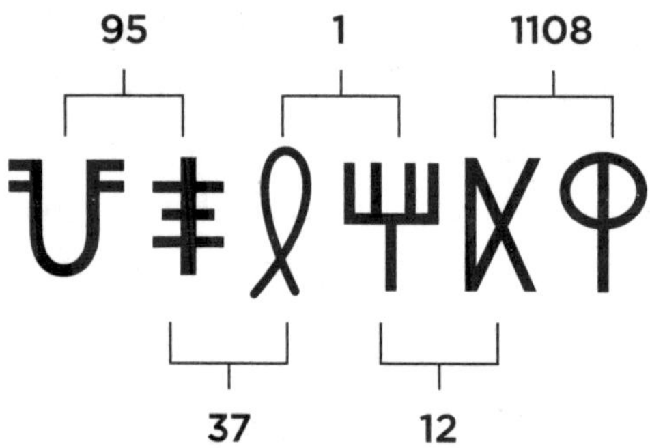

* For some reason, 1/15 of Indus texts run left to right. In addition, there are nine examples of so-called boustrophedon writing, where the direction alternates left to right and right to left line by line, the way you'd mow a lawn. The rongorongo flip-it-upside-down style is called reverse boustrophedon.

Here, you'd cleave the string into three words, chopping along the 1 and along the 12:  and  and . The fact that  is also common hints that it might be a word as well, with  as a suffix.

Unfortunately, the good news peters out there. Given the lack of long texts, scholars know virtually nothing about the language's syntax and grammar. They cannot agree on how many allographs exist (the a/ɑ variants), nor on what objects the pictographs represent: The ubiquitous  has been described as a cow head, a pot with handles, and a ficus tree, among other things. Compounding the problem, we don't know of any Rosetta Stone bilingual texts, we don't know the Indus calendar, and we don't know the names of any rulers or cities. (Harappa and Mohenjo-daro are modern names.)

Most daunting of all, we have no idea what language the Indus people spoke. Based on current evidence, it's probably a Dravidian tongue. But the oldest-known Dravidian texts are roughly 2,000 years younger than any Indus text, an eternity in language evolution. Given the size of the Indus empire, it's also possible that people there spoke multiple languages even while using a common script (similar to how British, French, German, and Spanish people all write in the Roman alphabet today). Or perhaps the Indus people spoke an extinct language, one that's left no trace in the modern world.

The political situation in India today makes the language question fraught. Again, Hindu nationalists desperately want to prove that the Indus script is early Sanskrit. It's not, but they howl at those who say otherwise, denouncing them as racists, imperialists, or sinister "leftists." Their critics don't pull punches, either, dismissing the supposed Sanskrit decipherments as "trash" and "propaganda," if not outright fraud. This overheated rhetoric has fueled suspicion and mistrust within the field, undermining the collaborative efforts that proved so fruitful with Maya glyphs.

Some scholars have even declared that the Indus script doesn't represent true writing at all. As previously noted, beyond using the stone seals to mark trade goods, the Indus people might have used them as identification badges. By this logic, the Indus "letters" might be akin to medieval heraldry signs, which certainly encoded meaning but didn't map onto speech the way true written scripts do. Moreover, although writing first arose in most places for boring commercial reasons (taxes, inventories), people usually saw exciting new possibilities pretty quickly and adapted the technology to record poems and prayers and historical deeds. So why didn't the Indus people? If they invented a written language, they sure didn't do much with it.

To be clear, most scholars do consider the Indus script a written language. The characters (almost) always read the same direction, and strings of certain characters usually appear together in a specific order, both universal traits of writing.

In addition, in 2009, a team of computer scientists and other researchers analyzed the so-called conditional entropy of the script. Conditional entropy measures randomness, or a lack thereof: Given one symbol-letter, how much flexibility do you have in choosing the next one? In English, *S* rates high on conditional entropy, since you can follow it with *A, C, E, H,* et cetera. *Q* rates low.

The team calculated the conditional entropy of both the Indus script and other written languages, as well as nonlinguistic information systems such as DNA sequences, musical scores, and Fortran. In the end, DNA and music had the highest entropy-randomness, Fortran the lowest. Languages clustered in between. And the Indus script sat square in the middle of the cluster—close to Sanskrit, but even closer to Old Tamil (a Dravidian tongue) and the language of ancient Sumer (an Indus trading partner).

Finally, while it's certainly not scientific, the Indus script just *feels* like a language to many scholars, who can't accept that such carefully crafted symbols are mere accounting icons. One moaned about "the gross mismatch" in his heart "between the artistic excellence of Indus seals and the notion that many were intended as receipts for fish." A few brave (or foolhardy) researchers have proposed tentative Indus words based on puns, including the names of the planets in the night sky. ( is a common symbol in Indus, and a Dravidian word for "fish," *meen,* can also denote "star.")

Still, the general mood among Indus decipherers is frustration. Given the Indus people's widespread trading routes, and the large number of Indus sites that remain unexcavated, perhaps a subcontinental Rosetta Stone will emerge someday. Until then, as the world's leading Indus expert admitted, "It looks most unlikely that the Indus script will ever be deciphered fully." He then added, wistfully, "That ... must not deter us from trying."

CHAPTER EIGHT

LOST KNOWLEDGE

Julius Caesar walked right into a holy hell of a mess in Alexandria.

This cosmopolitan city served as the seat of government for Egypt's 13-year-old pharaoh, Ptolemy XIII, a descendant of the Ptolemy mentioned in the Rosetta Stone. In 48 B.C., his kingdom was beset with controversy. According to his late father's will, Ptolemy was supposed to rule Egypt jointly with his 21-year-old sister Cleopatra. But Ptolemy's advisers—a scheming general named Achillas, a conniving eunuch named Pothinus, and a devious rhetorician named Theodotus—had convinced the teen to seize the kingdom for himself and banish Cleopatra to the desert.

The trio of advisers then did something even more audacious. In 48 B.C., Julius Caesar was fighting a heated civil war against a rival,

Pompey. After losing a battle in Greece, Pompey fled to Egypt seeking refuge—a request that put Ptolemy's advisers in a bind. Taking Pompey in would make an enemy of Caesar, who seemed likely to win the war. Then again, if Caesar lost, refusing Pompey would make an enemy of *him.* So, cleverly if cold-bloodedly, the trio met Pompey on his warship in Alexandria's harbor and lured him onto a dinghy. There, the general Achillas stabbed him. As his comrade Theodotus said, "A dead man cannot bite."

Caesar arrived in pursuit of Pompey four days later, at which point the advisers presented him with Pompey's decapitated head as a gift. Caesar shed a few crocodile tears—he had to show some respect for a fellow Roman citizen—then rowed ashore with his troops and took up residence in the royal palace.

This proved unwise. Egypt was touchy about its independence, and seeing the most powerful man in Rome strutting around the palace worried the Egyptian people. Did Caesar have designs on their kingdom? Caesar tried to appease them, receiving local dignitaries and going sightseeing; he no doubt took in the famous lighthouse near the harbor, one of the Seven Wonders of the Ancient World. But he couldn't defuse the tension. Riots broke out, and the mobs killed several soldiers.

Things grew even more tense when Cleopatra showed up. One night, she and a trusted guard slipped into Alexandria's harbor on a rowboat. Once ashore, the guard wrapped her in a bedroll, hoisted her over his shoulder, and gained entrance to the palace by pretending to be a traveling salesman.* Famously, he unfurled the roll at Caesar's feet, and Cleopatra popped out.

Caesar, 56, was smitten by her good looks and saucy wit. Exactly as she'd calculated, they became lovers. Moreover, he agreed to help

* Different versions of this story exist, with different details.

her reconcile with her brother and regain her kingdom. To paraphrase historian Irene Vallejo, she came, he came, she conquered.

Ptolemy's advisers were of course alarmed to see Caesar canoodling with the boy's rival to the throne. Caesar, in his postcoital daze, didn't realize the danger he was in and even threw a banquet to celebrate the reunion of Cleopatra and Ptolemy. During the feast, however, Caesar's barber wandered off and overheard the eunuch and general plotting about murdering the Romans. Acting quickly, Caesar ordered his guards to storm in and seize the advisers. Achillas and Theodotus escaped, but Caesar executed the eunuch Pothinus. Achillas then began amassing troops outside the city, and when Caesar sent two messengers out to negotiate, Achillas killed one and drove the other off. War was now inevitable.

Caesar hastily summoned reinforcements from abroad to aid his 3,800 soldiers, but the troops wouldn't arrive for weeks. In the meantime, the Egyptian general attacked with 22,000 men. The fighting that followed was fierce. At one point, in a pitched battle in the harbor, Caesar had to leap off his ship and swim for his life, even disrobing in the water to keep from drowning. The people of Alexandria fished his clothes out and paraded them around as trophies.

Caesar's troops held on until the reinforcements came a few weeks later, but the newly arrived Roman galleys found themselves stuck outside the city. Alexandria's harbor was C-shaped—a circular bay with a narrow mouth—and dozens of Egyptian ships were blocking the entrance. To remove this obstacle, Caesar had his troops sneak up and hurl torches at the ships. The canvas sails and pitch-soaked planks quickly ignited.

While the inferno blazed, Caesar's men rushed across a causeway to an island, allowing them to link up with the reinforcements. And while it wasn't easy, Caesar outfoxed the Egyptians over the next few months, defeating Ptolemy's forces and restoring Cleopatra to the throne.

However dramatic, the battle for Alexandria might have been a mere footnote in Caesar's career if not for one thing. The fire on the ships in the harbor grew so massive that embers began drifting ashore on the wind. Some of the warehouses there caught fire, and stores of highly combustible grain went up, sending sparks jumping between the buildings "like meteors as they cut furrows across the heavens," said one witness. And according to some ancient sources, the ensuing inferno destroyed the greatest concentration of wisdom in history: the legendary Library of Alexandria.

It's hard not to wince at the sheer scope of lost literature. Historians estimate that we possess just a third of Aristotle's treatises, a quarter of Aristophanes's comedies, and one-fifteenth of the tragedies of Aeschylus. Of Caesar's oeuvre, just two slim volumes survive. We're missing key works from Euripides, Archimedes, and Cicero, too—not to mention a few dozen lost books of the Bible and at least 10 gospels of Jesus.

The problem is not confined to ancient times, either. Two of Shakespeare's plays no longer exist, and works by Milton, Blake, Austen, and Melville have vanished as well. Even modern writers—Joyce, Hemingway, Plath, and others—have seen works disappear in whole or in part, in every conceivable way: lost in the mail, destroyed in bombing raids, seized by the KGB, puked on, scribbled over by children, accidentally burned as rubbish, stolen from cars, swiped by rivals, even crushed by steamrollers.*

---

* The near misses are equally scary. On his deathbed, Virgil asked friends to burn the manuscript of his not-quite-finished epic *The Aeneid*, but Emperor Augustus forbade this. Similarly, Max Brod saved the novels and stories of his friend Franz Kafka from the flames. The oldest extant copy of *Beowulf* almost burned in a fire in 1731, and its edges are still singed today.

Still, no loss of literature will ever sting as much as the destruction of the Great Library of Alexandria. Although not the world's first library (temples in Egypt and Anatolia had long been storing documents for priests to consult), Alexandria's library was vaster and far more ambitious than any predecessor, aiming to gather every last work in the known world. Some historians believe that Alexander the Great himself—who adored literature and slept with a copy of *The Iliad* beneath his pillow (a text personally annotated by Aristotle)—came up with the idea of the library after conquering Egypt. "All the Earth, I consider mine," he once declared, and a universal library in his namesake city was very much in keeping with this ambition.

Alexander died before he could enact such plans, so the task fell to his former general and successor in Egypt, Ptolemy I. Ptolemy and his heirs would build Alexandria into the largest and most vibrant city of its day—"the umbilicus of the world," one historian called it—and the library would play a key role in its rise. Much as the Medici did with artists in Florence, the Ptolemies bribed dozens of leading scholars to move to Alexandria to boost the city's prestige. A universal library also familiarized the kings and their advisers with distant lands: good practical intelligence for commerce and conquest. We don't know the date of the library's founding, but Ptolemy imported a Greek politician and philosopher to get the venture going. The library seemingly opened its doors after Ptolemy died in 282 B.C., under the reign of his son Ptolemy II, but no historical record survives.

The great archive sat within the city's Royal Quarter near the harbor. And properly speaking, it consisted of two institutions joined at the hip: the library itself, and a temple-shrine dedicated to the Muses of Greek mythology—a *muse*um. The library-museum's grounds resembled a college campus, with lecture halls, gardens, and a domed cafeteria. Sources hint that Ptolemy II also opened a zoo there, with lions, giraffes, rhinoceroses, peacocks, an immense python, and what must have been the world's most miserable polar bear. The library wasn't laid out like modern ones, with racks of materials broken up by open areas to sit and work. It probably looked more like the stacks of a research library, dense with bookshelves and cubbyholes. You'd grab what you needed, then head off to the gardens to read.

The library contained no books per se (i.e., texts divided into pages and bound together; those came later). Instead, scholars studied scrolls made of papyrus. This plant grew along the Nile, and its fronds were pounded, smoothed, and glued together into long sheets, which authors wrote on. As you read a scroll, you unfurled it with your right hand and rolled it up with your left. Most scrolls were 6 to 12 inches wide and extended 10 to 12 feet, although some ran well over 100 feet. After finishing, you were supposed to rewind a scroll to the beginning for the next person, as with old VHS tapes, but sometimes people were jerks and didn't do that.

A surviving bibliography hints that the library divided the scrolls by genre into history, rhetoric, philosophy, medicine/law, various types of poetry, and a miscellaneous category that covered everything else, including recipes. This was the first attempt in history to organize knowledge systematically, a major intellectual achievement. Unfortunately, papyrus was brittle, and the constant rolling and unrolling damaged the scrolls and caused tears. To combat that fragility, scribes were constantly recopying texts onto fresh scrolls to preserve them. Considering the sheer drudgery of the task, these scribes might have been white-collar slaves.

Some scrolls were stored in linen or leather sleeves for protection. Instead of listing the title and author first, they usually included such information (if at all) near the end, since the last lines of a scroll were

LEFT: In 1485, the much maligned King Richard III was killed at Bosworth Field in a skirmish with troops commanded by an upstart pretender to the throne: the future Henry VII. Richard became the last English monarch to die in battle; his body was severely abused after his death and dumped into an ignominious, unmarked grave rumored to lie beneath a modern parking lot.

BELOW: While crushing a revolt in Judea in A.D. 70, soldiers led by the Roman general Titus burned down a site sacred to the Jewish people, the Second Temple in Jerusalem, which had been built roughly 90 years prior. The Arch of Titus in Rome depicts the soldiers hauling away loot from the Temple, including a menorah, an offering table, and a pair of silver trumpets.

ABOVE: Even eight centuries after his death, the ruthless warrior Genghis Khan remains beloved in Central Asia, although his final resting place is unknown. This 130-foot-tall statue of the so-called Disturber of the Universe sits near Ulaanbaatar, Mongolia.

RIGHT: A fresco from the tomb of Nebamun, a middling grain accountant at a temple in Egypt who happened to select a brilliant but unknown artist to decorate his mausoleum, which is now lost. This panel shows a garden filled with birds, lotus flowers, palm trees, a sycamore fig, and a pool with fish.

TOP: The ruins of the fabled city of Troy, near the modern site of Hisarlık in Turkey

MIDDLE LEFT: The so-called Mask of Agamemnon, which Heinrich Schliemann discovered at Mycenae in Greece in 1876

MIDDLE RIGHT: Heinrich Schliemann, the German archaeologist who proved the world wrong by showing that the legendary city of Troy really did exist

RIGHT: Heinrich Schliemann's wife, Sophia, wearing gold jewelry discovered at Troy and mistakenly dubbed Priam's Treasure

TOP: A rendition of the ancient city of Çatalhöyük, which had no streets or open public spaces. People walked from house to house along the roofs, and entered and exited through skylights.

BOTTOM LEFT: Illustrations of a goddess and her handmaiden, based on the royal treasure of Dorak discovered by archaeologist James Mellaart

BOTTOM RIGHT: The British archaeologist James Mellaart. His publications on the mysterious Dorak treasure—a collection of jewelry, swords, figurines, and other items looted from Turkey—continue to confound historians.

TOP: A scrap of the Dead Sea Scrolls, a collection of roughly 900 fragmented manuscripts discovered between 1947 and 1956 that contain ancient biblical texts in various languages

MIDDLE LEFT: Two papyrus pages from the Nag Hammadi cache, a set of codices (early books) that include several apocryphal and even blasphemous accounts of the life of Jesus and other figures

MIDDLE RIGHT: The two halves of the Copper Scroll discovered near Qumran. Although considered part of the Dead Sea Scrolls, the Copper Scroll contains no religious texts, just lists of buried treasure.

ABOVE: Excavators searching for fragments of the Dead Sea Scrolls near Qumran. The scrolls represent the oldest known versions of many books of the Bible.

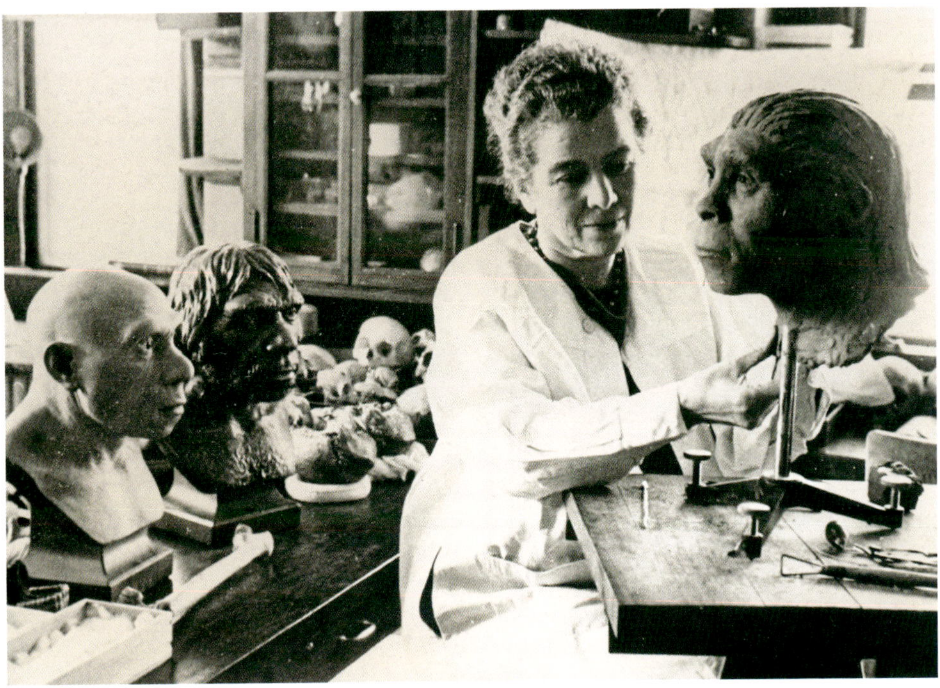

TOP: Workers digging at Longhushan—Dragon Bone Hill—in China, where the famous Peking Man fossils were unearthed beginning in 1929. The bones remain the most important lost fossils in history, although promising clues to their whereabouts have recently emerged.

BOTTOM: American sculptor Lucille Swan touches up her "Nellie" sculpture at Peking Union Medical College in China, where the Peking Man fossils were stored and studied. They disappeared from the campus in 1941.

TOP LEFT: The brilliant but flawed archaeologist and writer Rakhaldas Banerji, who first discovered the Indus Valley Civilization

TOP RIGHT: A small figurine of a young female dancer wearing arm bangles, excavated at the Indus Valley site of Mohenjo-daro

BOTTOM: An intricately carved Indus Valley Civilization seal from Mohenjo-daro featuring an elephant and the empire's mysterious script

TOP: The sarcophagus lid of the famous king Pakal from the Temple of the Inscriptions in Palenque, Mexico

BOTTOM: A wooden tablet featuring writing in *rongorongo,* an undeciphered script from Rapa Nui (Easter Island). Unusually, rongorongo is read in a so-called reverse boustrophedon style, which involves flipping the board upside down after finishing each line.

TOP: A painting of the Egyptian goddess Ma'at in the tomb of Nefertari, the wife of Ramses the Great. The text in the cartouche (the yellow circled portion) reads, "Nefertari, beloved of Mut," another Egyptian goddess.

BOTTOM LEFT: A seal from the Indus Valley city of Harappa. Archaeologist Rakhaldas Banerji noted similarities between Harappan seals and ones from Mohenjo-daro, and thereby realized he'd uncovered a lost civilization.

BOTTOM RIGHT: A portrait of Jean-François Champollion, the French Egyptologist who finally deciphered Egyptian hieroglyphs using the Rosetta Stone, which he never saw in person

TOP LEFT: The famous Rosetta Stone from 196 B.C. It contains the same message written in three different scripts: Egyptian hieroglyphs, demotic, and Greek.

TOP RIGHT: Michael Ventris, an English architect who studied the undeciphered Linear B script in his spare time

BOTTOM: A tablet of economic and administrative records written in Linear B. It dates from 1300 B.C. and comes from the ancient kingdom of Pylos in western Greece.

TOP: An illustration of the fire near the Alexandria harbor started by Julius Caesar's troops in 48 B.C. According to some sources, the blaze destroyed the famous Library of Alexandria.

BOTTOM LEFT: Fragments of a charred scroll from Herculaneum, a city buried in the eruption of Vesuvius in A.D. 79.

BOTTOM RIGHT: Hernando Colón, the illegitimate son of Christopher Columbus who grew up to become a noted book collector

ABOVE: Cocos Island off Costa Rica, where the Treasure of Lima supposedly lies. The treasure consisted of more than a billion dollars (in modern money) of gold, silver, jewelry, and other precious items that the colonial Spanish government smuggled out of Peru on a ship to keep out of the hands of rebel forces. But the crew spiriting it away turned pirate and buried it at an unknown location.

RIGHT: A detail from a map featuring the 14th-century Malian ruler Mansa Musa, who was likely the richest person who ever lived. Most of his wealth consisted of salt and especially gold, which Mali was rich in. His 1324 hajj to Mecca became legendary for his excessive spending and profligate generosity.

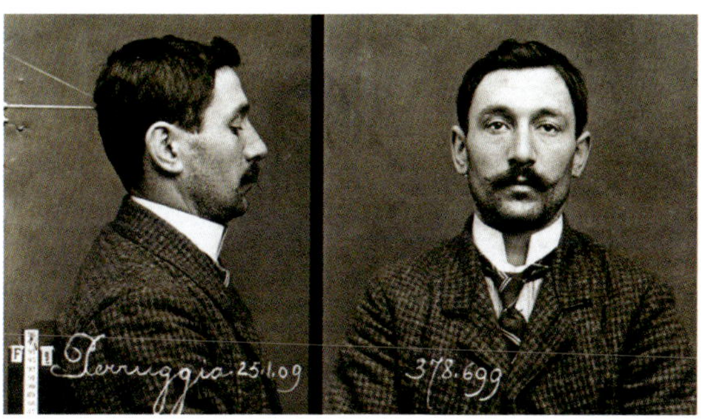

TOP LEFT: Parisians lined up by the thousands to see this empty space on the wall of the Louvre after the *Mona Lisa* was stolen in 1911.

TOP RIGHT: A modern reconstruction of Leonardo da Vinci's grandiose horse sculpture

MIDDLE: Peter Paul Rubens's copy of Leonardo da Vinci's ambitious but doomed mural in Florence, *The Battle of Anghiari*

BOTTOM: Vincenzo Peruggia, the Louvre employee who stole the *Mona Lisa* in 1911. These mug shots date from 1909.

TOP: The ruins of the castle in Königsberg where the Amber Room panels were stored after the Nazis plundered them during World War II

BOTTOM: A modern reconstruction in Russia of the legendary Amber Room, an architectural marvel that both Soviet Russia and Nazi Germany coveted

TOP: This Goldbergian contraption, designed by Hero of Alexandria in ancient times, automatically opened temple doors when priests started a fire on the altar.

BOTTOM LEFT: A fragment of the 2,100-year-old Antikythera Mechanism, history's first-known computer. It helped calculate eclipses and other astronomical events.

ABOVE: Sponge divers pose with a crusted-over statue recovered from the Antikythera wreck. Education Minister Spyridon Staïs stands on the upper deck between the ropes, in a fedora. Two rows below him, in a brimmed hat, sits diver Elias Lykopantis. To the left of him, just past the ropes, is captain Dimitrios Kontos.

TOP: Scientists assumed that the coelacanth had gone extinct 80 million years ago, until one turned up near South Africa in 1938.

BOTTOM LEFT: An ivory-billed woodpecker poses for the camera atop the hat of guide J. J. Kuhn in the Singer Tract in Louisiana in the spring of 1938. Very few of the birds were ever seen alive after this.

BOTTOM RIGHT: The skeleton of a dodo, a prime candidate for modern de-extinction efforts using genetic engineering wrapped in the center and were more protected. To aid identification, some scrolls had tags affixed to them, but if the tags fell off, you'd just have to start reading. Because papyrus was expensive, scribes filled each scroll completely, omitting all section breaks and even the spaces between words. Itwasjustlineafterlineofunbrokentext. Most works were in Greek, the language of scholarship then, but the library strove to include Persian, Hebrew, Buddhist, Georgian, Armenian, Egyptian, Indian, and Zoroastrian literature as well.

As the collection grew, Ptolemy II would stop by and ask the librarians, "How many now?" How many texts? Historians estimate that the library held 70,000 to 100,000 different titles and (counting duplicates) 500,000 to 700,000 scrolls overall—equivalent to 100,000 to 150,000 modern books. (For perspective, when Gutenberg's presses began running in 1456, there were 30,000 books in all of Europe.) The library eventually got so big that it opened an annex in a temple, with around 40,000 additional scrolls. Unlike the Great Library, which was restricted to scholars, the annex was open to the public. (That said, it wasn't convenient to access, as it sat on a promontory overlooking town, up a steep staircase; visitors arrived wheezing.)

Gathering together so many titles required some serious moolah. Alexandria had built its wealth on grain exports, and its 300,000 inhabitants also did brisk trade in glassware and textiles. The Ptolemies plowed a significant fraction of that wealth into buying new works, often sending armed warriors off on horseback with sacks of gold and silver to visit other centers of learning. These soldiers journeyed thousands of miles, crossing lands decimated by plagues and fires, and spent many a cold night shivering beneath their capes, scratching at lice and scanning the hills for bandits—all for a few precious scrolls.

Building the collection also required strong-arm tactics. Whenever a ship visited Alexandria's harbor, customs officials seized every scroll onboard to make copies. The ships then got the copies back, while the library kept the originals. Even more brazen, Ptolemy III once asked Athens to send him the original manuscripts of the plays of Aeschylus, Sophocles, and Euripides, the city's great tragedians. Wary of Ptolemy's intentions, Athens agreed, but first demanded a bond of 15 talents—a thousand pounds of gold and silver—to ensure the scrolls' return. Athens never saw them again. Ptolemy's scribes made lavish copies of each piece, then sent the copies to Greece. As for the gold and silver, Ptolemy snorted and told Athens to keep it; he could afford it.

In ancient times, the only collection to rival Alexandria's was the one in Pergamon in Anatolia. It held at least 200,000 scrolls in a state-of-the-art building with vents to circulate fresh air and prevent moisture from damaging the material. To squash this upstart, the Ptolemies banned the export of papyrus to Pergamon, which meant that scholars there could no longer recopy texts when they began crumbling. (Eventually, Pergamon got around this embargo by perfecting the art of making parchment, a more durable material.) Later, when Pergamon tried to poach the head librarian at Alexandria, the reigning Ptolemy had the man thrown in prison to make sure he didn't skip town. Indeed, the Ptolemies never hesitated to punish scholars who displeased them. One wrote a satire about the incestuous marriage between Ptolemy II and his sister, and according to lore, he was arrested, sealed inside a lead vase, and tossed into the sea.

Nevertheless, scholars rarely turned down invitations to work at the Great Library. Some were gadflies who'd been run out of other lands and were grateful to the Ptolemies for taking them in.* More commonly, scholars simply couldn't resist the eye-popping terms of employment: free housing, free meals, a generous salary exempt from taxes, and above all, unrivaled access to texts and the chance to collaborate with brilliant minds in every field. One historian described the library as "part think tank, part graduate school; part observatory and part laboratory." Given all these advantages, Alexandria acquired a critical mass of talent and saw an explosion of ideas rarely if ever surpassed in history.

Here's a selected list of things that scholars at Alexandria achieved. They invented latitude and longitude. They determined that Earth is round, nailed down its circumference to within 50 miles, and put forth convincing arguments that all its oceans are connected and that, à la Columbus, you could sail west to reach Asia. They discovered the nervous system, described the anatomy of the eye in detail, determined the liver's function, and ascertained that the heart pumps blood a thousand-plus years before Thomas Harvey. A thousand-plus years before Copernicus, they suggested that Earth revolved around the Sun, and later developed leap days and leap years to keep the seasons from drifting out of whack with the calendar. They invented the idea of organizing texts in alphabetical order by the author's name, as opposed to the previous filing system of dumping scrolls wherever there was room and memorizing their location. They pieced together the first definitive versions of *The Iliad* and *The Odyssey*—the versions we're still reading today—and also composed epic poems of their own. They compiled the first lists of the Seven Wonders of

* One vivid, if dubious, story holds that Ptolemy I hired 72 Jewish scholars from Jerusalem—six from each tribe of Israel—to visit Alexandria and translate the Old Testament from Hebrew to Greek. Rather than have them collaborate, Ptolemy ordered each scholar to render his own translation, at which point he would select the best. Miraculously, all 72 translations turned out identical, guided by divine intervention.

the Ancient World and the five simple machines that underlie much of physics. They constructed the world's first steam engines long before James Watt, and even built steam-driven robots, as well as self-playing musical instruments driven by wind. They fashioned the enormous mirrors that sat atop the giant lighthouse in Alexandria's harbor, which could cast light 30 miles out to sea. They did pioneering work in trigonometry and geometry, and Euclid wrote his *Elements* there. Archimedes did a tour, too.

In sum, Alexandria was the most electric city in the world in its prime, rich and fashionable and thrumming with new ideas. One historian commented on the almost "erotic thrill" of living there.

Then it all disappeared.

As far as we know, just one scrap of the library's hundreds of thousands of scrolls still survives today: a document from 235 B.C. that was later used to line a mummy's coffin. It's a list of the first lines of satirical poems, probably written as a finding aid. It's 28 inches long. Otherwise, every last one of the millions upon millions of lines in the greatest library of antiquity has vanished completely.

So what happened? We don't know exactly, since several key historical documents that could clear things up have, naturally, gone missing. But historians have identified a few suspects.

The most notorious is Julius Caesar. As we saw earlier, while Caesar was pinned down in Alexandria, he ordered his men to start a fire in the harbor that spread to land. And according to a few ancient sources, the blaze destroyed part if not all of the Great Library's collection. Pity the poor scholars! They came to Alexandria to debate Homer and draw maps and build steam engines. Suddenly, they're dodging Roman centurions in the street, and the next thing they know, their beautiful library goes up in flames. You can imagine them sprinting into the dark stacks, scooping up armfuls of precious scrolls, and stumbling around in the choking smoke. But they can save only a few, and are left watching in impotent despair as nine generations of irreplaceable work burns into ashes.

But did this actually happen? Some signs point to yes. A dozen years later, after Caesar's assassination, his ally Mark Antony reportedly raided the massive library at Pergamon and presented Cleopatra with 200,000 scrolls to make up for Caesar's arson. Furthermore, prominent visitors to Alexandria in later years neglected to mention the Great Library in their accounts of the city—even while they mention the attached museum. It's a puzzling omission, given the centrality of the library to life there.

Then again, some ancient sources do allude to the library, or at least seem to. After the eventual Roman conquest of Egypt, one emperor reportedly funded an addition to a sizable library there, while another sent scribes to some library to copy books. A third seemingly appointed a director. You'd also think that Caesar's many enemies would have trumpeted the destruction to discredit him. Yet not one says peep about it, so perhaps it survived Caesar. Furthermore, while most historians doubt that Mark Antony really shipped 200,000 scrolls to Egypt just to woo Cleopatra, some people back then apparently believed this story, which would make sense only if the Great Library still existed. Finally, as discussed, Alexandria did export papyrus to other cities and also seized scrolls from ships to copy them. Perhaps it was those scrolls—either copies of works or blank ones awaiting shipment—that burned in Caesar's fire, not the Great Library itself.

Given all that, some historians have absolved Caesar and turned the blame, however dubiously, on fanatical Christians and Muslims. One day in A.D. 391, a crew of Christian construction workers in Alexandria unearthed some pagan relics while building a new cathedral and decided to parade them through the streets for people to mock and spit on. This proved a dumb idea. Alexandria was a volatile place, thrumming with religious strife. As one historian commented, "Riots were something of a revered civic tradition" there, with mobs "often slaughter[ing] one another with gay abandon."

True to form, a horde of pagans murdered the blasphemous Christians, then fled to a temple on an outcrop overlooking town—the very temple that served as an annex for the Great Library. The affair ended with the Christians burning the temple and razing it. And somehow, in history's game of telephone, the destruction of the annex seemingly became the destruction of the Great Library itself. In truth, it's not even clear whether the annex held books at that time.*

The Muslim story is equally doubtful. Muslim armies conquered Alexandria in A.D. 642, and a general supposedly sent a message back to his ruler, the caliph, asking what to do with the mounds of scrolls moldering away in the library. (According to one source, the library had been neglected so long that you could gather cobwebs by the pound; it smelled as musty as a swamp.) The caliph's response was terse: "If those books contradict the Quran, they are heresy. If they agree with the Quran, they are superfluous. Either way, destroy them." Sounds pretty damning. Except no contemporary historian mentions this story; the earliest versions appear six centuries later. Moreover, the caliph says the exact same thing in another source about a cache of scrolls from Persia. In all likelihood, the scholars who recorded the Alexandria tale either got their facts mixed up or were deliberately falsifying history. As for why they might have done so, we haven't a clue—especially since these

* The story of fanatical Christians destroying the Great Library originated with historian Edward Gibbon, who never missed an opportunity to bash Christianity. Carl Sagan then introduced more errors centuries later by tying the destruction to the death of the scholar Hypatia. Hypatia was indeed murdered by Christians, but in 415—24 years after the temple incident. Her demise had nothing to do with the library.

historians were themselves Muslim and presumably weren't trying to cast their fellow believers in a bad light.

Overall, there are so many dubious, contradictory stories about the Great Library's destruction that it's hard to know what to think. Archaeological work could clear things up—finding a layer of ash circa 48 B.C. would look pretty bad for Caesar—but no trace of the library's footprint has ever emerged. (This is possibly because floods and earthquakes destroyed much of the Royal Quarter in medieval times, leaving it underwater.)

Still, one explanation, put forth by modern historians, offers a way out of this morass. It's possible that all of the above stories are wrong, and that the real culprit in the Great Library's demise was slower, subtler, and in many ways sadder: simple neglect.

Even historians struggle to tell the different Ptolemies apart sometimes. Vallejo admitted that, to her, reading about them "conjures the mirage of a single vampiric ruler who lives three centuries while the Hellenic world ... teeters and changes hands around him." But after the reigns of Ptolemy III, who read avidly, and Ptolemy IV, who dabbled in playwrighting, the Ptolemaic dynasty changed character. Ptolemy V, of Rosetta Stone fame, was battling rebellions in 196 B.C., and the troubles never let up during the reigns of his 10 successors. As a result, later Ptolemies neglected patronage and ruled like despots. In the 140s B.C., Ptolemy VII was murdered by his uncle Ptolemy VIII, who then banished all foreign scholars from his kingdom and installed a soldier as head of the library. And instead of pouring their riches into scrolls and scholars, the Ptolemies invested in their palace, adding rooms and wings and eventually whole buildings. By Julius Caesar's time, the palace swallowed a third of the city.

With the library already suffering from neglect, Rome then finished it off. Caesar's affair with Cleopatra scandalized Roman aristocrats, especially after she visited Rome and showed off her newborn son by Caesar. Rumors swirled that Caesar planned to marry this foreigner and make her his queen, then shift the empire's capital to Egypt.

After Caesar's murder and another civil war, Augustus took over as emperor and annexed Egypt, largely to secure grain. After this point, the library was doomed. For all their achievements, the Romans could be pretty philistine, and some of them balked at the idea of subsidizing a bunch of pointy-headed freeloaders. Roman governors in Alexandria instituted a spoils system instead, and began granting those coveted, tax-free jobs at the library to soldiers, athletes, and toadies. The quality of work among the few remaining scholars inevitably declined, and most of them shifted away from producing new knowledge to merely commenting on existing texts—what one historian called "parasitic writing." The very word *Alexandrian* became an insult, with connotations of pedantry.

Things deteriorated further when a new technology began spreading after A.D. 100: the codex, an early type of book with pages to flip. Scrolls suddenly seemed clumsy, passé, and the library had to update its collections to the new medium. Unfortunately, the scholars lacked the funds to convert everything, so they had to pick and choose. As with the shift in modern times from print to electronic texts, a lot got left behind, and the original papyrus scrolls eventually crumbled to dust. Equally bad, Rome secured new sources of grain from other territories, and Alexandria's fortunes slumped. By the 260s, the Great Library was moribund: There's no known list of members after this point. And if there was anything left of its collection, a series of Roman sieges, sacks, and invasions in the late 200s likely wiped it out.

It's hard to know what we lost with the death of the Great Library, but it's equally hard to resist speculation. Although only $1/18$ of Sophocles's dramas survive, even that meager fraction has given us immortal characters like Oedipus, Electra, and Antigone, and spawned a whole universe of metaphors in psychology. Just think if we had 18 times more Sophocles to draw on. Or consider how influential *The Iliad* and *Odyssey* have been. As we've seen, other epic poems about the war have vanished, some of which might have told the story of Troy's demise from the Trojan point of view or fleshed out details about the Trojan horse and other legendary scenes. Given all the foreign texts and translations in the library, we probably never would have lost our knowledge of hieroglyphs or cuneiform, saving a million hours of labor down the line. Most poignantly, the library boasted of experts in Indian history. If its collection had survived, could we read the Indus Valley script today?

In the sciences, the sting is keener still. Half the surviving literature from ancient Greece consists of the works of a single man, the physician and anatomist Galen. Unfortunately, most of the science in Galen is rubbish, and the same can be said of many scientific treatises from the time. We've far surpassed the ancients in terms of basic knowledge.

What we really lost was time, momentum. Scientific progress requires an interplay of theory and experiment, of thinking and testing. Historians talk incessantly of the Greek miracle of the 400s B.C., especially the flowering of thought in Athens. But the snooty Greeks disdained experiments as grubby and common, akin to manual labor. The Romans, in contrast, flexed their engineering might in the early centuries of the common era, but often betrayed a small-minded suspicion of theory as too highfalutin.

In between them was Alexandria, where thought and deed flourished together. Imagine what technological marvels will exist 2,000 years from now. If Alexandria and its library had pulled through and kept growing, we could be living in that world now. Instead, the greediness of the Ptolemies and especially the indifference of the Romans frittered it all away.

So in apportioning blame for the destruction of the Great Library and everything it represented, we might not know who, if anyone, burned it down. But in securing Roman rule over Alexandria, we really can fault Caesar. Just not for the reason most people think.

After Alexandria, libraries in the Western world suffered a shocking decline. In the 600s, the theologian Isidore of Seville managed to scrape together the largest collection of texts in all of Europe; scholars have estimated he had as few as 140 books. (James Patterson alone has published nearly 300.) Things improved enough by the 1100s that major monasteries could boast of 500 volumes, and in the 1300s, the Sorbonne in France topped 2,000. But even then, books were so expensive that libraries kept many titles chained to tables under the suspicious eye of the librarians on duty.

Not until the 1500s did anyone take up the mantle of the Great Library and attempt to collect all the world's knowledge in one place. This time, it wasn't an institution that tried but an individual—Hernando Colón, the bastard son of Christopher Columbus.

Despite Colón's illegitimacy, Columbus did right by the boy and arranged for a fine education—which came in handy after Columbus's disastrous third voyage to the Americas, when he was arrested in Spain and briefly imprisoned for torturing the natives of Hispaniola. To restore his reputation, Columbus hired a monk in 1501 to put together a book of "prophecies" based on Bible extracts; it aimed to convince the Spanish crown that he, Columbus, was a savior destined by God to lead a new crusade overseas. Columbus compelled his son to help write the book, and many passages were penned in 13-year-old Hernando's hand.

The book apparently did the trick—the Spanish monarchy funded Columbus's fourth voyage in 1502—and the navigator rewarded Hernando by taking him along. It proved an even bigger fiasco than the third journey. The 51-year-old Columbus was suffering from arthritis, gout, and malarial fevers, and his crew nearly mutinied and overthrew him. The sailors also endured a year-long marooning in Jamaica before finally limping home.

Having had his fill of adventure, Colón turned to a quieter life of scholarship and book collecting. But he didn't renounce his father's ambitions. To the contrary: If Columbus helped Spain establish a world empire, Colón wanted his burgeoning library to be its brain. And he proved no less rapacious than his father with regard to accumulating books. He sometimes visited a dozen cities a year, scouring every shop and market stall for new volumes. Unusually for the time, he focused not on manuscripts—books written by hand—but on titles produced with a technology new to Europe, the printing press. He eventually accumulated 15,000 to 20,000 titles, a collection five to six times larger than any other in the world.

To prevent this massive inventory from sprawling out of control, Colón hired several scholars, called *sumistas,* to read and summarize all his volumes. He also composed a list of authors and titles in alphabetical order (an abecedarium) and jotted down bibliographic information for each book on small sheets of paper—sheets he could then shuffle around and interfile with new entries as he purchased more books. In other words, he pioneered and perhaps invented the card catalog.

Had Colón collected during the 1400s instead of the 1500s, he might have surpassed Alexandria and achieved his ambition of collecting every book in existence. But with the rise of the printing press, books were multiplying too quickly, and no matter how many shops he ransacked, no matter how much money he poured into his quest, he simply couldn't keep up. He died in 1539, thousands of books short.

Then, Alexandria-like, his collection disintegrated. For unknown reasons he willed the collection to a nephew whom one historian called "a wastrel with no interest in books." The nephew was soon jailed for bigamy, and in his absence, other collectors swept in and pilfered titles. By the time the cathedral in Seville stepped up to manage the collection, half the volumes had disappeared; further attrition from moths, mold, and leaky roofs has whittled the total down to about 4,000 today. Among the items lost over the centuries were his father's original logs of his voyages to the Americas.*

Today, the most comprehensive collection of books in existence is the Library of Congress in Washington, D.C.—a remarkable achievement for an institution that suffered through several rocky decades after its founding.

A $5,000 grant from Congress in April 1800 netted LoC its first 740 volumes, mostly law texts. The collection was housed in the U.S. Capitol initially, since only members of Congress could access it. The folly of this arrangement became clear during the War of 1812, when British soldiers sacked Washington and the Capitol came under threat. As the redcoats bore down, a staff librarian ran into the streets, jumped in front of several carts of fleeing residents, and commandeered the vehicles in the name of the United States of

* Miraculously, the most important book in the collection reemerged in 2019, the so-called *Book of Epitomes,* the log in which the *sumistas* summarized each book. For 350 years, the *Epitomes* lay unrecognized in an archive in Copenhagen amid a collection of Icelandic and Scandinavian literature, shorn of the first hundred-some pages. Even then, it's a massive tome, a foot thick and about 2,000 pages long. The summaries, all in Latin, run from a few lines for obscure titles to 30 pages for the collected works of Plato. It also revealed the existence of a handful of books we never would have known about otherwise.

America's official government library. The owners laughed and drove on. Staff librarians did manage to secure at least one cart and save a few items, but the British soon set fire to the Capitol and burned all 3,000 books inside. The flames were visible from Baltimore.

To replenish the library, former President Thomas Jefferson sold the government his personal collection of 6,487 books, netting him $23,950 ($500,000 today). This was not a wholly selfless gesture on Jefferson's part, considering he had serious debts to pay. But his collection greatly expanded the library's scope, adding classic literature and books on art, architecture, science, and geography.

Jefferson's volumes nearly went up in flames during a second fire at LoC a decade later. One evening in December 1825, a congressman from Massachusetts spotted an orange glow through an upper window of the Capitol. He convinced a guard—who, incredibly, didn't have keys to open the library's door—to rouse the official librarian from his nearby home and investigate. Sure enough, a candle had set a stack of old, crumbling books on fire. Among other people, U.S. Representatives Daniel Webster and Sam Houston helped fight the blaze, and only a handful of books were damaged.

After that, Congress banned candles and oil lamps from the library. Members also held public hearings to address the matter. You know the drill: They denounced those responsible, provided several fabulous-sounding quotes, and solemnly swore to secure the library's future on their honor as gentlemen. Then, being Congress, they did exactly nothing—not until the worst fire yet forced their hands.

On Christmas Eve in 1851, two guards smelled smoke inside the Capitol. After poking around, they forced the door of the library open (they still didn't have keys, apparently) and saw that a table and a few shelves had started on fire; the cause was a blocked chimney. At that moment, a few buckets of water would have put the fire out, so they raced off to find pails. In their haste, however, they made a disastrous mistake and left the door open.

The library had been sealed off before this, and the modest fire inside was starved of oxygen. But with the door open and air rushing in, the flames began to feast. By the time the guards returned, they found a raging inferno. To compound the problem, the local fire department had battled another five-alarmer the previous night, leaving the crew sluggish and slow to respond. They'd also left their hoses outside overnight, and found them clogged with ice. By the time another crew arrived to put out the blaze, roughly 30,000 of the library's 55,000 books had turned to ash, including 4,300 of Jefferson's volumes. The library also lost several presidential portraits and its entire map collection. (The staff did manage to rescue the Declaration of Independence in Jefferson's handwriting.) After that, Congress finally got its act together and built a fireproof cast-iron room for the collection in the Capitol; the library was later spun off into its own building in 1897.

Over the next century, LoC grew into a colossus, and today owns more than 39 million books, plus 70 million manuscripts and 39 million DVDs' worth of digital data. There are 181 million items total, in 470 languages.* Pretty impressive. And yet, given the utter deluge of printed material since 1900, the library is floundering even more than Hernando Colón did, utterly incapable of keeping up. The situation with digital media is bleaker still, given the need for specialized hardware and software to read it. If you absolutely needed to, would you have any way to view the contents of a floppy disk today? Probably not, and internet information is more ephemeral still. If the attempt to collect

* The world's second-largest library is the British Library, with Russia's National Library coming in third. In Soviet times, all 32 million volumes on the shelves of the National Library had their spines turned inward, away from patrons, so they couldn't see what books were there. The card catalog was jealously patrolled by the KGB.

every text in the world was foolhardy in ancient times, it's laughable today. There's just no way.

Maybe that's for the better. Scholars of a contrarian bent have argued that quasi-universal libraries do little to preserve knowledge over the long term, and may even be harmful. To be sure, the concentration of works in a place like Alexandria can lead to unprecedented bursts of creativity. At the same time, those great libraries are built upon great wealth and power, and that same wealth and power makes the cities that house the libraries irresistible targets for attacks—at which point the libraries burn. It's the classic mistake of putting too many eggs in one basket. We owe the survival of most ancient literature today not to the concentration of works in Great Libraries, but to the scattering of works among thousands of monasteries and country villas, where nameless individuals squirreled them away in trunks and attics. One such villa near Pompeii, in fact, is currently our best hope for rescuing the many, many famous works that have disappeared since the days of Alexandria.

In 1709, a team of workers began digging a well near Naples, at the foot of Mount Vesuvius. Sixty feet down, to their bewilderment, they found a building. Specifically, a 2,500-seat theater, adorned with statues of horses and humans. More digging revealed other buildings nearby, and soon an entire town emerged. Its name was Herculaneum. It was buried in the same volcanic eruption that wiped out Pompeii in A.D. 79, then forgotten for 16 centuries.

In 1750, a team of treasure hunters began excavating an ocean-front villa in Herculaneum. In one room, they discovered what looked like misshapen lumps of wood, which they tossed aside. Thankfully, one digger took a closer look and realized they were actually blackened scrolls. The crew was standing in a library—the only intact library ever discovered from ancient times.

The library's roughly 1,800 scrolls and scroll fragments survived through luck and chemistry. The Vesuvius eruption buried Herculaneum under 60 feet of pulverized rock and hot ash, which reached temperatures of 900°F. That's hot enough to burn papyrus, but the density and sheer tonnage of ash entombed the scrolls and blocked out all oxygen—a necessary ingredient for fire. As a result, the scrolls didn't burn as much as bake, carbonizing into dark brown lumps. They've been described as looking like "saggy brown burritos" wrapped in cigar paper.

Disastrously, scholars tried unrolling several scrolls after their discovery. A museum curator sliced into one with a knife, as if attacking a bread roll; it disintegrated in his hands. Another tried dunking a scroll in mercury, perhaps believing it would slither between the rolled-up layers and magically unfurl them. This failed as well, and he probably poisoned himself to boot. The least-worst idea involved affixing silk threads to the ends of the scroll and unpeeling them with gentle tension, at a tenth of an inch per day. Every flake that crumbled off fell onto an adhesive backing formed from the membrane of a pig bladder, and waiting scholars would scribble down whatever text they could make out before it decayed into dust. The first scroll took four years. Overall, various teams opened, and destroyed, scores of scrolls before finally admitting defeat. Scholars more or less abandoned all hope of ever reading the rest. Until 2020.

During the pandemic lockdown, a bored, wealthy Silicon Valley bro began reading about the Herculaneum scrolls online. The story hooked him. He was further intrigued to read that, in 2019, a computer science professor in Kentucky had run two scrolls through a CT scanner, similar to what hospitals use to study patients' inner organs. The professor was trying to scan the internal layers of the scrolls to generate images of them. In essence, he would virtually "unwrap" them.

For technical reasons, the professor's project failed: He couldn't see any writing on the images that emerged. But the tech bro felt certain that the collective brainpower of Silicon Valley could overcome this problem. So after some discussions with the professor, on March 15, 2023—the Ides, natch—they announced a contest with a cash prize. The first programmer to coax four passages of 140 characters out of a scroll would win $700,000.

The first big step forward occurred when a physicist began examining blown-up images of the scrolls and noticed certain patches with a different texture, like dried mud. He called it "crackle." This crackling was faint in most places, like a watermark. But it often looked like fragments of letters.

Building on this discovery, a 21-year-old computer science student in Nebraska wrote a program in his spare time to map and enhance the crackle. One night in August 2023, he was partying in some dude's house when someone emailed him a link to a few new scans of some scrolls. He loaded the files into his home computer remotely from his phone, launched his program, and kept partying. A few hours later, walking to his dorm, he pulled out his phone to check the program's output. He unlocked his screen, took two steps, and froze. "Holy cow," he muttered. Staring back at him, on a background of papyrus fibers, was a ghostly image of three letters: πορ. It was the start of the word πορφύρας (porphoras), an ancient Greek term for "purple." He was the first person to read those letters in nearly 2,000 years.*

* Oddly enough, the student was an intern for SpaceX at the time and later worked for Elon Musk's DOGE group under Donald Trump.

Things moved quickly from there. An Egyptian computer science student in Berlin found the same letters a few days later. The Nebraska student teamed up with him, as well as a robotics student in Switzerland, and they began churning through images. The prize organizer had asked for four passages of 140 characters, but when the contest ended on December 31, 2023, the trio had excavated 2,000 letters over four columns of text. The passages came from an essay by an Epicurean philosopher named Philodemus, in which he discusses the joys of sensual pleasures. (He adored music, capers, and the color purple.) Although Philodemus's name was known before, the work was not; we had no inkling it existed.

After 250 years of frustration—of knowing the scrolls existed yet having no way to read them—classics scholars were astounded at the news, not to mention moved. The ceremony to announce the prizewinners was as nerdy as you'd expect: dudes in tennis shoes and T-shirts, a cheesy oversize check. But when they showed a slide of the writing onstage, one scholar in the audience nearly broke down crying.

Since then, another scanning technology that uses infrared light and artificial intelligence has decoded a second Herculaneum scroll. It relates brand-new details about Plato's life, including his final hours. (He spent them prostrate with a fever, while a slave girl played the flute for him. Grouchily, he snapped at her for her "scant sense of rhythm.")

Realistically, the unveiling of the rest of the Herculaneum scrolls will take years, maybe decades. Classics departments aren't exactly flush with cash, and it's expensive to take high-resolution scans and analyze them. But the sense of hope is palpable, and even the initial results have scholars' minds racing. What if the library contained the missing two-thirds of Aristotle's oeuvre? It's certainly possible, given how popular the big A's works were. Other scholars fantasize about finding lost verse by Sappho and Homer and others. And bear in mind, much of Herculaneum and other nearby villages remains unexcavated; more intact libraries could emerge someday.

Equally exciting, the same scanning technologies could expand our knowledge of the Dead Sea Scrolls, given the many fragments in that collection that are fused together. We could even glean texts from Egyptian mummies, whose masks were often made of layers of papyrus plastered together. The first known list of the Seven Wonders of the Ancient World turned up on a mummy wrapping from the 100s B.C., so who knows what other marvels await.

It's awfully easy to focus on what we've lost throughout history—all that's slipped through our fingers. But that's not the full story. Sometimes we should marvel at everything that still exists, the sheer miracle of its survival. Especially those rarest treasures of all: things that long seemed lost, but have now been found.

CHAPTER NINE

LOST GOLD

Who's the richest person in history? A few names probably leap to mind—Bezos, Musk, Gates. But if you take inflation into account, other contenders arise—Rockefeller, Carnegie. Or what about potentates from the past like Genghis Khan and King Solomon?

It's of course impossible to nail down the worth of historical figures to the last dollar, but historians can get a rough handle on their wealth by examining their kingdom's trading activity and economic output, then determining how much of that flowed up to the top. By that measure, Augustus Caesar, the Mughal emperors of India, and the emperors of the Song dynasty in China all controlled at least a quarter of the world's gross domestic product. By most metrics, however, one man stands alone as the single richest person to ever live: Kankan Musa, the Lion of Mali.

The origins of the Mali Empire date to the 1200s, when a neighboring kingdom invaded the region and slaughtered a noble family. Or most of it. The family had a dozen children, and while the invaders murdered 11 of them, they took pity on the sickly runt, Sundiata, and spared him. If you've ever seen a movie, you can guess what happened next. Sundiata grew up to become a powerful warrior, then gathered an army in 1235 to rout his enemies and seize their territory, laying the foundation of an empire.

Musa took over the empire in 1312 after the reigning monarch, his uncle, made a bold attempt to sail across the Atlantic Ocean and see what lay beyond the end of the world. Not a single one of his 3,000 ships returned. The more prudent Musa, around age 30, took the throne as the *mansa* (emperor) of Mali.*

Mansa Musa inherited a kingdom on the verge of fracturing. It covered parts of a dozen modern nations, stretching from the Atlantic coast to the Niger River 1,200 miles inland, and from the barren Sahara in the north to the lush rainforests of Ghana down south. Elites like Musa practiced Islam, but much of the population rejected monotheism for traditional animistic beliefs—a source of tension. Furthermore, Musa ruled over multiple ethnic groups, most of whom harbored ancient grudges against the others. Worse still, bandits and highwaymen roamed the countryside, attacking traveling merchants and choking off trade. A generation earlier, in fact, the Malian emperor Sakura had been waylaid and murdered while returning from the hajj in Mecca.

---

* The uncle's fleet would have had favorable winds sailing west, and scholars have speculated that, with a little luck, they just might have reached the Caribbean. More likely, their riverine craft got swamped on the open ocean and they drowned.

But Musa proved himself a wise and capable ruler, harsh when necessary and soft when mercy accomplished more. When miners in southern Mali went on strike to protest attempts to impose Islamic law there, Musa backed down. He valued stability, and if the miners believed that sacrificing birds and praying to their ancestors helped them find ore, who was he to oppose that? In contrast, with bandits, the Lion showed no pity: His troops rounded them up and punished them severely, medievally. And with the highways safe at last, trade boomed. Horses from Arabia, iron tools from Europe, silks and spices from China—all began flowing into Malian markets.

Mali in turn had several goods that Europe, Asia, and North Africa coveted: ivory, copper, cola nuts. Musa also squeezed plenty of taxes out of visiting merchants and did a brisk trade in slaves. But the Mali Empire built its wealth on two products above all: gold and salt.

Whenever foreign kings asked Musa where his gold came from, he always leveled with them. In a remote corner of his kingdom, he explained, gold grew on special plants and was picked like grain. And however much Musa wished he could give his fellow monarchs a few cuttings for themselves, alas: The crop was fickle, and if anyone but the natives of the region handled the plants, they withered and died. (It's a testimony to Musa's diplomacy, and acting skills, that anyone believed this.)

In truth, Mali was simply lucky: The kingdom had lots of gold, and most of it was easily accessible. People in southern Mali either panned for flakes in streams or sunk shafts into hillsides to mine nuggets. At the time, these were the richest gold deposits in the world, accounting for almost half the global supply. And every last ounce flowed into Musa's coffers. One historian, in trying to sum up Musa's fortune, could only marvel, "Imagine as much gold as you think a human being can possess, and double it." Musa was emperor of El Dorado.

The other pillar of his fortune rested on salt. It's hard to fathom nowadays, but for much of history, salt was one of the most coveted goods on earth. Sodium and chloride are essential nutrients, and salt played a key role in preserving foods, especially meats. For many, many centuries it was every bit as expensive as gold, and the very words *salt* and *salary* both derive from the same root. (Today, prices have diverged a bit. Twenty-six ounces of salt will set you back around $2, eight cents per ounce. Gold surpassed $5,000 per ounce over the past few years.)

Luckily for Musa, the dry lakebeds in his kingdom's northern deserts had acres of salt, along with natural outcroppings of it. In fact, given the lack of trees there, salt miners sometimes constructed homes from bricks of salt, with camel hides stretched over the top. It would be like 49ers building cabins out of gold bars.

At its peak, Musa's empire covered half a million square miles, roughly double the size of Texas. From his tall black ebony throne—with two giant ivory tusks arching over it—he commanded the fealty of two dozen kings and 400 cities. One historian pegged Musa's fortune at roughly $570 billion in modern money. Others threw up their hands and described his wealth as "incomprehensible." Regardless, given that salt and gold drove much of the Old World economy, it's easy to see how a man with vast stores of both would emerge as probably the richest person in history.

And yet, for all his wealth, due to Mali's isolation and the formidable barrier of the Sahara, Mansa Musa was barely known outside his kingdom until the 12th year of his reign, when he undertook a storied journey.

The journey began under sad circumstances. According to one chronicle, Musa accidentally killed his mother one day. Frustratingly, the chronicler fails to provide a single follow-up detail—narrative malpractice. Did Musa serve her a tainted meal? Knock into her and send her tumbling down some stairs? It's anyone's guess. But he felt so wretched that he decided to make the Islamic hajj to Mecca to atone. This was no light undertaking: The round-trip, across 9,000 miles of mostly desert, would last roughly two years. Recall, too, that an earlier emperor had been murdered on his hajj. But Musa was determined.

Some accounts of the journey are clear exaggerations. One claimed that Musa's camel caravan stretched so far that when the vanguard reached a certain town 500 miles from his capital, he himself had not left his palace. But according to other credible sources, the retinue had around 60,000 people. This included 8,000 soldiers; thousands of musicians, cooks, doctors, poets, camel herders, and messengers; and the 12,000 personal attendants—all dressed in silk—that Musa considered absolutely critical for his comfort. Most of the 60,000 walked, but Musa trotted along atop a black steed. According to the prevailing fashion then, the richer you were, the wider your trousers, and the mansa's pants were made from 20 pieces of material, a veritable hot-air balloon on each leg. To purchase supplies, each of the 12,000 attendants carried four pounds of gold, and a train of 80 camels staggered along under 300 more pounds each.

The caravan plodded along at three miles an hour, heading north and then east. The first few weeks on the kingdom's grasslands passed pleasantly, as people gawked at passing elephants and giraffes. Every Friday, the Muslim sabbath, Musa stopped and ordered his men to build a mosque. It didn't matter what type of ground they were on, or how few people lived nearby, or whether they'd even heard of Islam—they were getting a mosque.

Once the caravan entered the Sahara, the trip became more precarious. Trails and landmarks vanished, and sandstorms tore through their ranks, blinding people and threatening to suffocate them. Air temperatures reached 130 degrees, and the hot sands underfoot could top 170. Water was a constant worry. And of course they had to keep building mosques every Friday.

After months of trudging eastward, Musa's retinue reached Cairo. Residents there could reportedly hear its rumbling approach from miles away—men shouting, camels bleating, drums banging to keep time. After pitching his tents near the Sphinx, Musa made a grand entrance into the city, preceded by marching bands, dancing girls, servants waving colored pennants, and 500 slaves swinging four-foot-long staffs of gold whose luster blinded the crowds. Cairo was fairly rich then, but its residents had never imagined wealth on this scale. One exclaimed, "This caravan competes in glittering glory with the African sun itself."

Just because, Musa gave every local clerk and alderman a sack of gold coins, and every beggar received alms. Merchants would jack up prices fivefold whenever one of the Malians wandered into their stalls, yet the foreigners always paid without haggling, without even seeming to care. Musa's men flooded Cairo with so much gold that the price of the metal dropped sharply afterward, and the city's economy cratered.

After resting in Cairo for three months, Musa's crew pulled up their tents and marched the thousand miles to Mecca. Upon seeing the holy city, the mansa's eyes welled with tears, perhaps from thoughts of his slain mother. After performing the necessary prayers and ablutions, he purchased several homes in town so that any Malians who made the pilgrimage in the future would have a place to stay. He also gave away 20,000 more gold coins, and essentially bought several scholars, poets, and architects to bring back to Mali, as well as four sharifs (descendants of Muhammad), as if they were souvenirs.

Embarrassingly, by the time he reached Cairo on the journey home, the Lion was running low on gold. He also felt bad for destabilizing the city's economy, so he secured a loan from some bankers at a truly usurious rate: For every 300 coins borrowed, he had to pay back 700. But it sopped up the excess gold in town and gave Musa enough cash to return. (When the Egyptian bankers journeyed to Mali to collect the first loan payment later, Musa shocked them by paying everything back in one lump sum. Unfortunately, they lugged all the gold straight back to Egypt, where the economy collapsed again. It took 20 years to even out.)

On the way back to Mali, a messenger intercepted Musa's train with exciting news. A general of his had just conquered the legendary city of Timbuktu, adding it to Mali's empire. Musa diverted the retinue south to inspect his new province. Under his patronage, the city would become a leading center of Islamic art and learning, the Alexandria of West Africa.

A dozen years after his hajj, Mansa Musa died of unknown causes. Sadly, his feckless son lost several provinces to rebellion, and later kings cared more for wallowing in luxury than ruling wisely. All that Musa had done to promote peace and prosperity crumbled, and over the next several centuries, Mali's fortunes continued to sink. Today, the land that once boasted of the richest man in history is one of the poorest nations on earth—so poor that few people outside West Africa would likely even believe that such a place could produce a prince like him.

Mali is not the only civilization in sub-Saharan Africa that's disappeared from our collective memory. There's also Great Zimbabwe, namesake of the modern nation, which flourished between the 11th and 14th centuries. At its peak, it produced roughly 40 percent of the world's gold, and its rulers left behind massive forts with 32-foot-high walls, built with stones crafted so precisely that they didn't need a speck of mortar. Early European visitors refused to believe that Black Africans had built such structures; they attributed them to Persian, Arab, or Chinese colonists instead, or even to King Solomon and the Queen of Sheba. (To be fair, local Black populations also swore that their ancestors never built the forts; they credited devils.) Even when archaeological digs showed conclusively that Africans had built Great Zimbabwe, the ruling national government of Rhodesia banned the mention of this fact in guidebooks and school texts. Archaeologists recall threats of being fired for speaking the truth. "It was the first time since the Germans" under Hitler, recalled one, "that archaeology has been so directly censored."

This memory hole with regard to Africa seems all the stranger considering the fact that the wider world did not discount its wealth or achievements at the time. To the contrary, people in Cairo hailed Mansa Musa as the greatest king on earth, and news of his spectacular wealth swept through Asia and Europe. As one historian noted, Musa was "the first to penetrate the iron curtain of color prejudice ... and to win for the true African a small measure of the respect which, even today, is often grudgingly granted them."

Europeans especially seemed fascinated with Mali, as reflected on their maps. Given the Roman influence in North Africa, Europeans in medieval times had a decent grasp of the geography there. Beyond that, the details got sketchy. If they even bothered including sub-Saharan Africa on maps, they treated it more as a doodle pad for fantastical beings like ants the size of canines and humans without noses or mouths. But in 1339, Mali made its first appearance on a European map, along with Musa's likeness, and more details emerged over the next few decades. One famous picture of Musa, from 1375, shows a bearded man with a regal flowing robe sitting on a cushioned throne. He's holding a golden orb and wielding a golden scepter, with a crown of gold atop his head. The emperor grew so prominent in the European imagination that he continued to appear on maps for two centuries after his death.

Throughout the 1300s, Malian gold flowed into Europe through merchants in North Africa, who made long sojourns across the desert and dragged the heavy metal back. They charged ridiculous prices for their troubles, which left European monarchs and merchants grumbling. How could they cut out these middlemen? Eventually, after a century of staring at Musa on their maps, and tracing their fingers along the rivers and byways, a few bold sailors started making sojourns down the coast of Africa, trying to reach Mali themselves. The Portuguese proved especially persistent, and by 1446 they were making sallies into the Gambia River, which led to within shouting distance of Musa's old gold fields. El Dorado was in reach.

Over the next century, much of that gold flowed directly back into Europe. And, emboldened by the trips to Mali, Portugal used that gold to finance excursions to even more-distant places, eventually reaching India. Meanwhile, Spain grew alarmed at its rival's prowess and began financing its own voyages—eventually culminating in the fateful Columbus expedition to the Americas in 1492. There, the Spaniards would encounter more gold than they ever could have imagined. And they would devise increasingly ruthless ways of extracting it.

In the early 1530s, the Spanish military invaded Peru and captured the Inca king Atahualpa. Sensing his life was in danger, Atahualpa offered the Spanish a ransom. He'd noticed their peculiar obsession with shiny metals, and during a meeting with the conquistador Francisco Pizarro, he took a piece of chalk and drew a line approximately eight feet high around the walls of the room they were in. He offered to fill the room up to that line with gold, and then twice more with silver, all within a year. Given the size of the room, 17 feet by 22 feet, this was a generous offer—the richest ransom in history—and Pizarro accepted. Atahualpa's countrymen scoured temples and palaces across the empire for treasure, and fulfilled their obligation four months early. Pizarro thanked Atahualpa profusely, then executed him anyway.

By the early 1800s, after countless such atrocities, the treasuries of Spanish Peru were groaning with gold and silver. But South America was a tumultuous place at the time, with countries declaring independence left and right. In 1821, revolutionaries in Peru laid siege to the colonial capital of Lima. The local viceroy feared that the $60 million in his vaults (around $1.5 billion today) would fall into enemy hands.

In a spirit of fair play, the revolutionaries were allowing foreign merchants to sail in and out of Lima's harbor. So the viceroy sought out William Thompson, the trustworthy but foulmouthed captain of the British brig *Mary Dear.* He asked Thompson to sneak Lima's gold and silver out of the city, along with 200 chests of gems. Aware that he'd be hanged if the rebels caught him, Thompson quadrupled his normal fee; the viceroy agreed without hesitation. Catholic churches in Lima caught wind of the plan and entrusted their treasures to Thompson as well—chalices, crucifixes, a life-size gold statue of Mary. The viceroy also sent four guards and two priests along to keep Thompson honest.

Thompson had orders to sail around in circles for a few months while Spanish soldiers attempted to subdue the revolutionaries; if they couldn't, Thompson would sail to Mexico and rendezvous with Spanish agents there. Thompson, however, had other plans. Shortly after departing Lima, he plied the guards and priests with wine, then huddled with his crew and pointed at the treasure chests: "We can work ... the rest of our lives, boys, and not all of us together can ever produce for ourselves as much wealth as there is in one of those big boxes." (He no doubt added a few salty words for emphasis.) Thompson then made a clinching argument. The Spanish had stolen all that gold from the natives anyway, so they had every right to steal it from the Spanish.

In a flash, the crew turned pirate, slitting the guards' throats and dumping them overboard. The priests went into the drink, too. Then the *Mary Dear* hightailed it north for Cocos Island, which sits roughly halfway between the Galápagos Islands and Costa Rica. Although just four miles wide, this spit of land is dotted with 200 waterfalls and supposedly inspired the setting of both *Treasure Island* and *Jurassic Park.*

Upon arrival, Thompson's men began hauling the loot ashore on boats. After 11 such trips, they concealed everything inside a cave, burying it in three locations in the red soil at depths of four to 10 feet. Their plan was to head to the mainland, lie low for a year, then return to claim their prize.

Things didn't work out that way. A Spanish galleon spotted the *Mary Dear* on her way to the mainland and pulled alongside. Its captain knew about the arrangement between Thompson and the viceroy in Peru, and wondered what on earth the ship was doing near Cocos. When Thompson couldn't account for the treasure, the galleon's crew arrested the pirates and sailed for Panama, where they hanged them one by one. Finally, just Thompson and first mate James Alexander Forbes remained. The two men begged for mercy and, probably more effectively, promised to reveal the treasure's location if the Spanish spared them. The contingent set sail for Cocos.

There, Thompson outfoxed his captors. Given their long history of duplicity in the New World, he probably didn't trust the Spaniards to release him, so he and Forbes made a big show of tramping around and measuring the distances between some local landmarks. Just when they seemed to be getting their bearings, the Englishmen bolted. Most of Cocos is dense jungle, clogged with thickets and vines and drenched in rain year-round. Thompson and Forbes darted into this Jurassic landscape and vanished.

The Spanish gave hot chase, but a platoon of angry, thrashing sailors stood little chance of finding two lone men running for their lives. The Spanish kept at it for weeks, but when their supplies ran low, they gave up and sailed off.

Thompson and Forbes survived for the next year on coconuts, bird eggs, and fish. In 1822, a whaling vessel happened by and they screamed themselves hoarse flagging it down. They told the crew they'd been shipwrecked there, and by the smell and ragged look of them, the story seemed credible. The whaler dropped them in Costa Rica.

After all that, Thompson up and died soon after his escape. The Treasure of Lima was now Forbes's alone to claim, but he migrated to California instead and married into a wealthy Mexican family. He opened a flour mill and a quicksilver mine, and got so stinking rich that he lost all motivation to return to Cocos and unearth the treasure.

But before his death in 1881, Forbes allegedly sketched a map of its location for his son, which got passed down through several more generations. The tale of the lost gold, meanwhile, got passed around far more widely: To date, more than 300 expeditions have tromped through the jungles of Cocos Island in search of it. Bugsy Siegel and Errol Flynn reportedly tried, and when President Franklin Roosevelt went deep-sea fishing near Cocos in 1935, he let his crew have a go. One German fellow spent 19 years scouring every cave and thicket. In total, he found six doubloons.

The person who got closest to finding the treasure, at least according to him, was James Alexander Forbes IV, who inherited his great-grandfather's map and became obsessed with it. In 1939, he swore he found the very X marking the spot. But just as he was about to dig, he spied a few menacing ships offshore—including one with machine guns. Forbes played it cool and left. According to one source, the filmmaker John Ford had accompanied him on the expedition, and on the voyage back, Ford drew up plans to return and film an adventure flick in which John Wayne "discovered" the treasure on camera. But Forbes, naturally, died immediately upon returning home, and nothing ever came of the idea.

Costa Rica eventually tired of people uprooting the pristine Cocos landscape and declared the island a nature reserve. Today, landslides and storms have so remixed the topography that even if the ghost of William Thompson himself arrived to hunt for his loot, he likely wouldn't recognize a thing. The Inca and later gold that disappeared from Lima was no myth. But for all we know of its location now, it might as well be just another empty legend of buried pirate treasure.

Compared with the looting of the Nazis (see chapter 11), Japanese looting during World War II has received scant attention. Which is strange, because Japan stole plenty: everything from art and priceless artifacts (including the Peking Man fossils, possibly) to pigs from farms and carp from decorative ponds. One photograph from the war shows Japanese soldiers hauling pilfered goods away in baby strollers.

But above all, the Japanese plundered gold. In fact, according to a few controversial accounts, the value of the gold that Japan stole exceeds anything the Nazis got their talons on.

Those claims rest largely on the work of Sterling and Peggy Seagrave, a husband-and-wife team of historians. The Seagraves open *Gold Warriors,* their main book on Japanese war looting, with the melodramatic claim that they'll likely be assassinated for what they're about to reveal. (They weren't, although Sterling was run off the road on Christmas night once after the publication of the Spanish edition of the book; he careened into a ravine, where he lay unconscious for 14 hours until a helicopter rescued him.)

To be clear, the majority of the Seagraves' colleagues doubt that Japan stole as much as the duo claims. But they back up at least some of their assertions with written documents, and some scholars do buy their general argument that Japan pilfered far more than standard histories allow. Suffice it to say that pretty much every sentence in the account that follows should include a big, flashing *allegedly* at the beginning. Rather than clutter up the text, I'll simply note that here.

According to the Seagraves, after Japan invaded China in 1937, Emperor Hirohito and his brother Prince Chichibu founded an organization code-named Kin No Yuri—the Golden Lily—after a poem the emperor wrote. It aimed to siphon gold to the royal family and ensure that invading Japanese forces didn't pocket too much for themselves.

Such measures proved necessary because the Japanese reportedly employed some pretty unsavory characters abroad. This included the top don in the Japanese mafia, the yakuza, who was sprung from prison solely to travel to conquered territories and ply his dark talents there. He and his henchmen used several tactics to squeeze people. Most notoriously, they'd stroll into a defeated town, ask to speak to the mayor, and shoot him in the face first thing. The message was clear: cooperate or die. One army colonel also kidnapped people for ransom. If the family dithered about payment, his crew began chopping off body parts, starting with ears and escalating to testicles and breasts. In other cases, the occupying military would raise food prices sky-high. This forced food onto the black market, which the yakuza controlled; their agents would then demand gold or other precious items for payment, draining families of their riches. Finally, the yakuza traded this gold to the Japanese government for heroin, then turned around and sold that to people, to wring every last ducat out of a city. They even shook down the dead, tearing gold chains off corpses and extracting gold teeth. And Golden Lily made sure the emperor got the lion's share of everything.

The looting accelerated after Pearl Harbor. On December 8, 1941, Tomoyuki Yamashita—a stout, balding Japanese general with a push-broom mustache—invaded the Malay peninsula, pitting his 30,000 troops against 80,000 British soldiers. Yamashita's men clobbered them, conquering the whole territory in 69 days. Winston Churchill called it the worst disaster in British military history, and Yamashita became known as the Tiger of Malaya. Even after the Tiger fell victim to political bickering back in Japan and was banished to Manchuria, that hardly slowed the Japanese steamroller. Bataan, Java, the Philippines, and other territories fell in short order, making Japan the unquestioned master of Asia. And Golden Lily was determined to seize every gold coin, every watch and statue, every gold tooth from the Pacific Islands to Siberia: millions upon millions of pounds.

Still, Japan's empire proved fragile. The people they conquered loathed them, and underground armies sprang up to fight back. Most consequentially, in June 1942, the U.S. Navy defeated Japan at the Battle of Midway. This knocked Japan onto its heels, and it spent the rest of the war backpedaling. As island after island fell to the Allies in 1943, Golden Lily officials grew nervous, and shifted focus from plundering gold to concealing it.

For various reasons, these efforts centered on the Philippines. Its islands had many natural caves and tunnels that could be enlarged for storage. And perhaps the Japanese government believed, however delusionally, that the Allies would let them keep the Philippines after the war. So Golden Lily began transporting lucre to Manila on ships, including several painted to look like hospital vessels.

Prince Chichibu, the emperor's brother, supposedly oversaw the construction of the hiding spots himself, 175 in all. Many were dug in remote mountain areas, but plenty appeared in Manila as well—especially beneath churches and other landmarks that they knew the Americans would not bomb.

By late 1944, Japan's military was reeling, and the desperate Japanese government plucked the Tiger of Malaya out of Manchuria and installed him in Manila. His directive was to repel the coming Allied invasion. But even Yamashita could see his chances of victory were slim. He focused instead on helping Golden Lily excavate tunnels.

Most of them reached at least 90 feet underground, for protection from bombs, and some had dozens of miles of tunnels overall; like Theseus in the Labyrinth, visitors gripped a red cord as they groped their way forward to avoid getting lost. The diggers were either Allied POWs or local Filipinos that the Japanese enslaved. They worked 12-hour shifts seven days a week, subsisting on rice gruel and seaweed soup. Some took to eating charcoal just to fill their bellies and stop the hunger pangs.

The treasures often arrived in trucks: gold, platinum, oil drums filled with tiny gems of all colors. (Witnesses recall Japanese officials scooping the gems up and letting them run between their fingers like glittering rainbow sand.) One 13-foot-tall Buddha statue made of solid gold was so heavy it required two bulldozers to move, one pushing and one pulling simultaneously.

Usually, the workers who'd dug the tunnels would unload the trucks, but this was merely a ruse to distract them. Once Golden Lily officials had inspected a cache and documented the treasures on hand, Shinto priests would bless the site. Then, the priests and officials would quietly withdraw, and the officials would collapse the tunnel with dynamite or have it sealed off with construction equipment, burying the workers alive. It was a page right out of Genghis Khan's funeral. In one sad case, 1,200 POWs were unloading trucks in a tunnel when they heard the throaty rumbling of diesel engines; bulldozers were backfilling the only exit. The workers stampeded, desperate to escape, but waiting machine guns mowed down the first wave. The pile of bodies soon grew high enough that the second wave had to climb up and over their dead comrades, only to fall themselves in a hail of bullets. The very last men—the stragglers drooping with hunger—were too weak to climb the mountain of dirt and corpses now barring their way. They were still screaming when the tunnel was closed off.

After the tunnels were sealed, the military booby-trapped them. They connected stacks of dynamite to trip wires and thousand-pound bombs to springs that detonated them when disturbed. They blocked off narrow passages with massive terra-cotta pipes; if broken, the water inside would flood the tunnel and drown anyone there. Along those same lines, they filled shafts with several tons of fine sand, which would pour out and suffocate any would-be looters. They also mixed vials of cyanide into the sand, which people struggling to extricate themselves would break, hastening their demise.

For rural sites, the military would either spread dirt over the tunnel entrance and plant fast-growing papaya trees on top, or seal it off with concrete dyed to look like rock. Surveyors then mapped the area, although not in a straightforward way: A flag in the map's corner facing left or right indicated whether you read the map as is or needed to examine it in a mirror. (Mysteriously, some maps contained clocks with up to four hands pointing at different numbers, a probable code. But what the numbers mean, no one alive knows.)

For urban caches, Golden Lily officials employed other tricks. Prince Chichibu once sealed a hoard behind a false wall in a monastery. He then ordered an artist to alter a painting on the opposite wall that showed a man stretching out his hand—adding a sixth finger that pointed directly at the entrance.* It was an effective, if creepy, reminder.

Golden Lily continued hiding loot until June 1945, when Yamashita and Prince Chichibu held a farewell banquet in one underground vault for the 175 engineers who'd labored for years to hide gold for their emperor. The men drank whole barrels of sake, sang patriotic tunes for hours, and saluted each other with cries of *banzai*—long life. Around midnight, Yamashita and the prince slipped outside and callously dynamited the place shut, burying their countrymen alive to ensure extra secrecy. The prince evacuated

* Two anecdotes show how fanatical Golden Lily was about keeping the tunnels a secret. In one case, a Chinese slave bolted from a tunnel before it was sealed and eluded capture. Rather than risk compromising the tunnel's location, Golden Lily officials had his fellow workers remove all 270 boxes of gold inside and hide them in another tunnel. In another case, an official was checking a map of the tunnels when he realized an engineer had altered it subtly to conceal the real location of the entrance. The official had the man beheaded on the spot.

to Japan on a submarine a few days later, leaving Yamashita in charge of guarding all the loot in the Philippines against the advancing Allied forces. Yamashita actually held off surrendering until September 1945, three weeks after the atomic bomb attacks on Japan. Soon after his capture, rumors began rocketing around the Philippines about the vast sums of treasure there—Yamashita's gold, people called it.

According to the Seagraves, two people took the rumors especially seriously: one Filipino man and one American. Severino Santa Romana had fought the Japanese army as an underground commando during the war. He once observed, from a concealed position, a slave brigade loading heavy crates into a tunnel and then being dynamited inside. It wasn't hard to guess what the Japanese were hiding.

After the war, Santa Romana joined the staff of a general who served under Douglas MacArthur, the de facto military governor of Southeast Asia. In this capacity, he decided to pursue the lost treasure. Yamashita was the obvious person to interrogate. Unfortunately, the Tiger had been arrested for war crimes; he'd soon be hanged. So Santa Romana targeted Yamashita's staff instead, torturing his driver to reveal the location of the loot.

Before long, an American officer in the Philippines, Capt. Edward Lansdale, heard about Santa Romana's illicit interrogations and grew fascinated with the tales of Japanese gold. He decided to get his own licks in on the driver. He and Santa Romana finally broke the man, who agreed to take them to all the hiding spots he knew, a dozen total. Lansdale and Santa Romana swore they busted into two of them, albeit without explaining how they avoided any booby traps. Regardless, they emerged stunned, babbling about stacks of gold higher than their heads. A good soldier, Lansdale reported his discovery to MacArthur, then allegedly flew to Washington to brief President Harry Truman.

Now, if you buy the account of Sterling and Peggy Seagrave, here's where things get wild. They claim that a top deputy to the secretary of war flew to the Philippines and inspected the loot alongside MacArthur. And allegedly, allegedly, allegedly, the U.S. government decided to seize as much of the treasure as possible—billions upon billions of dollars—and keep it secret from the world.

They reportedly had several motivations for doing so. First, in July 1944, Allied leaders had held a meeting in New Hampshire to map out the economy of the postwar world. One resolution required the U.S. government to guarantee an exchange rate of $35 per ounce of gold. That seemed reasonable at the time, but the Seagraves claim that Yamashita's gold made the U.S. antsy: It would supposedly flood the world market and crash the price of gold in the same way that Mansa Musa's riches had destabilized Cairo. This would gravely wound not only the American economy but the economies of several other nations that had pegged their currencies to the U.S. dollar. The world had clawed its way out of the Great Depression only a few years prior, and American officials did not relish slipping back down that hole. Best, then, to keep Yamashita's gold secret.

Second, even as World War II was winding down, American leaders already had their eyes on the incipient Cold War. They saw Japan as a potential bulwark against communism in Asia and wanted to rebuild the Japanese economy quickly. Many of Japan's ruling elites were conservative and hated communism as well, making them convenient allies. Inconveniently, however, the most fanatical anticommunists were war criminals, and it wouldn't look good to support them with taxpayer-funded aid. The illicit gold provided a workaround—a way to prop up the anticommunists in secret.

The last motivation that the Seagraves cited is even darker. In short, they charged that the U.S. government wanted a slush fund to bankroll illegal cloak-and-dagger operations during the Cold War. To this end, the secretary of war's deputy ordered Santa Romana to deposit the gold under several aliases in 176 banks across 42 countries. The slush fund's name was Black Eagle, and over the next few decades, the CIA allegedly used this money across the world to smuggle arms, bribe politicians, throw elections—even murder people. The Seagraves trace much of this mischief to Lansdale, an anticommunist fanatic who eventually rose to become a major in the U.S. Air Force.

While relating these nefarious deeds, the Seagraves sound at times like they're playing left-wing-conspiracy Mad Libs: At one point they reference "senior U.S. Government officials and Pentagon generals [who] hoped to use Golden Lily treasure to create a new private FBI and a military-industrial complex controlled by them, in partnership with the John Birch Society, the Moonies, and far-right tycoons." They also claim that imperial Japan's most implacable foe, Douglas MacArthur, laid aside his animus and opened a joint his-and-his checking account with Emperor Hirohito: one so large that it paid out close to a billion dollars per year in interest alone.

So was any of this real? Most experts are dubious, especially about the CIA slush fund. Many even doubt that the Yamashita treasure troves existed. One reporter stationed in the Philippines during the war remarked, "We heard rumors, but we couldn't track any of them down. As far as I know ... it was a lot of hogwash." It doesn't help that the Seagraves often relied on single or anonymous sources for information.

Still, they have unearthed nuggets that support their case. A geologist from the Smithsonian Institution once said in an interview that General MacArthur invited him to Japan to examine gems that American troops had seized. He valued them at $50 million (over $750 million today). And MacArthur's own staff published a report stating, "One of the spectacular tasks of the occupation dealt with collecting and putting under guard the great hoards of gold, silver, precious stones, foreign postage stamps, engraving plates, and all currency not legal in Japan." Postage stamps aside, that sounds a lot like Golden Lily stashes. And while these "great hoards" were found in Japan, not the Philippines, the report did add, "Even though the bulk of this wealth was collected and placed under United States military custody ... undeclared caches of these treasures were known to exist."*

Plus, a Filipino man did seemingly recover some gold. As a teenager in the early 1960s, Rogelio Roxas met the son of a soldier who'd served under Yamashita; the son mentioned that his father had once drawn him a treasure map from memory. Roxas also talked gold with an interpreter for Yamashita who'd witnessed the loading of several tunnels. Roxas eventually settled into a career as a locksmith, but never forgot about the supposed stashes. In 1970, at age

* The European counterpart to Yamashita's hoard is the fabled Nazi gold train, a story that has zero basis in fact. The train supposedly fled Breslau (now Wrocław, in Poland) in early 1945, carrying 300 tons of looted Nazi gold. It promptly vanished. No trace of it emerged until 2015, when a Polish fellow and his German buddy claimed to have found traces of a hidden underground tunnel using ground-penetrating radar. (In a soap-opera twist, they knew where to look thanks to the deathbed confession of someone whose anonymity they swore to keep.) The press went bananas, and the Polish military began clearing out trees around the area and searching for booby traps. Digging began in August 2016. But—womp, womp—the "secret tunnel" turned out to be a natural cavity formed by an iceberg. Still, the hoopla in the media delighted the nearby town of Wałbrzych, which reckoned that the cockamamie tale won them close to $200 million in publicity; tourism jumped 44 percent the next year. "Whether the explorers find anything or not," beamed a town spokesman, "the gold train has already arrived [for us]."

27, he began digging in an abandoned mineshaft in a mountainous region 150 miles north of Manila. After seven months of toil, he uncovered a hidey-hole two yards wide and ten yards deep. Inside were two dozen gold bars and a gold Buddha that weighed, he estimated, 2,200 pounds. Its head screwed off to reveal a chamber packed with diamonds.

Roxas quietly sold several bars. But he wasn't quiet enough, and before long, a platoon of soldiers was pounding on his door, demanding he turn over the loot; they had orders from Ferdinand Marcos himself, the dictator of the Philippines. Roxas tried to flee, but the soldiers captured him and tortured him with cigarettes and electric shocks. They finally seized the Buddha and remaining seventeen bars of gold. Roxas was freed after that, but he later got arrested on trumped-up charges of carrying an illegal gun and received two years in prison.

After that, the Seagraves insist that the "pathologically greedy" Marcos grew obsessed with finding more Japanese gold. He recruited a mining engineer from Nevada and a psychic from Sweden, who in 1975 supposedly helped him break into a tunnel beneath Manila with $8 billion of gold inside; they also located a sunken hospital ship containing $6 billion more.* Given the steep rise in the price of gold since then, this $14 billion would be worth perhaps 20 or 30 times as much today. Marcos's wife Imelda later corroborated these accounts by saying that her husband's vast wealth derived mostly from

* We know of at least one clandestine Japanese mission that involved smuggling gold. In 1944, the Japanese submarine I-52 slunk out of port on its way to Germany carrying various commodities as payment for Nazi war goods: 2 tons of gold, 22 tons of molybdenum and tungsten, 60 tons of raw rubber, 3 tons each of quinine and opium, and, oddly, 119 pounds of caffeine. But I-52 was sunk off the coast of France and never arrived. A salvage team located the wreck in 1995.

recovered stores of Japanese treasure. (Then again, Imelda had strong reason to say this: to deflect attention from her husband's systematic embezzlement as president of the Philippines.)

The Marcoses were eventually deposed and fled to Hawaii. The dogged locksmith Roxas followed them there and sued Ferdinand in court for theft and for violating his human rights. Both Roxas and Marcos died before the case was resolved. But for whatever it's worth, the court sifted the evidence and witness testimony on behalf of their estates, and concluded that Marcos had indeed stolen a cache of hidden gold from Roxas, as well as tortured and falsely imprisoned him. The jury ordered the Marcos estate to pay a staggering $40.5 billion in damages. (It was later reduced to $19 million.) To be sure, the court did not weigh in on whether Roxas had found some of Yamashita's gold per se, or just a random cache of loot. But in referencing the case later, a U.S. court of appeals did state, "The Yamashita Treasure was discovered by Roxas and stolen from Roxas by Marcos's men."

As with the Inca gold on Cocos Island, treasure hunters from Japan and the United States have scoured the Philippines for decades for any trace of Yamashita's gold. (They often hire local Filipinos as guides—some of whom secure down payments from the foolish foreigners, then skip town.) People have excavated beneath fountains, forts, government offices, and churches; graves have been desecrated as well. Some speak of loot hidden behind waterfalls, or of glyphs carved into stones (hearts, arrows, pyramids) that they're convinced point to nearby gold. Most dramatically, a few claim to have actually drilled into sealed underground chambers, only to recoil, retching, at the geysers of putrid gas that erupted from inside, due to dead bodies. Sadly, several treasure hunters have died when the tunnels they were excavating collapsed.

But as far as the world knows, not a nickel's worth of Yamashita's gold has turned up since Roxas. Perhaps a few caches still exist out there; you never know. But after eight mostly empty decades of searching, the odds of anyone finding more gold in them thar hills seem slimmer every year.

CHAPTER TEN

LOST ART

It's a moment historians drool over. One day in the early 1500s, Leonardo da Vinci was strolling through a piazza in Florence when he spotted a few friends. They were discussing Dante's *Divine Comedy*, and they asked Leonardo a question about a certain passage. He stroked his long red beard, thinking, and admitted he was stumped.

Then, none other than Michelangelo entered the piazza—head down, striding fast. As usual, he was wearing filthy clothing and muttering to himself. Michelangelo adored Dante, and Leonardo's face lit up to see him. He nudged a friend and said, "Ask Michelangelo. He'll explain the passage to you."

Imagine that. Two titans of the Renaissance, about to swap opinions on Dante. What a moment.

Except, things went sideways. Michelangelo, around age 30, heard the comment and scowled at the 50-something Leonardo. Michelangelo had a pugnacious streak—his twisted nose was the result of someone socking him after he levied an insult, in church—and he assumed Leonardo was mocking him. He snarled, "Explain it yourself." Then he tore into Leonardo. "You, who designed a giant horse to cast in bronze and failed, and then abandoned it out of shame."

Leonardo blushed, and ducked his eyes in embarrassment. Michelangelo stomped off. And that ended that.

Historians nevertheless cherish the encounter for what it reveals about the two artists. Michelangelo was feisty and confrontational. Leonardo was chatty and generous of spirit, but as the insult about the horse sculpture shows, he was also sensitive about his less-than-flattering reputation—as a dilettante, a bungler, someone worthy of contempt. Indeed, despite the reverence for him today, you can make a strong case that this prototypical Renaissance man was brilliant, groundbreaking, and wildly overrated. And future generations lost several would-be masterpieces on account of it.

Leonardo's fame rests on two things: his art and his scientific work. Although in truth, it's hard to separate the two.

He was born in 1452, the illegitimate son of a notary and a maid. Beyond a little training on the abacus, he never attended school and could read Latin only haltingly, which cut him off from most scholarship of the time. He nevertheless won an apprenticeship at 14 with the top artist in Florence, Andrea del Verrocchio. His tasks likely included grinding pigments, preparing canvases with primer, and fetching Verrocchio's lunch.

After enough training, Leonardo earned the right to fill in landscapes and background features in Verrocchio's pieces. Eventually the day came when the master let the youth paint a kneeling angel in a baptism scene. Leonardo rendered the angel so beautifully, so evocatively, that Verrocchio reportedly tossed his brush down and quit painting—humiliated to know that he could never top his pupil.

The angel already showed signs of Leonardo's innovative sfumato technique, from the Italian word for "smoke." It involved swirling wet paint with a brush to fuzzy up the edges, leaving them hazy. This technique, along with his habit of surrounding figures with shadows, gave his subjects the appearance of depth and even movement. (In contrast, Michelangelo, a sculptor at heart, surrounded his figures with lines, which gave them a static, posed look.)

Perhaps most importantly, after becoming an independent artist in 1477, Leonardo adopted oil paints. Before this, artists typically painted on wet plaster using tempera, a blend of water, pigments, and egg yolk. (Painters often kept chicken coops to ensure a ready supply of eggs.) Tempera forced artists to work quickly before the plaster dried. Oil paints could be applied to dry surfaces, which allowed for the slow, painstaking brushwork that sfumato demanded. These new materials and methods would both win Leonardo renown and lead him into disaster.

In 1483, at age 31, Leonardo applied for a position with the Duke of Milan. In doing so, he submitted perhaps the most over-the-top résumé in history, claiming expertise with an absurd number of technologies—bridges, catapults, covered wagons, cannons, canals, aqueducts, flamethrowers, and more. He also boasted of his architectural prowess and declared himself the best artist in Europe, before later adding that he sang like a nightingale, too. That bit about his artistic talent was at least true, so the duke welcomed him to Milan and commissioned a portrait of his mistress, while also putting his new prodigy to work designing fireworks and planning parades for royal pageants.

Finally, the duke tapped Leonardo for a major project: a statue of his (the duke's) late father on horseback. Leonardo proposed the most ambitious project Milan had ever seen. The statue would stand 26 feet tall—double the size of any metal statue before then—and require roughly 75 tons of bronze. However intrigued, the duke expressed skepticism about its size. But Leonardo insisted he could pull it off.

His initial sketches called for the horse to rear on its hind legs, a dramatic pose. But as other sculptors noted, this pose would also render the statue unstable, with far too much weight perched on those skinny limbs. Leonardo modified his vision by including a fallen soldier and then a tree stump, which he could connect to the horse's feet for stability. He also toyed with having the rider stretch a weapon behind him for better balance. But he eventually abandoned the rearing steed for a more conventional pose on all fours.

Even before his design was set, Leonardo threw himself into preparatory studies. He began by drawing horses, plopping down in local stables to sketch them for hours. Then he decided to dissect a horse, to better understand their musculature. It was a novel approach, and might have served him well—except he got sidetracked writing a treatise on horse anatomy. Stranger still, he began designing a new type of stable, with machines to automatically fill feed bins and sluice away manure. A fine idea, but not what the duke was paying him for.

When he finally got back around to the sculpture, Leonardo let his imagination roam again and devised a new method for casting metal. Daringly, instead of the traditional method of casting a statue in pieces and forging them together, he decided to cast his statue in one go, to avoid the scars that resulted from welding the sections.

This plan required him to build a huge clay model of the horse first. He'd use that to create two concentric molds of the horse, one inside the other, with an inch and a half of wax between them. Next, he'd bury the whole thing upside down in sand and pour molten bronze into the horse's belly through tubes. The bronze would melt the wax and force it out through channels in the molds; steam would also shoot cartoonishly out of the horse's feet. As the bronze cooled, it would anneal into solid metal and render, in one gleaming piece, the most spectacular statue in the world.

It was innovative stuff. But artists with more experience had doubts. Designing the channels to remove all the wax would be tricky. They also suspected that the terrific heat of 75 tons of molten bronze would crack the mold and ruin everything. Similarly, the bronze seemed unlikely to cool evenly, which could mar the final work. Such rumblings made the Duke of Milan nervous, as did the fact that Leonardo spent far more time dissecting horses and designing feed machines than actually sculpting.

But in November 1493, Leonardo shut every last doubter up. He buckled down and finished the clay model of the horse, which he revealed at a wedding. The guests were stunned. The giant beast looked brilliant, utterly lifelike. You could trace every muscle and sinew, and practically hear its snorting breath. Poet Baldassare Taccone marveled that "neither Greece nor Rome ever saw anything grander." The duke couldn't wait to see the final thing.

And wait he would. The next step in Leonardo's plan involved preparation for casting the sculpture. But the Christmas holidays passed, and he still hadn't done anything. Then January slipped by. February and March, too. The exasperated duke learned that Leonardo was having trouble with his grandiose scheme. The water table in Milan was shallow, and digging down far enough to bury the horse upside down would plunge its head into a puddle and ruin the mold. So Leonardo decided to bury the horse sideways instead. But that new orientation would require redesigning the channels to pour the metal in and drain the wax—a frustrating delay. Outside the studio, he also got distracted with plans to paint a mural at a monastery in Milan, *The Last Supper*.

Finally, in November 1494, a year after the model went on display, the duke had had enough: Leonardo was nowhere near ready to begin casting. More pressingly, the powerful French army was threatening to invade Milan. The duke seized the allotted 75 tons of bronze and melted it down to make cannons. However disgusted Leonardo must have felt, he had no one but himself to blame. To add insult to injury, the French army steamrolled Milan anyway, extra cannons notwithstanding. When French soldiers swarmed the city, they gaped at the giant horse—then got drunk and used it for archery practice. They punctured dozens of holes, allowing rain to seep inside and eat at the clay. It melted in slow motion into a pile of muck, and became a punch line among artists like Michelangelo.

The horse statue was not Leonardo's only failure. His most notorious flop involved a mural in Florence, another doomed blend of artistic ambition and half-baked science.

In 1500, Leonardo moved back to Florence, a city jam-packed with painters—Michelangelo, Botticelli, Raphael. But Leonardo outshined them all. People adored his wit, and his dandyish clothing caught everyone's eye, especially his rose-colored tunics with fur collars. And while aloof at times, he had many warm acquaintances, including Niccolò Machiavelli.

In 1503, city leaders gave Leonardo the commission of a lifetime: a mural in their majestic city hall. It would stretch 66 feet wide and commemorate the Battle of Anghiari in 1440—a rare victory for the hapless Florentine army. (Florence won in part because the invading Milanese drummed up clouds of dust while approaching and cost themselves the advantage of surprise.) To be frank, the battle was hardly epic: Just one person died, after falling off a horse. Still, its memory lived on in the heart of every red-blooded Florentine, and given the scale, the subject, and the prestigious location, the mural seemed destined to be Leonardo's masterpiece.

Leonardo had been musing a battle scene for a decade by then—the gorier the better, as far as he was concerned. In notes on how to render such a scene, he wrote, "There must not be one level spot that is not trampled and saturated with blood ... The dying will be grinding their teeth, their eyeballs rolling heavenward as they beat their bodies with their fists." You can almost hear them scream. Despite the less-than-Homeric scale of the Battle of Anghiari, Leonardo decided to take some poetic license and depict plenty of carnage in his mural.

Based on prior experience—a quarter century earlier, Leonardo had flaked out and failed to finish an altarpiece for the city—the government in Florence gave him a hard deadline to complete the mural by February 1505. To help him along, Machiavelli's secretary provided a long narrative of the battle, which Leonardo dutifully sat down to read—until he got distracted partway through and drew a flying contraption in the margin. He also returned to some notes he'd written years before about the physics of dust and smoke and how they mingle to produce subtle gradations of gray and tan and blue. Six months after being hired, Leonardo still hadn't finished the preliminary step of sketching a full-scale drawing on paper, a so-called cartoon. City leaders began grumbling. Would he burn them again?

One official, however, had an idea. Leonardo's friend Machiavelli decided to commission a second mural in the same room as Leonardo's. And the artist he selected for the mural was none other than Michelangelo.

Leonardo was steamed. He'd recently been pressed into serving on a committee to decide where in Florence to display Michelangelo's newly completed *David,* which was already being hailed as a masterwork.* Leonardo vowed to not let this young punk upstage him in the great hall. As a motivational ploy, it was pure Machiavellian genius.

And it did light a fire under Leonardo. For a while. He finished his full-scale cartoon on 400 sheets of paper. It offered a panoramic view of the battle, with a skirmish for a military standard as the scene's focal point. The scrum was every bit as vicious as Leonardo's notes promised, with snarling soldiers, a pool of blood, and all the rearing horses his heart desired.

But even the threat of Michelangelo couldn't tame Leonardo's mind, and before long—you'll never believe it—he got sidetracked. One distraction involved the platform he'd stand on to paint the mural's upper reaches. As a self-proclaimed engineering genius, he couldn't just use a regular old scaffold—no, no, no. He designed an intricate machine instead, with an accordion lift to raise him up and down.

He also began experimenting with new methods of applying paint. Sadly, his mural *The Last Supper,* less than a decade old, was already flaking off the wall of the monastery that housed it—in large part

* Pushy as always, Michelangelo insisted on displaying his sculpture in a public piazza outside a palace. In contrast, several people on the committee suggested tucking it beneath a portico in the piazza's corner, which would have protected it from the elements but also effectively hidden it. Guess which option Leonardo favored? Michelangelo got his way, but Leonardo won another argument to cover up David's twig and berries with copper leaves.

because Leonardo, instead of painting on wet plaster, as every other artist did, had tried to innovate and paint on dry plaster with a mix of oil and water paints. This allowed him to slow down and add color in thin layers, using innumerable brushstrokes. (Witnesses recall him gazing at the mural for hours sometimes, doing nothing. Other days, he'd rush in, add a few frenzied daubs here and there, then hurry out.) No one could deny the result: *The Last Supper* is a stunning achievement, especially for its sense of movement. (Critics have called it less painted than choreographed.) But mixing oil and water paints on a dry surface proved foolish: The pigments refused to stick to the wall and began flaking off like dandruff.*

Leonardo didn't want his new masterpiece suffering similar damage. So he improvised a primer for the wall, coating the plaster with what he called "Greek pitch": probably either concentrated turpentine or resin blended with wax. If it held on to pigments, he could continue painting at his preferred pace. He ran some small, hasty experiments, and his test panels seemed to retain pigments well. Leonardo declared himself satisfied and raced ahead.

Unfortunately, the technique didn't work at scale. The plaster-pitch mix failed to set, and paint started dribbling down the wall. He had to hang flaming braziers perilously close to the surface to dry it.

By this time, Leonardo's deadline had long passed. Then, in June 1505, disaster struck. A torrential thunderstorm swept in, and dirty water leaked into city hall. The cartoon tore, and the already damp wall was left soaked and smeared. To salvage the painting, Leonardo

---

* By 1652, *The Last Supper* was crumbling so badly that the monks at the monastery gave it up for lost and chopped a door in the wall through Jesus's feet. Restoration efforts over the centuries have mostly done more harm than good, and only 20 percent of what we see today is original. Some details, like Judas knocking over a saltcellar, have disappeared entirely.

would have to start over. Except he didn't. He got distracted yet again with other projects, and despite the prestige of the commission, he soon abandoned it.* The wall was eventually painted over with a new mural in the 1560s, and no trace of his would-be masterpiece remains today.†

Regrettably, the horse and mural fiascoes were not the exceptions in Leonardo's career, but the rule. As a little quiz, how many works of his can you name? There's the *Mona Lisa,* obviously, and *The Last Supper.* Beyond that, it gets tricky. Arguably, his next-most-famous piece is the *Vitruvian Man,* that dude spread-eagled inside a circle—a striking image, certainly, but more a sketch than a fully realized work.

Now, guess how many paintings Leonardo completed over his career. Just 15—over four decades. With scores of other pieces, he got distracted and abandoned them partway through. Indeed, his flightiness was notorious among dukes and other would-be patrons; many began to refuse payment until he actually completed a piece. Even that couldn't always spur him, and he squandered enough

---

* To be fair, Michelangelo didn't even begin his mural. He reneged after realizing that his side of the great hall sat in shadows most of the time, which he considered insulting. Still, Michelangelo did complete a cartoon for it, which would have portrayed a different skirmish in Florentine history: the Battle of Cascina in 1364. He focused on a moment before the battle started, when soldiers were bathing in a river. Then an alarm sounded, and the soldiers scrambled out to dress. It's an odd choice for a "battle" scene, but as one writer commented, "as a rare event in military history that centered on nude wet men, it was suited for Michelangelo." The cartoon also provoked Leonardo's famous put-down that the grotesquely swole soldiers look like "sacks of walnuts."

† Giorgio Vasari painted that new mural. Intriguingly, a few soldiers in it carry a banner that reads CERCA TROVA—"seek and you shall find," the only words on the entire painting. One modern scholar interpreted this as a hidden message, a clue that part of the lost Leonardo mural lies beneath. His theory builds on the fact that the 1560s also saw extensive renovations to the hall, with new walls going up. So perhaps the wall Leonardo painted on was simply concealed behind a facade and is preserved today. It's a thrilling conjecture.

commissions that he went broke several times. At one point he was reduced to decorating clocks in exchange for firewood.

These stories aren't meant as a slur against Leonardo's talent. He was one of the most talented artists in history. He wasn't lazy, either. He worked hard, and constantly had a dozen different projects going at any one time. But inevitably, one by one, he'd abandon them. What was going on?

In short, Leonardo's problem was temperamental, even psychological. He lacked what the Germans call *sitzfleisch,* or "sitting flesh." It's a slang term for the buttocks. But metaphorically, it means sitting your buttocks down to get some work done. It's what one wag meant in defining writing as "the application of the seat of the pants to the seat of the chair." Sometimes, you just have to plop down and concentrate.

Consider Michelangelo. He was a moody prick, but boy, could he focus. In the throes of a project, he gnawed on bread crusts for meals, and refused to stop working to bathe or wash his clothes. He wouldn't even remove his shoes from his increasingly rank feet. Leonardo lacked such commitment. He'd hunker down before some deadline—intending to work, needing to work—then fritter away hours on some urgent triviality. The margins of his notebooks teem with random, scribbled thoughts on sneezing and yawning and woodpecker tongues. All of which is charming. But his flitting, magpie mind also prevented him from finishing anything. Time after time, he either drew up grandiose plans without thinking them through or wandered away from a project and never found his way back.

(A few historians have suggested that perhaps Leonardo had ADHD, attention deficit hyperactivity disorder: "We can only imagine," said one, "what he would have accomplished had Ritalin been available in the fifteenth century." It's an intriguing thought. That said, it's impossible to retro-diagnose someone with a psychological condition five centuries after their death, and Leonardo might have rejected the label anyway. But you do wonder.)

Similar flaws hobbled Leonardo's scientific work. He did make real contributions to anatomy, determining what the aortic valve does and how the pupil of the eye contracts or expands in response to light. But he also dabbled in botany, geology, ballistics, optics, linguistics, and physics without making any real contributions.

The same goes for his forays into engineering. Over the years, he sketched out plans to build automobiles, looms, lathes, diving suits, oil presses, submarines, parachutes, and more. But guess how many of those inventions he actually built. Zero. They were just fleeting thoughts, and in some cases, not even good thoughts. His flying machines, for instance, are arresting images: strap-on wings, helicopters powered by treadmills, that age-old dream of flight! But they were laughably impractical. He failed to grasp the basic truth that, compared to birds, human beings have far fewer muscles in proportion to our size and can't generate enough power to lift off. Other "inventions" of his show the same shortcoming: He didn't reason things through.

Now, I realize I'm being a Scrooge in criticizing Leonardo like this. But even his admirers can't deny that he fell far short of his promise. It's trendy nowadays to talk about creativity in terms of range. Explore—roam—jump from passion to passion. Develop your range. And no one in history had more range than Leonardo. But there's something to be said for grit as well. For focus, for single-mindedness. For applying the seat of the pants to the seat of the chair, and seeing a painting or two through.

In the end, perhaps we should just be grateful for the few masterpieces he managed to complete—*Virgin of the Rocks*, *Lady With an Ermine*, and of course the *Mona Lisa*. But most people don't realize how close we came to losing that last painting as well. And for once, the loss wasn't the result of anything Leonardo did, but of one of the most audacious, if harebrained, crimes the world has ever seen.

In 1495, 15-year-old Lisa Gherardini married a 30-year-old silk merchant in Florence and thereby became Lisa del Giocondo. Formally, she sometimes went by Madonna Lisa, or Mona Lisa for short.

When she was 24, her husband commissioned Leonardo to paint her portrait; it was one of the projects that distracted him from the battle mural. Leonardo rendered the work on a poplar board, 31 inches tall and 21 inches wide. It's a consummate sfumato painting, all blurs and wisps. Lisa lacks eyebrows in it, although most people don't notice that, bewitched as they are by her sad smile. The background—crags, a lake, a bridge—looks oddly alien, but in 2024 a historian identified the landscape as a real place, near the village of Lecco.

We don't know whether Leonardo and Lisa ever met again after she sat for him. Nor do we know why Leonardo never delivered the portrait to her. Perhaps he did deliver one version, and what we have today is a copy. Perhaps she crinkled her nose and rejected it: As one scholar noted, she's "darker and earthier than the ideal beauty at the time." Or perhaps the Giocondos got sick of Leonardo's flightiness and cut ties. Regardless, Lisa never saw the version that survives, since Leonardo continued to rework the piece for more than a decade.

After the battle mural fell apart, Leonardo bounced around between Milan, Florence, and Rome. In 1516, the French monarch François I tried to lure Raphael and Michelangelo north to be his court savants. When they declined, François settled for Leonardo, who lugged the *Mona Lisa* along atop a donkey. He died three years later, at which point the portrait seemingly passed to his assistant and probable lover Salai. In 1524 Salai died in a crossbow duel, and sometime over the next half dozen years, François snatched the painting up and hung it in a castle south of Paris. It moved to Versailles in 1695, then adorned Napoleon's bedroom for a spell before ending up in the Louvre.

Artists copied the work roughly 60 times in the 1500s and 1600s, indicating deep admiration. After that, fashions changed and its reputation sank, to the point that the caretakers at Versailles yanked it off the wall in 1760 and dumped it in storage. (At the time, Raphael and Jan van Eyck were held aloft as the greatest artists in history; Leonardo and his crumbling frescoes appeared well down the list.)

By the mid-1800s, Leonardo's stock was rising again, and in 1869 a critic penned an embarrassingly effusive essay about his obsession with the *Mona Lisa,* babbling about "Greek goddesses" and "the lust of Rome." He concluded that "she is older than the rocks among which she sits; like the vampire, she has been dead many times, and learned the secrets of the grave." If you say so, dude. Swept away by such rhetoric, art snobs began to champion the portrait again. Still, it was not well known outside such circles as late as 1911—when a single deed transformed it into an icon.

August 21 of that year was a Monday, the day the Louvre closed each week. At 7:15 a.m., a slim craftsman with a sweeping black mustache was huddled in a closet inside, dabbing sweat from his brow and listening for guards on their rounds. Vincenzo Peruggia was an amateur artist himself. But that morning, he wore the white smock of the Louvre maintenance staff, a job he'd held for several months. Specifically, he cut sheets of glass to mount in front of framed paintings—a step deemed necessary after a dressmaker had slashed a picture of a pope with her scissors a few years prior. Although it was good work, Peruggia found the job infuriating; every hour in the galleries left him seething.

Peruggia tensed to hear the clicking footsteps of a guard. Once they receded, he slipped out of the closet and made for the Salon Carré, where the museum kept its most prized paintings. He passed by the Rembrandts, van Dycks, and Velázquezes without a glance. More gratingly, he eyed Italian masterpieces by Raphael and Titian and Veronese. Peruggia had grown up in Italy and had endured mockery in France as an immigrant "macaroni eater." Colleagues thought it hilarious to steal his tools and dump salt in his wine. He'd also heard that every Italian painting in the Louvre had been looted by Napoleon a century earlier. Now Peruggia would get his revenge. He would liberate a masterpiece, return it to his motherland, and humiliate the Frenchmen who'd made him feel so small.

In plotting this revenge, Peruggia did have a point. Napoleon had pilfered countless artworks during his rampage across Europe. In his froth of rage, however, Peruggia had not bothered learning the provenance of the painting he'd settled on stealing. He had no idea that the *Mona Lisa* was a rare piece France had come by honestly.

With the coast clear in the Salon, Peruggia made his move. Paintings in the Louvre hung on the wall in a special way: The nails that supported them had fat heads that fit into brass loops mounted on the back of the painting. So you first had to lift a piece straight up and then pull it out from the wall; otherwise, it wouldn't come free. But Peruggia knew the trick and freed the *Mona Lisa* in seconds. Although small, the picture weighed nearly 200 pounds with its bulky frame. He lumbered over to a door and ducked into a stairwell. There, he sliced the wooden panel free and discarded the frame. Then he grabbed a white sheet he'd brought along and shrouded Lisa's face.

Now to escape. He hurried down the steps, found the exit, and twisted the knob—only to nearly bang his forehead on the door. It was locked. He had no key.

Peruggia felt panic rising in his throat. Then he remembered his tools—he'd brought a small kit just in case. Setting the painting down, he disassembled and removed the knob with a screwdriver, figuring the door would swing open. It didn't. He rattled the knobless door, thumped it with his shoulder. It remained stubbornly locked.

That's when he heard footsteps.

Peruggia wheeled around to see a plumber ascending the stairs. He crammed the doorknob into his pocket and tried to think. How could he explain this?

Luckily for him, the plumber was perhaps the least curious man alive. He'd just caught a Louvre employee dismantling an exit door while standing next to a painting-size object concealed in a sheet—and thought nothing of it. After a beat, Peruggia croaked, "Open the door." The plumber shrugged, pulled some pliers off his belt, and sprang the lock. He then turned and merrily went about his day.

Alone again, Peruggia crept out into the courtyard. A security booth stood right there, but the guard had left to fetch a bucket of water to scrub his booth. A delighted Peruggia hurried past and merged into the foot traffic of Paris. He immediately pulled off his smock. He also felt the doorknob banging around in his pocket, so he tossed it into a ditch. (A shopkeeper actually witnessed him doing all this, but didn't realize what was happening.) And just like that, Peruggia was free. Upon reaching his apartment, he shoved the *Mona Lisa* into a cubbyhole next to an umbrella and piled some firewood in front. Then he doubled back out the door, late for his shift at work.

Around 8:30 a.m., a gaggle of Peruggia's colleagues in maintenance strode through the Salon Carré. One noticed a gap where the

Mona Lisa normally hung and cracked, "They took it down so we wouldn't steal it." They all had a good laugh before heading off to that day's tasks.

The museum opened bright and early the next morning. Although large and prestigious—with half a million artworks on display over 49 acres—the Louvre was pretty sleepy back then, attracting just a few hundred visitors per day. Most people had fled Paris anyway for the countryside amid a stifling 90°F heat wave.

While patrolling the empty rooms, a guard noticed the gap in the Salon Carré straightaway. But the Louvre security staff was hardly an elite force. Most were creaky, retired military officers seeking an easy paycheck. Indeed, a newspaper story had recently exposed just how pathetic they were. A reporter had eluded their sweep at closing time one afternoon and spent the night wandering the museum alone; he'd slept in a mummy's sarcophagus. But no one at the Louvre seemed to care.

That morning in the Salon, the guard spied the gap and narrowed his eyes. Then he nodded. The Louvre had been taking official photographs of its paintings, and the *Mona Lisa*'s turn must have come. No need to inquire further.

Given this indifference, days or even a week might have passed without anyone realizing the truth, if not for a pushy artist. He'd been painting a scene in the Salon Carré that included the *Mona Lisa* and was annoyed to find it missing from the wall. He inquired with the guard, who explained about the photographs. After lunchtime, the painter pestered the guard again. *How long does it take to snap a photo?* And he kept pestering him until the guard finally harrumphed and waddled off to check. The nerve of some people.

When asked about the painting, the staff photographer frowned. He wasn't shooting the *Mona Lisa* that day. The guard corrected him: He must be, given that it's missing from the wall. After a few more

"Who's on First?" exchanges, the guard blanched and felt his knees wobble. As one historian noted, "He'd spent all morning guarding a room that had already been robbed."

The guard summoned the Paris police, who shut down the Louvre, citing a fictitious plumbing crisis. A hundred officers fanned out to search every closet and crawlspace, to make certain the painting hadn't simply been misplaced. They found the empty frame within an hour.

Having no immediate leads, the top detective on the case ran an experiment. He had the Louvre staff hang a dummy painting on the wall, then asked two policemen to remove it. They spent five minutes banging and swearing, raising an awful ruckus. Then the detective had a Louvre employee try. This man knew the trick about lifting the painting off the nails, and freed it from the wall in seconds. The conclusion was obvious: Someone with inside knowledge had committed the crime.

Over the next several days, the police fingerprinted and interviewed each of the Louvre's 300 employees, including Peruggia. In fact, they interrogated the Italian twice—including at his apartment, just yards away from the cubbyhole. Peruggia initially claimed he couldn't have stolen the portrait because he'd been working at the time of the theft. But his boss undermined that alibi, noting that Peruggia had been late that morning. When confronted with this testimony, Peruggia got sheepish, claiming he'd been out late carousing the night before and had simply overslept—an outright lie.

However, the detectives didn't press him. Romantically, they assumed that the theft of a masterpiece painting required a criminal of similar caliber—a mastermind thief. It's not clear how they squared this with their initial, and correct, assumption that someone inside the Louvre had stolen the portrait; perhaps they never noticed the contradiction. Regardless, they decided that a mere maintenance man—and a macaroni eater at that—simply could not be the criminal genius that the robbery demanded.

Another clue had turned up in the meantime: a fingerprint on the frame, a left thumb. And it just so happened that Peruggia had been arrested twice before, once for theft and once for possession of a knife during a row over a prostitute. As a result, the police had his fingerprints on file, ready to match with the print on the frame. Unfortunately, the filing system for prints was complicated and allowed for searching only via right-hand prints. Lefty prints were useless. And, having already dismissed the lowly Peruggia as a suspect, the police never thought to take his prints and compare them with the one on the frame. As one observer noted, "If the *Mona Lisa* had been something else, anything else—a stolen purse, a set of second-rate jewels—the thief would have been found far sooner."

After admitting they had no leads and no suspects, the police were flooded with useless tips, from as far afield as Peru. The banker J. P. Morgan, who had an appetite for art on par with Napoleon's, was spotted at a train station in Italy around this time with a painting-size crate. A mob surrounded him, howling that he'd arranged for the *Mona Lisa*'s theft and was now smuggling it to, god forbid, America. Morgan had to beat the crowd off with a cane to reach his train.

Meanwhile, newspapers couldn't believe their luck. This was the sexiest story in a decade—a heady swirl of art, scandal, bumbling bureaucrats, and (according to the police) a criminal mastermind. Stories about the robbery would run on the front page of every Paris daily for a month.

Then another scoop ratcheted the drama even higher. On August 29 and 30, a man about town named Honoré-Joseph Géry Pieret wrote two letters to a newspaper boasting that he had also stolen some art from the Louvre recently: three small limestone idols from ancient Andalusia. He'd fenced them to a local painter for 50 francs, which he'd promptly gambled away at billiards. When reached for comment, the Louvre staff admitted it had no idea the idols had vanished. Just how much art was the museum missing?

Why Pieret penned these letters isn't clear. He could politely be described as eccentric, more accurately as mad. But the editions with his letters soon made their way to a cabin in the Pyrenees, where Pablo Picasso read them on vacation and choked on his ham. He was the "local painter" Pieret had sold the statues to. And while Pieret claimed to have swiped them on a whim, that wasn't true. Picasso had paid him to rob the Louvre.

He'd done so to slake an obsession. The idols—one man, two women, about 15 pounds each—came from his homeland, and he adored their exaggerated features, which evoked the new type of art he wanted to make. He had to possess them. In fact, while he mostly stashed them in his sock drawer to hide them, he did use the idols as models for two faces in his 1907 masterwork *Les Demoiselles d'Avignon*, one of the most influential paintings in history.

At that time, however, Picasso was a nobody, and he faced prison time or deportation for the theft. He scurried back to Paris to rid himself of the idols. To this end, he concealed them in a suitcase and headed out one midnight to dump them in the Seine, slinking from bridge to bridge. But he lost courage and couldn't follow through.

A day or two later, on September 5, he finally convinced his friend, poet Guillaume Apollinaire, to drop the idols off at a newspaper where Apollinaire had connections. Picasso hoped their return would end the affair, but no. The Paris police were taking daily floggings in the press for incompetence. The madman Pieret had skipped town by then, so after Apollinaire relinquished the idols, the police browbeat the newspaper for his name. The next day, they arrested the poet and strip-searched him in prison. To Apollinaire's shock, the police then charged him with theft—not of the idols, but of the *Mona Lisa*. They figured he and his little painter friend must have *something* to do with it.

Within days, Apollinaire cracked and gave up Picasso. The next morning at 7 a.m., five hours before he normally rose, the police banged on Picasso's door. When they announced his arrest, he began shaking so violently that his lover, Fernande Olivier, had to dress him; he chose a polka-dot shirt and tie. At the courthouse, he spotted Apollinaire looking roughed-up, with a torn collar. Picasso promptly swore he'd never seen the man in his life. But bully him as they might, the police couldn't link Picasso to the *Mona Lisa* and eventually let him go.

In the meantime, the Louvre had reopened for visitors. And with newspapers hammering the story, the once sleepy museum now had thousands of people parading through to gape at the missing painting: four nails on a blank patch of wallpaper, with a faint outline of dust and discoloration marking the old frame. Franz Kafka was among them. A journalist went down the line asking questions, and most people admitted they'd never heard of the painting before. But they sure had now. Some left flowers in tribute.

Outside the gallery, vendors hawked reproductions and postcards of Lisa. Her face appeared in lingerie ads and on boxes of chocolates and cigarettes. As one wag noted, "The world could now see the *Mona Lisa* everywhere *but* the Louvre." Only the sinking of the *Titanic* eight months later drove the story off the front pages for good. By then, the French government had given up: "There is no ground to hope that *Mona Lisa* will ever resume her place in the Louvre," said one minister. The museum replaced her on the wall with a Raphael.

In December 1913, a plump art dealer named Alfredo Geri opened a letter in his office in Florence, skimmed the first few lines, and rolled his eyes. Since the *Mona Lisa*'s disappearance, cranks and crazies across Europe had been claiming to know the painting's location. This letter, signed "Leonard," sounded nuttier than most. The writer claimed to *have* the painting, and to want to return it to Italy to avenge Napoleon. Geri was about to crumple it up when he hesitated. It was almost certainly nonsense, but he felt duty-bound to at least follow up.

After consulting with the director of the nearby Uffizi Gallery, Geri wrote back to Leonard, praising his courage and adding that he longed to see Mona Lisa "smile again in Florence." Could Leonard bring her to town? To his surprise, Leonard agreed. After a flurry of telegrams and two canceled meetings, Leonard suddenly arrived in town on December 10 and asked to see Geri straightaway. The dealer lowered the shades in his office and welcomed in a slender man with a sweeping black mustache. Leonard claimed to have the painting in his hotel room and asked for a reward of a half million lire (close to $1 million today) for its liberation from France. Geri stalled; he needed the Uffizi director on hand to confirm the painting's identity, but the man was out of town. Geri told Leonard to meet him at his home at 3 p.m. the following afternoon.

The next day, the Uffizi director arrived at Geri's home early, and the two men settled in to stare at the clock. Three o'clock passed, then 3:05. No sign of Leonard. Then 3:10. At 3:15, the director grabbed his coat to leave. Another hoax.

At that moment, Leonard bounded up to the door. He explained that he'd never visited Florence before, and had been taking in the sights. He didn't seem nervous—more excited—and told the others to follow him to his hotel.

His room was so cramped that they had to stand shoulder to shoulder inside. Leonard locked the door and pulled a trunk from beneath his bed. Geri's heart quickened; it was large enough to hold a painting. What it held instead was junk. Leonard removed some old shoes, a crumpled hat, a smock and brushes, a mandolin. Before long, the trunk was empty.

Then Leonard started fiddling with something inside. To Geri's astonishment, he lifted away a false bottom. A rectangular object emerged from the cavity, wrapped in red silk. With a magician's flourish, Leonard yanked it off—and presented the *Mona Lisa*.

The Uffizi director compared the painting to a photograph he'd brought, then checked the Louvre's identification stamps on the back. There was no question. Yet, however hard it was, he played it cool and frowned. He said he just couldn't tell. Could he take the painting to his office and study it there, for confirmation?

Leonard once again surprised them, saying of course they could. He rewrapped Lisa and they descended the stairs—only to suffer a tense moment at the exit. The eagle-eyed concierge saw Leonard leaving with a painting-size object and darted from behind his desk. The hotel had artwork throughout, and no one was going to steal anything on his watch. He tried to seize the red silk bundle. The Uffizi director finally intervened and assured the hothead that everything was under control. As they made their way out, Geri had to shake his head; if only the staff at the Louvre had been so conscientious.

After dropping the painting off at the Uffizi, "Leonard" strolled back to his hotel, practically whistling as he walked. He was feeling radiant. Everyone in Italy would soon know his name—Vincenzo Peruggia. He might even get to meet the king! So imagine his shock when the police barged into his hotel an hour later and arrested him. Didn't they know he was a hero?

The Uffizi director called up his counterpart at the Louvre and triumphantly announced the return of the *Mona Lisa.* Or tried to. The Louvre director hung up on him mid-sentence and returned to his dinner; he, too, was tired of hoaxes. It took another call, and several rounds of assurances, to convince him.

The next day, the story broke in the newspapers. A heated session of the Italian parliament happened to be underway then—so heated that a fistfight broke out on the floor. But when someone rushed in yelling that they'd found the *Mona Lisa,* the assailants lowered their dukes and hugged each other.

Italy agreed to return the painting, but not before indulging a bit. The government displayed it in three cities, starting with Florence. So many people showed up the first day—about 30,000—that a near riot broke out; windows were smashed, and the harried guards had to pull sculptures aside to prevent them from being stampeded. Then came Rome and Milan, where tens of thousands more filed past. Newspaper reporters saw men removing their hats, soldiers saluting, little old women crossing themselves in tears.

After an armed escort back to Paris, the painting drew even bigger crowds at the Louvre. From that moment forward, the *Mona Lisa* was far and away the most famous artwork in the world—all thanks to one slightly unhinged glass cutter and a crime that never should have succeeded, but somehow, miraculously, did.

The *Mona Lisa* next left Paris just before World War II. She was not alone this time. With the Nazi army likely to invade France soon, the Louvre's directors decided to evacuate their most valuable pieces. And unlike the bumbling 1911 crew, the museum staff of 1939 proved a crack outfit, packing up and removing 3,690 pieces in just three days. A system of stickers helped workers know which ones to prioritize. Yellow stickers indicated valuable art. Green stickers indicated masterpieces. Red stickers indicated world treasures to save at all costs. The *Mona Lisa* got three red stickers. After the evacuation, the Louvre galleries looked like a lumberyard, spookily empty and piled with blank frames.*

The artwork ended up in castles throughout western France. To ensure that Allied planes didn't bomb those castles, Louvre officials relayed their coordinates in encoded radio messages, prefacing the information with the phrase, "The *Mona Lisa* is smiling."

The *Mona Lisa* itself had an initial layover a hundred miles southeast of Paris, then shifted location five more times during the war. For transport, the portrait was carried on an ambulance stretcher to an armored van that was hermetically sealed to provide consistent humidity. (During the first trip, the poor guard riding along with it nearly suffocated.) Although rumors persist to this day that the Nazis got their clutches on Lisa at one point, there's little hard evidence for that; if anything, they grabbed a copy. She returned to the Louvre for good on June 16, 1945.

But her travails were not over. In 1956, a vandal threw acid at the painting, splattering the lower half. Then in late 1956, a homeless man hurled a stone at her, chipping off some paint by her elbow,

* Two pieces proved especially difficult to move. The delicate *Winged Victory of Samothrace* had to be eased down a flight of stairs on a wooden ramp as a half dozen men crowded around, scarcely daring to breathe. Then there was the gargantuan *Raft of Medusa*. At 16 feet tall and 23 feet wide, it wouldn't fit in any normal vehicle, so officials propped it on a trailer used by a theater company to haul scenery around. On its journey, it got tangled in electrical wires and was nearly fried in the shower of sparks. After that, it traveled with some postmen carrying insulated poles, to lift any wires they encountered.

reportedly because he hoped to spend the winter in a warm prison cell. The painting was put behind strong glass at that point—and good thing, because in 1974, while the piece was touring Japan, a woman in a wheelchair tried to spray-paint it red to protest the Tokyo National Museum's lack of accommodations for disabled people to view the painting.

Nowadays, the painting resides in a bulletproof case with a seismic cradle to protect against earthquakes, as well as a personal air-conditioning unit to control the temperature and humidity (65°F, 55 percent). But that hasn't stopped the assaults. In 2009, a Russian woman denied French citizenship hurled a ceramic mug at the painting; it shattered harmlessly on the bulletproof glass. In May 2022, a man donned a wig and rolled into the Louvre in a wheelchair, taking advantage of the museum's policy of letting disabled patrons get closer than others—at which point he threw off the wig, leaped up, and smeared cake on the glass, to protest climate change somehow. Finally, environmental protestors struck again in 2024, hurling pumpkin soup at Lisa to highlight food insecurity in Europe. Through it all, Lisa continued smiling.

The destruction of art is sadly common throughout history. Sometimes the cause is natural (earthquakes, floods, fires), other times not (plane crashes, shipwrecks, car bombs, mobs of religious zealots, the 9/11 terror attacks). In one case, an avant-garde filmmaker recorded Pablo Picasso painting several pieces and then (accounts differ) either burned most of them in an alley afterward or allowed Picasso to tear them up. That way, his footage would be the only record of their existence.

Art theft continues today, too. Picasso alone has had 1,100 pieces stolen. The most stolen individual work is the *Ghent Altarpiece,* which has been nabbed seven times since 1432. The costliest heist occurred early on March 18, 1990, when two thieves dressed as cops took advantage of St. Patrick's Day revelry in Boston to relieve the Isabella Stewart Gardner Museum of 13 works by Rembrandt, Vermeer, Degas, and Manet. Collectively, those paintings are worth hundreds of millions of dollars, and empty frames still hang in the gallery as a tribute. One theory holds that a two-bit mobster stole them to negotiate the release of his don from prison. But really, we have no idea.

(More happily, several missing artworks have been recovered in recent decades. A Titian robbed from a mansion in England in 1995 was mysteriously found in 2002 sitting at a bus stop in a blue-and-white plastic bag. Sometime around 2010, a man in the American Midwest, who chose to remain anonymous, bought a three-inch gold orb at a junk shop for $14,000 and decided to melt it down for scrap. Luckily, he searched online first, and discovered it was a Fabergé egg worth $34 million; the Bolsheviks had seized it during the Russian Revolution and sold it for tractors, after which it vanished. The scholar who rushed over to authenticate it found it sitting on the man's counter next to a cupcake. Another piece—a painting lost in the chaos of World War II—appeared as a prop in the background of the kiddie movie *Stuart Little.* The art historian who spotted it nearly dropped his daughter off his lap in shock. Oddest of all, a retired bus driver in England stole a portrait of the Duke of Wellington in 1961 to protest a British television tax. He returned it four years later out of guilt, but not before a copy of it appeared as a joke in Dr. No's lair in a James Bond flick. Ironically, the fake was subsequently stolen after filming and remains missing today.)

The potential mob connection in the Boston heist brings up an interesting point. Peruggia stole the *Mona Lisa* to restore it to his homeland, which doesn't excuse the crime but does have a noble ring to it. Picasso, meanwhile, commissioned the theft of the stone idols to quench an aesthetic obsession. But such exalted motives are rare. Most art crimes are ugly deeds undertaken for ugly reasons—either to make a quick buck or to keep as a plea-bargaining chip if the crooks are ever nabbed on other charges. Worse still, organized crime syndicates sometimes use stolen art as collateral in drug and gun deals. Terrorists have exploited art, too. ISIS relied heavily on looted art for funding. And Mohamed Atta's original plans for 9/11 called for trading looted Afghani pieces for his own plane to smash into the World Trade Center; hijacking a commercial flight was the backup option.

Even Peruggia's motivations might not have been so pure. For whatever reason, France never extradited him to stand trial, so Italian courts handled the matter instead. It soon emerged that Peruggia had tried to sell the painting several times before surrendering it in Florence, including once to J. P. Morgan. Peruggia downplayed these incidents in court, claiming he simply wanted to bank enough money to ensure a comfortable retirement for his parents. In reality, given all the hoopla over its disappearance, he never could have offloaded it without incriminating himself. In which case, we're lucky he didn't destroy it to save his skin; we easily could have lost another Leonardo.

Regardless of his true purpose, the Italian people hailed Peruggia as a folk hero, exactly as he'd hoped. Supporters mailed him cheese, wine, and cigarettes in jail before his sentencing, and attempted to purchase as souvenirs the paintbrushes, mandolin, and other junk he'd kept in the trunk with Lisa. Given his popularity, and seemingly honorable intentions, he received just twelve and a half months in prison and served only seven. Even that was too harsh in his mind: As his lawyer argued, who'd been hurt by his crime? He'd made Lisa del Giocondo immortal, and the Louvre had received its painting back without any damage. Indeed, the museum received a *superior* painting back. Thanks to Peruggia, the Louvre now possessed the most famous piece of art the world has ever known. He also made millions of people care, deeply, about art for the first time in their lives. Maybe he was a hero after all.

CHAPTER ELEVEN

LOST LOOT

The summer of 1941 lasted just one day in Leningrad. The morning of June 22 bloomed clear and bright, and everyone in town grabbed their hats and rushed over to the riverfront to paddle around in boats, spread picnic lunches, and luxuriate in the sunshine. Then, sometime after noon, a winter chill descended: News swept in, first spread in whispers, then moaned and shouted, that Nazi Germany had invaded the Soviet Union. Four million stormtroopers—the largest invading force in history—were marching their way.

Over the next month, the citizens of Leningrad (modern St. Petersburg) threw up barricades and dug 16,000 miles of trenches to frustrate German tanks. Meanwhile, museums prepared to evacuate the country's cultural treasures: gems, coins, paintings, sculptures, icons, chandeliers, well over a million items. The logistics were overwhelming. Museum directors shanghaied anyone they could—students, artists, old pensioners—to help pack, jamming everything into crates and heaving them onto trains.

Some of the most feverish work took place in the town of Pushkin, a former summer retreat for the tsars that sat a dozen miles south of Leningrad. Workers there spent several days packing up literal tons of portraits, vases, carpets, and lavish furniture, often working past dawn. When they ran out of packing material to cushion the items, they wadded up dresses from the old tsarinas and stuffed those into the crates. When the dresses ran low, they mowed the grass outside and used that. A few people spent so many hours hunched over the boxes that they developed nosebleeds. But no one quit, or even paused. The Nazis were drawing nearer every day, as the impotent Soviet military proved little more than a speed bump on the blitzkrieg east.

Overall, the evacuation teams did heroic work. Entire trains left for Siberia laden with nothing but art. Still, there was one thing the curators at the Catherine Palace in Pushkin could not evacuate, despite it being the most precious item in the entire Soviet Empire: the Amber Room.

Amber is fossilized tree resin—"petrified vegetable juice," people once called it. It's surprisingly light and soft for a gemstone, only as hard as fingernails and only as dense as water. Historically, 95 percent of the world's supply came from the hills and seabeds near the city of Königsberg in Prussia, where a dense forest thrived more than 40 million years ago.

In centuries past, amber was sometimes worth a dozen times more than gold. Beginning in medieval times, a religious sect called the Teutonic Knights dominated the amber trade; slaves collected nuggets for them by trawling the seafloor with nets. (Regular citizens who collected it were hanged from trees.) With their monopoly, the knights grew disgustingly rich, and in 1255 they erected a grand castle in Königsberg with towers and dungeons; its walls soared 60 feet high.

Due to its dear cost, people generally used amber in tiny amounts, for objects like earrings and rosary beads. But in 1701, to honor his coronation, the king of Prussia commissioned an entire chamber of amber—six tons' worth, to be fashioned into panels and mounted on walls. The project became known as the Amber Room.

To create the panels, craftsmen heated amber nuggets over flames to make them pliable and sliced them into translucent shards. Then they dipped the shards into solutions of honey, cognac, or linseed oil to enrich the color, producing every shade from lemon yellow to reddish gold to fiery topaz. After the pieces hardened, workers cut them into jigsaw shapes and arranged them into pictures like in stained glass windows—flowers, royal crests, biblical scenes, windmills. As a final step, they glued the pieces onto wooden panels coated with gold leaf for extra sparkle.

Altogether, the team constructed a dozen 12-foot-tall panels; 10 more panels that were a yard square; and two dozen amber-studded skirting boards to circle the floor. Meanwhile, another team of sculptors carved hunks of amber into rococo figurines to mount on the panels: eagles, mermen, trumpets, swords, bunches of grapes—each one a triumph of miniature artistry. Amber smells sweet in powdered form, and as the craftsmen hunched over their nuggets, etching in the intricate details, the studio must have smelled like the world's most expensive confectionary shop.

Still, you can have too much of a good thing. Plans for the Amber Room grew so elaborate that the king died in 1713 before the panels were complete. The new Prussian monarch, Frederick Wilhelm—who reportedly "despised all forms of art, culture, or finery" and preferred pouring money into his military—scrapped the project as frivolous.

Three years later, when the tsar of Russia swung through on a diplomatic junket, protocol demanded that Frederick bestow a gift. He used this opportunity to offload the Amber Room. (He also handed over a comely looking yacht that was so riddled with leaks it nearly drowned the tsar's men when they sailed off in it.) The tsar's retinue packed the amber panels into 18 crates with straw and rattled them back to Russia in carts. In exchange, the tsar gave Frederick a barge, a lathe, a goblet, and 55 men with pituitary gigantism to serve in a special military regiment.*

Frankly, the tsar thought the amber a bit much—too flashy—but his daughter adored it, and eventually had the panels installed in the so-called Winter Palace in St. Petersburg. The room she chose was too big for the panels, so she commissioned mirrors and busts of nymphs to cover the gaps—as well as, when funds ran low, colored glass mounted on panels with yellow foil backing: a cheap trompe l'oeil imitation.

In 1755, Catherine the Great moved the Amber Room to her palace in Pushkin. Catherine had been born in Prussia, near where most amber came from, and despite the ruinous cost, she imported 900 more pounds to replace the glass with the real deal. She also commissioned four stone mosaics from Italy to hang alongside the panels, each of which had a scene depicting a different human sense (sight, taste, etc.). Naturally, each came with its own elaborate amber and bronze frame.

Under Catherine, the Amber Room became the most stunning piece of architecture in Europe—perhaps the world—worth nearly $450

---

* A half-mad sadist, Frederick was obsessed with giant soldiers for some reason. Many stood seven feet tall, and he dressed them in pointy hats to make them seem taller still. Most served in the regiment against their will, as his officers had kidnapped them around Europe. No profession was safe—they snatched doctors, lawyers, priests, even diplomats—and he eventually accumulated 2,000 of these Goliaths in Potsdam. Predictably, they made terrible soldiers; many could barely walk. But Frederick drilled them mercilessly and beat them when they faltered. The poor men led miserable lives, and several tried to burn down Potsdam once to escape. Others committed suicide.

million today. Over the next two centuries, tsars and tsarinas used it for different purposes: a meditation hall, a meeting space, a trophy room. But often they just plopped guests down and let them gawk. When lit by candles, the panels glowed from within, as if they possessed their own aura. Sitting there was like visiting an orange autumn forest at sunset while warming your hands by a glowing fire—a prism of refulgent light in every earthy hue imaginable. One visitor gushed, "Only in *1,001 Arabian Nights* and in magic fairy tales, where the architecture of palaces is trusted to magicians, spirits, and genies, can one read about rooms made of ... jewels." But here was such a room in real life.

Many people declared the Amber Room to be no less than the Eighth Wonder of the World. Which is exactly why the Nazis were determined to seize it.

The original Seven Wonders of the Ancient World were a motley crew. One was so modest (a 40-foot-tall statue of Zeus at Olympia) that it hardly deserved the name. Another lasted just 54 years (the Colossus of Rhodes), while a third was as much an engineering feat as anything (the Lighthouse of Alexandria). Just one wonder remains standing today (the Great Pyramid of Giza, although it's lost its sparkling white facade), while one perhaps never existed (the Hanging Gardens of Babylon, whose archaeological ruins have never surfaced). And while several were felled by earthquakes (including the Mausoleum at Halicarnassus), one succumbed to a dastardly crime (the Temple of Artemis, set afire by a man named Herostratus who burned to go down in history but, lacking any discernible talents, decided that torching the temple was his ticket).

Since ancient times, dozens of other monuments have been dubbed the "eighth wonder," some of them plausibly (the Taj Mahal), others less so (the Houston Astrodome). But perhaps no place has earned the appellation more than the Amber Room. Even after the Bolshevik Revolution, when the tsars of old were demonized and declared Enemies of the People, the new leaders of communist Russia dared not touch the room, and turned it into a museum. Despite its fragility by the 1940s—the stress from the various moves had caused cracking and crumbling, as had the temperature swings between the Russian summers and winters—it remained one of the most renowned masterpieces in the world.

Given that, the Nazis thought it would look splendid in the Reich. They also resented the fact that so much German amber had ended up in the hands of Russians, a race of people that most of them considered akin to apes. Before sneak-attacking the Soviet Union in 1941, Adolf Hitler raged to his advisers that the invasion "must be conducted with unprecedented, unmerciful, and unrelenting harshness"—and it was. Nazi armies wiped out 30 whole cities and every soul in them on the drive east, ravaging thousands of churches and libraries and destroying 110 million books. After capturing Soviet soldiers, the Nazis often starved them to death in prisoner-of-war camps, then burned the bodies and distributed the ashes as fertilizer.

The Nazis also plundered Russia. This was part of a larger scheme to pilfer art throughout Europe for a planned Führermuseum in Hitler's hometown in Austria. The thefts began in Germany after the Nazis took power in 1933 and initially concentrated on Jewish families who'd fled the country or been arrested. (Bizarrely, Nazi officials sometimes left receipts in people's homes after stealing things; the German mania for recordkeeping extended even to pillaging.)

The thefts ramped up as the Nazis invaded nearby countries, where they often seized art under the guise of "protecting" it while a war was underway—a war they'd started. A staggering 20 percent of all art in Europe, millions upon millions of pieces, ended up in Nazi hands. Much of it was piled into salt mines, warehouses, or remote castles. (That hangar of Nazi art at the end of *Raiders of the Lost Ark* was more truth than fiction.) Photographs of this plunder run the gamut from heartbreaking—a trough of wedding bands ripped off people's fingers—to simply baffling: mounds of paintings and rare books stacked up in some empty château with no one to look at them, seized out of sheer greed. In trying to put this aspect of the Nazi legacy into perspective, one observer noted that "history's greatest mass murder has long concealed history's greatest robbery." Even today, some 100,000 pieces of art remain missing.

Russian art stood high on the Nazi wish list, and well over a million pieces disappeared into the Reich: paintings, sculptures, crowns, icons, porcelain figurines, chalices, crucifixes, and more, objects worth perhaps a billion dollars today. Part of this tally can be traced to the Soviet leadership's bungling reaction to the initial invasion. In their panic, some museum directors near the front lines evacuated only brass candlesticks and other metal objects—things that could be melted down into arms—and left masterpieces hanging on the walls to poach. In other cities, officials refused to evacuate anything, because doing so would encourage "defeatist" attitudes among the proles. Did they really think the mighty Red Army could lose to imperialist swine? Such towns lost everything.

Wiser heads prevailed in Leningrad, the cultural heart of Russia, and museum directors there acted quickly to remove items. But the Amber Room presented another problem entirely. How do you evacuate a whole chamber, especially given how fragile the panels and mosaics were? The lead curator of the Catherine Palace—a clumsy, thick-necked, bespectacled man named Anatoly Kuchumov—had thousands of pieces of cigarette paper pasted over the panels to keep them intact. But when his crews tried prying the first one off the wall, the amber splintered and cracked. In despair, Kuchumov decided the

Amber Room would have to stay in place. His only consolation was that if he couldn't move it, the Nazis wouldn't be able to, either.

A bit pathetically, the staff did try hiding the room by covering the panels with cloth and padding, then wallpapering over them. By this point, in September, the Nazis were within shouting distance of Leningrad. Kuchumov finally gave up trying to save everything and spent his last frantic hours in the palace tending to various tasks: boarding windows, filling vases with water to absorb the blast of explosives, strewing sand on the inlaid wooden floors to protect them from German jackboots, and running from room to room with scissors to snip swatches of curtains and upholstery, to help re-create the furnishings someday if worse came to worst. Among the last items he grabbed were 28 shards of amber that had crumbled off the panels. Then he boarded a train to accompany 17 boxcars of palace art to Novosibirsk in southern Siberia, a journey of 1,900 of the bleakest miles on earth.

The Nazi siege of Leningrad, which began September 8, was one of the grimmest incidents of the war. Over the next 872 days, 1.5 million people would starve to death or succumb to disease. When food supplies ran low, residents hunted cats and dogs. Up next were pigeons and rats. Soon they were stewing leather belts to slurp out the gelatin, and were finally reduced to eating petroleum jelly and melting lipstick to get at the fat. Everyone who survived remembered it as the most depraved period of their lives.*

* The most poignant story to emerge from the siege involved some scientists in Leningrad who'd spent decades collecting grains, nuts, beans, tubers, and fruit from around the world for a seed bank, to preserve the global food heritage of humankind. Every day they reported to work, their stomachs stabbing with hunger pains, and had to stare at the bins of rice, barley, beans, peanuts, and potatoes in their offices. But their sense of duty was strong enough that none of them ever took a nibble, and nine ended up starving to death. You can hear this amazing story in the "Seeds of Starvation" episode of my podcast from June 2023. See *samkean.com/podcast.*

But at long last, in January 1944, the siege lifted. Kuchumov returned in March. "Our favorite beautiful city still looks the same," he reported, "but advanced in age, like an old man after a wasting disease." It took another month to secure permission to visit the Catherine Palace; he hitchhiked down, a bleak trip. His car passed burned-out homes, piles of gas masks, skeins of barbed wire, a birch tree turned gallows, and multiple dead bodies in the road. On the palace grounds, Kuchumov nearly retched from the smell, the air rank with human filth and piles of sweat-soured clothes. Broken beds and munition crates littered the lawn, and a chapel had been converted into a motorcycle garage.

The grand marble steps in front were mangled, so Kuchumov climbed a side staircase to the administrative entrance. Inside, he found the roof partly collapsed. The walls bore shrapnel wounds, and several doors had been hacked off with axes. He held his breath as he hurried down the scuffed corridors, wincing at the decapitated statues and gargoyles missing noses. If he caught his reflection in any mirror, he would have looked red-faced and sweaty with worry.

He finally reached the Amber Room, and nearly crumpled to his knees. He'd feared the panels would be damaged. Instead, there were no panels at all. He saw only bare brick walls streaked with soot. Had the amber been burned? Pilfered? If so, where was it? He would spend the rest of his life trying to answer those questions.

The Nazis had arrived at the Catherine Palace in 1941 in high spirits, fresh off a string of victories across western Russia. Soldiers swarmed the rooms inside, tromping about in muddy boots and doing what every museum visitor secretly longs to do: pushing past the velvet ropes and plopping down on the beds and chairs.

A cheer soon went up on the first floor, and everyone raced off to see what the fuss was. They walked into a poorly wallpapered room to find two privates peeling the layers back and gaping at the amber beneath; Kuchumov's camouflage hadn't even survived the afternoon. And whereas the Russian had thrown up his hands and declared the panels impossible to move, his Nazi counterparts proved less feckless. According to their records, they had all the many tons of panels, mirrors, and mosaics stripped from the walls within 36 hours.

Everything was shipped to Königsberg, where the amber had originated. There, curators installed it all on the third floor of the Teutonic Knights castle. The Amber Room's "repatriation" became a point of pride throughout the Reich.

At least for a few years. By August 1944, the war had turned against the Nazis, and Königsberg was on the front line of the pummeling. Multiple times that month, Allied planes dropped nearly a million pounds of bombs on the city. The Soviet army was also closing in on land. City officials knew that it was not a matter of whether the Russians took Königsberg, but when.

The top curator at the Königsberg castle was Alfred Rohde. Acquaintances recall being spooked by how much he resembled Heinrich Himmler; he also had a noticeable tremor, likely due to nerve damage from chemical weapons during World War I. Eyeing the Red Army's progress, Rohde dismantled the Amber Room and packed the panels and mosaics into crates. He then took several scouting trips in the fall of 1944 to other castles deep inside Germany, to find somewhere to ship them. These were frustrating errands, as he was repeatedly denied permission for space. One castle was being used to test biological weapons; others were already stuffed with items of infinitely less value, like grand pianos and Otto von Bismarck's furniture. At last, Rohde found two workable options and hurried back to Königsberg.

Unfortunately, the Germans had other evacuation priorities, and before Rohde could ship the Amber Room anywhere, the Soviet pincers snapped shut around the city in January 1945. While Rohde scrambled to smuggle the amber out, or at least find a good hiding spot, the crates were trundled into the castle's feasting hall, a vast chamber with a ribbed roof.

After a few months of siege, the Russian army battered its way into Königsberg, hammering buildings with shells and clearing them of people with flamethrowers. Before long, the castle was about the only building that hadn't been toppled. The German military command surrendered the city on April 9.

Strangely, even though Soviet cultural commissars had made the recovery of the Amber Room a top priority, they didn't send anyone to Königsberg to search for it until late May. Equally curious—perhaps they were angry over his failure to safeguard the panels back in Leningrad—the commissars barred Anatoly Kuchumov from leading the search. Instead they sent Alexander Brusov, a balding man in his 60s with white hair and a perpetually exhausted look. Brusov normally worked as an archaeologist—a background that proved handy on his mission, because by the time he arrived in Königsberg, the castle where the Amber Room had last been seen had mostly burned down and was a heap of smoking ruins. Just a few rooms remained standing, and the 60-foot walls seemed liable to topple at any moment.

While awaiting permission to excavate, Brusov tried interviewing the citizens of Königsberg. The effort proved futile. Ninety percent of the city's 2.2 million inhabitants had died or fled, and the remainder were shuffling around like zombies, half starved and smeared with soot. (The smell of smoke pervaded everything, but at least masked the stench of corpses.) One man did hint to Brusov that he knew where the Amber Room was, but for unknown reasons, Brusov put him off. The next day, the man was found swinging from a tree, lynched by his countrymen for collaborating with the enemy. His hands were tied behind his back to make it clear he didn't commit suicide.

Brusov began picking through the castle ruins on June 2. Despite his mission's high priority, his small team had just two shovels to dig with, and no paraffin to burn for light, making it impossible to see anything as they tunneled deeper. Brusov was also troubled by signs that someone else had been digging there before him. Indeed, security at the site was atrocious. One man in particular—a bespectacled fellow who looked suspiciously like Heinrich Himmler—kept wandering through and breaking into tears upon seeing the ruins. Brusov took him for a local drunk and tried to chase him off, only to discover that he was the castle's curator, Alfred Rohde. Brusov interrogated him about the amber, but Rohde remained tight-lipped; Brusov sensed he was hiding something.

After three days of digging, Brusov punched through the rubble to the floor of the giant feasting hall and began crawling around on his knees, squinting in the darkness. He saw several stone cornice pieces that resembled elements of the Amber Room, as well as iron bands often used to secure wooden crates. But no amber.

The next two weeks held more of the same. A handful of charred and broken items turned up that might have belonged to the Amber Room, but Brusov never found anything conclusive. One night, unable to sleep, he took a stroll around the ruins under the moonlight, fretting over his failures. Suddenly, he noticed smoke. Had another fire broken out? He scrambled over the rubble to investigate—and was stunned to find Rohde there, burning a cache of letters. Brusov snatched them from the flames and had them translated. One in particular grabbed his attention. In it, Rohde mentioned losing the key to an underground bunker where he intended to store some castle treasures. Brusov summoned Rohde and questioned him. Rohde admitted that he'd since found the key and agreed to take Brusov to the site.

Upon arriving, they descended four stories to a cellar, where another stairway led farther down. At the bottom sat a sizable air-raid shelter with several rooms, as well as stacks of paintings and sculptures. Brusov examined them, relieved that he'd finally turned up something of value. But there was no sign of the Amber Room there, nor anywhere else in town. When he left Königsberg a few days later, Brusov concluded that the panels and mosaics had likely burned in the fire that destroyed the castle.

After Brusov returned home, Anatoly Kuchumov tracked him down in Moscow to debrief him. But as they talked, Kuchumov grew alarmed over certain details. For example, Rohde's letter mentioned that he'd lost the key to the underground bunker. Yet when Kuchumov had Brusov walk him through their visit, Brusov admitted that Rohde had strolled right into the bunker with a simple twist of a doorknob—no key was necessary. Was Brusov sure that Rohde had led him to the correct place?

Furthermore, Brusov admitted that he'd explored only the main room of the bunker, not any side rooms. Brusov also let slip that Rohde had wandered off at one point and disappeared for a spell. But when Kuchumov asked where Rohde had gone and what he'd done, Brusov could only shrug. He hadn't thought to ask. Kuchumov walked away from the interview gnashing his teeth, convinced that Rohde had pulled a fast one. The Eighth Wonder of the World was still in Nazi hands somewhere, he was sure of it.

In March 1946, Kuchumov won permission to visit Königsberg himself to continue the search. To render him inconspicuous, the big brains in Moscow gave him a muted dark suit to wear. Unfortunately the scheme backfired, as the suit was brand-new and stuck out badly in a city populated by refugees wearing rags. Kuchumov hoped to interrogate Rohde immediately upon arriving, but couldn't find him. He sent word to Soviet authorities to track him down, then began exploring the castle ruins.

This proved a dangerous task. He inspected the castle's flooded cellars, which reeked of gangrene from dead bodies. Several passages down there were booby-trapped with electricity or poisoned water. None held any amber. Next, Kuchumov began clambering about on the ruins of the upper stories. Suddenly the boards beneath him gave way, and he crashed down through two more floors. He likely would have fallen farther, splattering into the cellars, had he not thumped down on a thick oak beam, which broke his fall by nearly breaking his back.

A gimpy Kuchumov stuck to the main floor after that—and good thing, because he soon found some enticing clues. Recall that Catherine the Great had commissioned four framed mosaics from Italy to help cover up gaps in the room where the amber panels ended up; they depicted the human senses. While digging through the rubble in the castle's feasting hall, Kuchumov saw a flash of bronze. It was a frame, and the metalwork looked Italian. Sure enough, he pawed away the debris to find the mosaics. They were scorched and brittle; when he touched one, the stone tiles crumbled into powder. But they unquestionably came from the Amber Room.

The odd thing was, Kuchumov found only three of the mosaics. Where was the fourth? Moreover, the amber panels had contained some bronze elements, as well as metal mirrors. Wouldn't those have survived the fire, too? He also found it suspicious that no bits of amber turned up amid the ruins, not a single sliver. From this, Kuchumov concluded that most of the room—in particular the fourth mosaic and the giant amber panels—had been removed from the castle. He had to find out what Rohde knew.

The only problem was, Rohde was dead.

At least it appeared that way; the Soviets looking for him heard different stories. Some townsfolk said he'd starved or committed suicide. Others swore that vigilantes had hanged or poisoned him to prevent him from revealing where the Amber Room was. But no one could confirm anything, nor locate his grave. A death certificate eventually turned up claiming he'd died of typhus, but no one could find the doctor who'd signed it, either.

Kuchumov did track down a few men who'd worked with Rohde, including a fellow who'd run a restaurant called Blood Court in the castle's old torture chamber. He claimed to have seen Rohde packing the amber panels in crates, and said Rohde later told him he'd shipped them out via train. But Kuchumov didn't trust these tales. Would Rohde really have blabbed about top-secret plans to some restaurateur? Ultimately, Kuchumov left Königsberg frustrated: optimistic that the panels had survived, but unsure where to look now.

The next October, in 1947, he flew to Berlin to investigate another lead. Kuchumov landed wearing his dark suit, which wasn't looking so natty anymore after slogging through water tunnels and crashing through floorboards the previous year. In Berlin, he met with a Soviet general at an imposing building near the riverfront—a warehouse of looted Russian art. The general unlocked the giant steel doors, and Kuchumov wilted when he walked inside. He'd understood in the abstract that the Nazis had thoroughly pillaged Russia. But seeing the sheer scale of the theft in one place left him dizzy. There were whole mountains of crates stacked up—in fact, a veritable mountain *range* of them, running from the front door all the way to the back wall a third of a mile distant. Kuchumov's job was to open every last one to find the amber panels and missing mosaic.

He hired a hundred local German men, who got to work with hammers and crowbars. They went through tens of thousands of crates, often laboring overnight by lamps; many brought lunch and dinner along so they could keep searching during meals. They found zero trace of the Amber Room.

As the best leads petered out, the search for the Amber Room deteriorated into black comedy. The secret police in both the Soviet Union and East Germany—the KGB and Stasi—conducted independent investigations, scouring at least 1,500 sites between them. (Although some of the excursions hardly deserved the name, as the parties involved lacked even basic equipment like flashlights.) Agents nevertheless crawled through mines, catacombs, and caves all throughout Germany, and all for nothing.

Meanwhile, rumors swirled that the panels had been whisked off to North America, or that Stalin had secretly constructed a fake Amber Room before 1941 and that the Germans had stolen only the decoy during the war. Another rumor emerged that Rohde had ferried the panels out of Königsberg on a steamship called the *Wilhelm Gustloff*, which a Soviet submarine quickly torpedoed, killing more than 9,300 people. (It remains the deadliest maritime disaster in history.) Multiple teams of divers combed the wreck to no avail.

One of the major players in the search was a baron in Liechtenstein who was Vladimir Nabokov's cousin. Another was the Soviet equivalent of Ian Fleming, a spy novelist whose James Bond was named Max Otto von Stierlitz and who penned classics such as *Diamonds [Are] for the Dictatorship of the Proletariat*. The nuttiest character was a West German strawberry farmer who grew obsessed with the Amber Room and began printing exclusive reports based on baloney information that the Stasi fed him. Alarmingly, the farmer soon reported that a group of thugs had ransacked his home and drugged and tortured him, trying to bully information from him. He also got stabbed, twice, in separate incidents, and spent time in a psychiatric ward. His body was finally found naked and disemboweled in a forest in 1987; a scalpel and scissors lay nearby. It later emerged that he'd actually staged the first two knifings by forcing his wife to stab him. (She killed herself after the second incident, rather than keep playing his sick games.) In all probability, he'd faked the third and fatal "attack" as well. The reasons behind his actions remain inscrutable.

Eventually, the official KGB and Stasi searches lost momentum and expired. For his part, Anatoly Kuchumov kept poking around for decades, his dark wool suit looking shabbier every year. In the meantime, he preserved those 28 pieces of chipped amber that he'd shoved into his pocket on his way out the door during the 1941 evacuation, mounting them on cardboard. He never lost hope that the rest of the Amber Room had escaped destruction, too. But to everyone else, the odds of its survival seemed slim.

Kuchumov finally died in 1993. That turned out to be bad timing. Because a few years later, the very thing he'd longed to see more than anything else in the world—a lost section of the Amber Room—actually turned up in Germany.

In the summer of 1997, an art curator in recently unified Germany received a suspicious phone call in the middle of the night. The man on the other end muttered something about the Amber Room. He wanted to meet right away.

However sketchy this sounded, the curator dragged himself out of bed and tramped over to a seedy bar nearby. Half an hour later, a jumpy middle-age man slunk in and dropped a bomb into his lap. He said his father, a soldier, had accompanied the Amber Room from Pushkin to Königsberg in 1941, then remained stationed there. And at some point before Königsberg fell, he'd filched part of the room as a keepsake—the missing stone mosaic from Italy, with a scene depicting a man holding a rose out for a woman to sniff. It had sat in his parents' attic for decades until they'd died. After some dithering, he tried shaking the curator down, demanding 400,000 deutsche marks for its return (more than $1.4 million today). The curator bargained him down to 250,000, and they wrote up a contract on a beer mat.

Then, inexplicably, the man bolted before signing.

The curator reported the meeting to the police, who announced plans to arrest the man for harboring looted art. He eventually slunk back and agreed to take 210,000 deutsche marks. After its surrender, curators authenticated the mosaic. A Russian minister then flew in, and Germany turned it over in exchange for 101 drawings that the Russian army had looted from Germany in 1945. Meanwhile, the story set Amber Room fanatics aflutter. If the mosaic had survived, why not other pieces? This was the biggest break in the case in a half century.*

It was also a dead end. The man had no information about any other pieces of the Amber Room. Worse still, some heroic sleuthing by two British journalists a few years later—they spent months trawling through every relevant archive in Germany and Russia, bribing sources left and right for access to hidden files—unearthed a massive cover-up that all but quashed any hope of finding more.

---

* Publicity from the case soon turned up another item from the Amber Room: a chest of drawers that a woman in Berlin had bought from "Stasi art dealers" in the 1970s. She'd kept it in her living room, to store tablecloths and napkins. The chest was made of wood, not amber, and it's not clear where it disappeared to after 1941. Regardless, it proved no help in tracking down the panels.

To understand what the duo discovered, it helps to know the Soviet mindset during the war. As noted, the Nazis treated the Soviets with savagery during the 1941 invasion, killing wantonly and looting and destroying art at unprecedented scales. So when the war turned the Soviet Union's way, the nation wanted revenge, and the Soviet high command authorized special military units to seize German artwork.

In theory, these brigades had a limited scope: They would repatriate looted pieces and, in the case of destroyed ones, commandeer rough equivalents as payback—a one-to-one exchange. In practice, the art units deteriorated into trophy brigades that roamed Germany like Mongol hordes, snatching treasures by the armful. Masterworks by Monet, Renoir, El Greco, Velázquez, Dürer, Rembrandt, van Gogh, and Cézanne all allegedly disappeared behind the Iron Curtain, as did a Gutenberg Bible, several important stained glass windows, and thousands of Greek vases and statues. In all, the Soviets pilfered an estimated 2.5 million artworks and 10 million books, a trove worth $8 billion today.

(Alas, the Soviets reported failing in their attempts to rescue the only goods at stake with a worth comparable to that of the Amber Room: Priam's Treasure, the hoard of diadems, earrings, daggers, vases, gravy boats, and cauldrons that Heinrich Schliemann had smuggled out of Troy in 1873. Given that these were the most valuable archaeological goods in the Reich, the Germans had packed Priam's Treasure into crates even before the first bombs fell on Berlin in August 1940. At that point, some of the crates were moved to a bank vault for several months, others to the cellar of the mint, before everything was reunited and transferred to the stoutest keep in the Reich: a giant antiaircraft tower of concrete and steel near the Berlin zoo. Unfortunately, the tower got pummeled in 1945, and while the Russian trophy brigades hurried over as soon as they could, they announced finding no trace of Priam's Treasure.)

Although no fan of Germany, Joseph Stalin opened an investigation into the Soviet trophy brigades, and at least two generals were arrested for overzealous looting. But as the British journalists found, the true extent of the army's crimes never came to light.

In the account of the fall of Königsberg above, you might have noticed a few important but initially overlooked details. For one thing, when the German military surrendered Königsberg in April 1945, most of the castle was still standing; film footage proves this. By the time the archaeologist Alexander Brusov arrived in late May, it was mostly smoking ruins. Someone, then, burned it down. Perhaps German saboteurs did—although the Soviets surely would have trumpeted this to the world. Instead, the silence surrounding the deed implies that the occupying Red Army was at fault: They either burned the castle themselves, accidentally or not, or proved too inept to stop its destruction. Remember, too, that the trained eye of the archaeologist Brusov had noticed signs of someone digging through the ruins before him—probably the trophy brigades. This would also explain why no mirrors and very few bronze pieces from the Amber Room turned up, because looters had already cleared them out—perhaps even before the castle burned. If so, perhaps they grabbed the amber, too.

The emergence of the Italian mosaic in 1997 also forced people to revise their assumptions. Anatoly Kuchumov had cited the missing mosaic as proof that the Amber Room had been divided up and secreted away in multiple locations. But if a German soldier had simply swiped the mosaic from the main hoard in the castle, there was no reason to suspect that any other pieces lay elsewhere. As for why no amber slivers turned up in the castle ruins, that was easy. As resin, amber melts between 400°F and 700°F. The fire consumed it.

All in all, here's what likely happened. Try as he might, Alfred Rohde probably never succeeded in evacuating any part of the Amber Room from Königsberg; the Soviet army had closed in too quickly. Then, after the Soviets conquered the city, a trophy brigade or two ransacked the castle. They either overlooked the amber or realized they'd never get away with plundering so famous a treasure. At some point, the castle started on fire, and before the archaeologist Brusov arrived, Soviet soldiers picked the ruins clean of anything valuable. It's still possible, just, that Rohde had evacuated the panels to somewhere else in Königsberg before the city fell; that could explain why he set fire to his letters. But most evidence points to a simpler conclusion: that the panels were all in the castle together, and that they all burned.

The world never learned this because the Soviet Union lionized the Red Army after the war, hailing it (with reason) as the liberator of the Russian people. Plus, in the incipient Cold War, Soviet leaders glorified the army as a symbol of Soviet strength. Admitting that its officers were a pack of greedy goons who'd burned and/or stolen one of the most cherished treasures in history wouldn't exactly be a publicity coup. So the Soviets covered things up. There are shades here of Caesar allegedly burning down the Library of Alexandria—the difference being that the Soviets had enough control over their people to suppress the crime.

As the wounds from World War II healed, the nations involved began making efforts, however halting, to restore pilfered artwork. In the 1950s, the Soviet Union "donated" 1.5 million German pieces that they'd looted to their communist allies in East Germany as a goodwill gesture, including such archaeological gems as the Pergamon Altar.

More dramatically, in the glasnost period following the collapse of the Soviet Union, the Russian government revealed that it had been lying all along about Heinrich Schliemann's artifacts from Troy. Priam's Treasure had not been destroyed in the Battle for Berlin but looted by trophy brigades, brought to Moscow, and stuffed into the basement of the Pushkin Museum.

In 1996, the museum flexed its muscles and put 260 Trojan artifacts on display. Naturally, Germany cried foul and demanded them back. But they weren't alone in doing so. Given that Schliemann had illegally smuggled them out of Troy in the first place, Turkey also claimed the goods—a claim complicated by the fact that the government Schliemann was dealing with, the Ottoman Empire, no longer exists. Additional claims were filed by the descendants of Frank Calvert, the wannabe archaeologist who owned half the Troy-Hisarlık mound. Given Russia's recent descent into despotism, all talks about repatriating Priam's Treasure have broken down. Worse, Russia is reportedly using its war with Ukraine to loot artifacts there; at least 3,000 cultural sites have been damaged, and at least 15,000 objects have gone missing.

Other nations have done a better job repatriating stolen art—especially pieces from Holocaust victims that ended up scattered across the world. In 2023, a few American museums surrendered works valued at $10 million. And while some institutions continue to resist these efforts, often with mealymouthed excuses about "gaps in the provenance" of their works (well, no shit), most are coming around. Rather than stonewall investigations, they're more forthright about providing information that can identify past owners, such as photographs of the backs of paintings, where tags, stamps, and other distinguishing features are often found.

Meanwhile, the Catherine Palace in St. Petersburg has not had much luck recovering its lost works. Of the estimated 30,000 items stolen—the list runs 300 pages—officials there claim that only 400 have been recovered, and a substantial fraction of those were too damaged to restore. That figure includes a score of items that former Nazi soldiers seized as souvenirs long ago and returned voluntarily out of guilt.

As for the Amber Room, nothing more has turned up since the stone mosaic in 1997. But using that mosaic as a guide, along with several old photographs of the panels, the Russian government managed to re-create the Amber Room within the Catherine Palace, using six more tons of amber from the Königsberg area. (It helps that Russia now owns the surrounding territory. Königsberg's name today is Kaliningrad.) The refurbished Amber Room opened in 2003 to celebrate the 300th anniversary of St. Petersburg. Luciano Pavarotti sang at the dedication, and the Russian government spent 29 million rubles to have fighter jets spray chemicals into nearby clouds to dissipate them and ensure a glorious sunset—all to recapture the entrancing liquid-honey glow of the original room.

Still, even today, amateur sleuths continue to search for the missing panels. And every so often, a shaky news story pops up about treasure hunters tracing them to some abandoned bunker or sunken ship. As Boris Igdalov, a stone carver who helped re-create the new Amber Room, said, people "are looking for [the room] everywhere, probably on the moon." It's easy to scoff at such attempts. Why bother, if they're almost certainly never going to find anything? But I think that misses the point. It's the quest that matters, the hope. As Anatoly Kuchumov once declared—in what could serve as an epithet for every lost treasure in this book—"Lovers of beauty, you must not reject the continuation of the search."

CHAPTER TWELVE

LOST TECHNOLOGY

Dead bodies. The moment the diver breached the surface, he began raving about dead bodies on the seafloor. Men, women, horses—piles of bodies down there, a veritable graveyard.

The ship's captain, Dimitrios Kontos, could only sigh. It had already been a frustrating week, and he didn't need another hassle. But sailors are a superstitious lot, and however ridiculous the tale sounded—who ever heard of an underwater graveyard?—he knew it would likely spook his crew. To reassure them, he'd have to go down there himself and investigate.

It was spring 1900.* A few days earlier, on Holy Tuesday, Kontos and his crew of Greek sponge divers had been sailing for North Africa

* Different accounts of the discovery vary in certain details.

when a storm swept in and hammered their ship. They'd scrambled for the shelter of the nearest island: a six-mile-long speck called Antikythera that sat between Crete and mainland Greece. They'd anchored off the northwest coast, near a cliff with a streak of red rock.

They hunkered down there, and the weather finally cleared after a few miserable days. Kontos sent one of his two ships to a nearby port to buy seafood for the days of fasting ahead. While his own ship waited, he decided to send a few men diving. They probably wouldn't find any sponges, but they could work off some nervous energy. A veteran named Elias Lykopantis went first—only to surface minutes later, babbling about dead bodies.

Kontos suspected Lykopantis was suffering from "dive drunkenness" (nitrogen narcosis), a condition that arises when divers breathe high-pressure air underwater. (The excess gas interferes with brain function. After about 65 feet, every 10 additional yards of depth equals one martini.) Kontos ordered his crew to treat Lykopantis with the usual remedy, cigarettes, then donned the dive equipment himself.

In previous generations, sponge divers usually descended naked, holding their breath, but Kontos ran an advanced outfit. He snaked his legs into the canvas dive suit and soaped his wrists to jam them into the snug rubber cuffs for the gloves. A cabin boy lashed steel-soled boots onto his feet, to weight him to the seafloor. Then Kontos slipped a copper helmet over his head, with a glass viewport; the helmet's umbilical would provide him with air. After double-checking everything, he tromped over to the edge and splashed in.

Despite their proximity to shore, the water was deep, nearly 200 feet. Kontos found himself on a gentle slope, which ran for roughly 40 yards before plummeting into an abyss. He got right to work exploring, his boots squishing on the muddy seafloor.

The glint of something green caught his eye. A closer inspection left him gaping. It looked like an arm.

Then everything clicked. Kontos was staring at a statue. It was made of bronze and half buried in muck. He saw other statues nearby as well, both people and horses. He just about melted with relief. And to prove to his men they had nothing to fear, he grabbed hold of the mottled green and yellow limb—bent at the elbow, missing two fingers—and wrenched it back and forth until it snapped off. Then he tugged on the umbilical three times to signal his crew to winch him up.

Back on deck, they passed the arm around for inspection, and everyone no doubt had a good laugh at Lykopantis. Dead bodies! When the other ship returned with provisions, they took off for Africa, where they made quite a haul of sponges; they'd be living fat for months.

All the while, though, Kontos's mind kept chewing over those statues. They likely came from an ancient shipwreck, and he was mighty tempted to return and salvage them. Antiques sold for a pretty penny on the black market.

But after some more thought, his conscience got the better of him. Nineteen hundred was a low point in Greek history. A few years earlier, the Ottoman Empire had clobbered Greece in a war, with Turkish soldiers nearly overrunning Athens. Kontos's crew, while ethnically Greek, all hailed from an island under the yoke of Ottoman control, and their patriotism was fierce. It angered them that the Ottomans had been blithely allowing foreigners to plunder Greek cultural treasures. (The Elgin Marbles being a prime example.) The statues off Antikythera could be a major find—a way to recapture some lost heritage. So upon returning to Greece that fall, Kontos did the honorable thing and wired government officials in Athens to alert them of the discovery.

The government did nothing. It's not clear why, but you can imagine the officials receiving the message and rolling their eyes. They knew sailors: A fish jumps out of the water, and a dozen of them swear they saw a mermaid.

Thankfully, Kontos persisted. He and Lykopantis met with an archaeology professor in Athens, who in turn arranged a meeting with the man in charge of archaeology throughout Greece: Spyridon Staïs, the minister of education. Kontos made sure to bring along the bronze arm he'd dredged up, which got Staïs's attention. Kontos offered his crew of two dozen to lead the salvage efforts; as he well knew, few other divers could handle the operation, and only they knew where the wreck was anyway. (According to one account, Kontos initially gave out false coordinates for the location, in case the government double-crossed him.) Although Greece was floundering financially, Staïs promised that the ministry would sponsor the operation and provide support from the Royal Hellenic Navy.

The work commenced in November of that year. Given the extreme depth—this was the deepest salvage operation in history until then—the divers couldn't linger on the bottom for more than a few minutes or they risked getting the bends. And that was just the start of the complications. One historian compared the work to excavating "the tomb of Tutankhamen ... in five-minute shifts by [nitrogen-] drunken stevedores who had never seen an Egyptian tomb, working in semidarkness, dressed in American football pads with coal scuttles over their heads."

The constant storms didn't help. The first day, the crew had to cease work after just three hours. But even in that narrow window, they managed to recover several elegant fragments of statues, including a sword tip and bearded head. The excitement among the divers was palpable.

Over the next few months, the team recovered dozens of statues of both marble and bronze. The marble ones were in rough shape. Mussels and urchins had latched on and pitted them on every square centimeter that wasn't buried in seafloor muck, like some awful skin disease; some were barely recognizable as human forms. The bronze statues fared better: Although crusted over with sea critters and minerals, the metal beneath remained intact. The divers also found other cargo from the shipwreck: glass bowls, cutlery, a fancy bed, dice and board game pieces, gold earrings, a flute, a silver wine jug, a creepy carving of Medusa. The ship also probably carried slaves to sell, although just four skeletons emerged from the deep—three men and one woman. (Lykopantis wasn't totally wrong about the dead bodies.)

Several statues on the bottom were trapped beneath massive boulders, which the archaeologists supervising the operation figured had tumbled down from nearby Antikythera during an earthquake long ago. Removing them was difficult, dangerous work, requiring the divers to tunnel into the mud beneath each boulder and snake ropes around it as a sling; some boulders needed 20 separate dives to secure. The ship above then winched the rocks up several yards and, listing dangerously under the weight, chugged over to where the slope dropped off underwater. There, the crew slammed their engines into reverse, causing the ship to judder; this shook the boulder from the sling and dropped it into the bottomless fathoms below. Between the bone-crushing weights and inherent danger of working underwater, it was a miracle no one got hurt. In fact, sailors stood on the deck above with axes, ready to hack at the five-inch-thick ropes if the divers had bound them too tightly and the ship seemed in danger of sinking with them.

Education Minister Spyridon Staïs happened to be onboard during this operation—he'd stopped by to observe the work—and after several boulders had been dumped, he had a horrifying thought. He ordered the next boulder raised up to the ship, and even before it broke the surface of the clear water, he groaned. Just as he'd feared, the "boulder" was actually an encrusted statue. This one depicted Hercules with a lion skin, and it's now one of the most famous artworks from the Antikythera trove. But that hardly consoled Staïs: What other masterpieces had the nitrogen-drunk divers failed to recognize in the dim water and flung into the abyss?

The long hours of work—days sometimes started at 6 a.m.—took a serious toll on the divers. As the months dragged on, they sometimes looked pale and weak as they emerged from the water. On multiple occasions, someone nearly passed out before surfacing. It didn't help that they smoked cigarettes for "breakfast" and regularly got smashed on wine after shifts.

In late April, the inevitable happened. After a late-night bender, one diver woke up feeling wobbly. He refused to call in sick, perhaps out of pride, and completed one dive. But he came up gasping after the second, felled by an acute case of the bends. Kontos applied an age-old sailors' remedy, dumping him in a cold bath and then chopping a live chicken in half and smearing its guts on his chest. It didn't work; the man died that night. Sadly, two other divers ended up paralyzed later after their own bouts of the bends.*

The operation finally wrapped up in September 1901, and the recovered statues are now considered some of the most important Greek art ever found. Still, few people today would know the name

---

* Despite such dangers, the crew and Kontos received just 150,000 drachmas (around $1.1 million today) as payment for a year of work—which didn't even take into account lost wages from not sponge diving, nor the cost of equipment that Kontos had to foot. Sadly, Kontos soon suffered an accident on another dive and ended up paralyzed himself.

Antikythera if not for one item. Near the mission's end, a naval officer was inspecting a small boulder hauled up from the seafloor and encrusted with shells. He'd decided to toss it back as useless when another officer onboard spied a bit of metal sticking out the side. After conferring, they decided to keep it—and thank god. That corroded hunk of rock would prove the single most important artifact in the entire Antikythera hoard, and arguably the most important artifact ever discovered from ancient times.

Based on coins amid the wreckage, archaeologists now believe that the ship carrying the Antikythera trove sank circa 67 B.C.* on its way to ports farther west. It was a large freighter stretching around 130 feet and holding roughly 300 tons of cargo, including grain and luxury goods (wine, oil, statues, glassware). The waters around Antikythera were often overrun with pirates, so perhaps some scurvy blackguards attacked the ship and sent it to its doom. More likely, it blundered into a storm and crashed into the cliffs of Antikythera, killing everyone onboard and strewing the treasures along the seafloor.

After chiseling the mineral crusts off the statues and restoring them, archaeologists put them on display in a museum in Athens. They included portrayals of Zeus, Achilles, and Hercules; Odysseus in a scene from the lost epic *The Little Iliad;* plus four horses, two dancers, a lion, a dolphin, and the head of a scraggly-bearded philosopher. However rough some pieces looked, the intimate details on the undamaged ones left people gaping: the bulging

* Nailing down this date took some time, as the coins emerged only in 1976 during a salvage operation led by Jacques Cousteau.

veins on the horses' legs, the hangnail on a fragment of hand, the supple folds in the thongs woven around the knuckles of a boxer. People came by the thousands to view them, burning with patriotic pride. One bronze nude in particular, the six-foot-five-inch *Antikythera Youth,* quickly became a Greek icon. Local newspapers ran at least 440 articles on the statues and the salvage and restoration efforts.

Yet the most important artifact received scant attention at first. Accounts of its discovery vary. In the most colorful one, Spyridon Staïs was treating his wife and her sister to a day at the museum in May 1902. While the women fawned over the *Antikythera Youth,* Staïs began examining some chunky rocks at its feet. These rocks had also been raised from the Antikythera wreck, and were perhaps included in the display to add some nautical flair. Regardless, the minister's eye strayed over the hunk that had nearly been tossed back into the sea, except for the bit of metal sticking out. The hunk had since cracked into four pieces, and the minister found himself staring at the glistening innards—a rainbow of green, chocolate, blue-black, and yellow. Strangely, he also noticed the faint outline of a gear.

Museum security was a bit casual in those days, so he hopped over whatever rope or railing was in place to scrutinize the hunk up close. He confirmed the presence of a gear—several, actually—and also noticed some writing in Greek. Stunned, he alerted the museum director, his cousin, who quickly had his archaeologists remove the pieces to examine them.

The innards of the hunk were corroded bronze—most of the actual metal had oxidized after 2,000 years underwater—and they were alarmingly delicate, the consistency of phyllo dough; they crumbled at the slightest pressure. The writing, a few fragmentary inscriptions, mentioned the rays of the Sun and also Aphrodite, the Greek name for the planet Venus. The archaeologists deduced that they were looking at an astronomical instrument. Perhaps an astrolabe, a device that sailors used to calculate times, dates, and positions at sea. But if so, its gears made it vastly more complex than any astrolabe ever discovered.

In fact, it seemed vastly more complex than any *object* ever discovered from ancient times—so much so that a few scholars eventually denounced it as fake. Another suggested that a ship in modern times must have jettisoned it overboard on a trip past Antikythera, and it just happened to come to rest amid the ancient statues. But even those who didn't subscribe to conspiracy theories had no idea what to make of the thing. It was soon dubbed, deliberately vaguely, the Antikythera Mechanism.

Given this bewilderment, nothing much happened with the mechanism until 1958, when a 36-year-old British physicist and clock buff named Derek de Solla Price undertook a detailed study of it and proposed a radical idea. A rather formal fellow, Price arrived each day at the museum in Athens dressed in a suit and tie despite the torrid summer weather. He'd gingerly remove the crumbling fragments from the cigar boxes they were stored in and begin measuring the gears and studying how they fit together. Based on those details, Price concluded that the Antikythera Mechanism was an astronomical computer.

Today, we think of computers as electronic devices, but mechanical contraptions can perform the exact same calculations, albeit more slowly. (Charles Babbage designed a mechanical computer back in the 19th century, and Vannevar Bush constructed a computer using wheels and discs in 1931.) Still, no one had dared imagine that the ancient Greeks built computers. Price compared this discovery to opening King Tut's tomb and finding an internal combustion engine inside: a baffling, miraculous anachronism. Corrosion limited how much of the mechanism Price could see, but x-rays of the interior over the next several decades provided a much clearer picture of how it worked.*

The mechanism's primary purpose was to chart the movement of the Sun, Moon, and planets, as well as predict eclipses. Just 40 percent of it survives today, in roughly 80 fragments, some as small as the broken cornflakes at the bottom of a cereal box. When new, the device was the size of a fat telephone book and weighed maybe 20 pounds; it had a wooden case around the outside and front and back covers made of bronze. The writing inscribed on the covers included an instruction manual and was quite tiny, ranging from roughly three-point to eight-point font. The shape and style of these letters would have looked old-fashioned to people at the time of the shipwreck, like elaborate cursive does to us today. Paleographers have dated the writing to between 150 and 100 B.C., meaning the device was decades old when it sank.

Inside, the device contained five or six dozen thin, interlocking bronze gears, some with more than 200 teeth. To operate it, you turned a knob or drive-crank on the side, which sent the gears whirring. (Modern re-creations are surprisingly quiet; they sound like someone softly rattling a chain.) By turning the crank backward or forward, you could set the mechanism to any date you wanted, past or future, to see what was happening in the heavens then. Conversely, if you wanted to know when an astronomically determined religious festival would take place, you could crank the dial to the right configuration and note the date. Or if you wanted to launch a project

* Given the fragmentary, corroded nature of the Antikythera Mechanism, everything that follows is conjecture, but it's based on solid evidence and close scrutiny of the surviving pieces.

on an astronomically propitious day—a military campaign, say—you could scroll ahead in time for an arrangement in the heavens that looked promising.

A single large dial dominated the front face. Imagine a clock, except with seven hands instead of two. One hand each represented the Sun, the Moon, and the five planets known in ancient times. (To see beyond Saturn, you need a telescope.) On the end of each hand sat a colored bead to differentiate one planet from another. The dial face also had a half-white, half-black ball that rotated to show the phases of the Moon.

Around the outside of the dial ran two concentric rings. One had the names of the months inscribed in it, as well as holes to mark each date; it could likely rotate and shift for leap years. The inner ring was divided into 12 sections for the 12 zodiac constellations. This allowed you to determine when Mars was in Pisces, or what have you. Around this ring, there were also a series of Greek letters etched in: *alpha, beta, gamma,* et cetera. Each letter corresponded to a certain astronomical event, often the first or last appearance that year of an important star above the horizon. In this way, the ring of letters acted as a sort of mini-almanac for stargazers.

The hands rotated at wildly uneven rates. Each full turn of the drive-crank sent the Moon hand zipping around the dial three times; meanwhile, a complete circuit for Saturn required 140 turns. As you can imagine, getting all seven hands to move in perfect sync required pretty intricate gearwork, as well as precisely crafted components. And keep in mind that most ancient astronomers didn't realize that Earth and other planets revolved around the Sun. They built the mechanism using a clumsy geocentric view of the cosmos—yet it was still accurate enough to compute the positions of the planets even a century into the future.

Equally impressive, the gearwork could handle variable speeds. Although it's subtle, the Sun and Moon travel at different velocities across the sky throughout the year. By using a pin and slotted-arm combination with certain gears, the mechanism could reproduce these variations. It could also handle retrograde motion, when planets appear to travel backwards through the sky compared to their normal direction. (This illusion occurs because Earth and other planets all orbit the Sun simultaneously, and do so at different speeds.) The mechanism captured retrograde motion by reversing the direction of a given planet's hand from clockwise to counterclockwise during the appropriate period, even while all the other hands kept moving the opposite direction. Pretty slick.

The back face of the mechanism was more crowded, with two large dials and three small ones. Each had a pointer that turned concurrently with the hands on the front. One of the large dials predicted when eclipses would occur, both lunar and solar. The details about the other large dial get pretty gnarly, but it essentially helped you translate between a lunar calendar and solar calendar. (Many ancient societies used lunar calendars because the regularity of the Moon's phases provided an easy way to track time.) As for the three small dials, one made subtle corrections to the lunar-calendar-to-solar-calendar conversion; one refined the prediction of eclipses; and the last, fancifully enough, noted the years in which the Olympic Games* and other athletic festivals took place.

---

* The Olympics began on the first full moon of the first lunar month after the summer solstice. Other notable games (at Nemea, Delphi, Corinth) occurred at different times. Confusingly, each city used its own calendar, which made it a pain for competitors to figure out when to travel to the sites. The best athletes—like the stud boxer and wrestler Menodoros, who won 32 prizes at 14 games—practically had to become amateur astronomers to keep their schedules straight.

Various lines of evidence point to the mechanism being constructed on the island of Rhodes. Rhodes boasted of many talented craftsmen, and the days of the year when certain stars appear and disappear on the horizon correspond to a place at the island's latitude. Furthermore, in the 70s B.C., the orator Cicero referenced a device in Rhodes that "at each revolution, reproduces the motions of the Sun, Moon and five planets"—exactly like the mechanism. Each gear would have been cut from a sheet of bronze, and each tooth filed by hand. Overall, the mechanism probably took a craftsman a month or two to make, not counting the intricate inscriptions: a significant investment of time and labor.

The most contentious mystery of the mechanism involves its purpose. What did people use it for? It seems too big and complicated to be a navigation aid; sailing from one island to another hardly requires converting from lunar to solar calendars or foresight about the next Olympics. Beyond that, scholars disagree. Perhaps ancient auguries used it to cast horoscopes or track eclipses, which were ominous events in centuries past. Perhaps priests used it to plan religious festivals, whose dates were often determined by celestial happenings. Perhaps astronomers used it as a research or teaching tool. Perhaps all these groups used it, or none of them. We just don't know.

Regardless of its purpose, the mechanism is an astounding object. Devices of similar complexity don't appear again in the historical record for 1,400 years, until the clocks of medieval times. Heck, we don't know of a single other *gear* from ancient Greece beyond it. And if the ancient shipwreck off Antikythera had occurred a little farther north and spilled the device into the abyss beneath the waves, we still wouldn't. Historians would be declaring, with full confidence, that building a computer in ancient times was impossible.

Scholars once considered the mechanism a one-off miracle, as if Zeus himself had handed it down from Olympus. Few still subscribe to that theory today, because that's not how technology works. The mechanism couldn't have been the first and only device of its kind, any more than you could suddenly build a sleek Ferrari without the clunky Model Ts of yesteryear. Predecessors must have existed. Sadly, its brethren were likely melted down for the valuable bronze inside, perhaps during times of war or economic hardship. But the survival of the Antikythera Mechanism forced scholars to reappraise ancient sources and admit that they had systematically underestimated what the Greeks and other ancient people were capable of.

Take the case of Hero (aka Heron), the son of a cobbler who worked at the Great Library-Museum of Alexandria in the first century A.D. Hero was arguably the greatest engineer of ancient times, having mastered the use of air pressure, heat, gravity, and simple machines to power a wide variety of devices. He even built the world's first steam engine, a good 1,700 years before James Watt.

Here's an example of one of his contraptions, a device that rivals anything Rube Goldberg dreamed up. (See the diagram in the photo insert.) Religion was a competitive sport in ancient Alexandria, with Roman, Egyptian, and Anatolian cults all vying for worshipers. So Hero invented an automatic door opener for one temple to impress potential converts. Outside the temple door, a priest would burn a sacrificial offering—some incense, maybe, or a small animal. He did so atop a tall, skinny altar reminiscent of a modern podium. The podium-altar was hollow, and a hidden pipe inside ran into an underground chamber. There, the pipe was connected to a sphere filled with water. Hot air expands, so as the fire warmed the air in the altar, it applied pressure on the water in the sphere. This pushed some of the water out the sphere via a second pipe on the side. The water poured into a bucket suspended from the chamber's ceiling. The bucket was connected via chains to two posts that controlled the temple doors above. As the bucket filled with water and grew heavier, it sank and pulled on the chains. This turned the posts and cranked open the doors. A blast of trumpets would sound, and the priests would declare that the gods were pleased with the offering. The gobsmacked crowds—thinking they'd witnessed a miracle—would rush inside.

Hero built dozens of gizmos like this: mechanical birds that warbled as they twirled; vending machines that dispensed holy water for coins; a statue of Hercules that shot arrows at a hissing dragon; a rolling podium with a Dionysus robot and six dancing girls that automatically wheeled itself onto a stage, poured slugs of wine, lit a small fire on a brazier, produced a bouquet of flowers from a hidden compartment like a jack-in-the-box, played drums and cymbals for the crowd, and then wheeled itself offstage again after its seven-minute performance, no doubt to raucous applause. Design-wise, none of these devices was as sophisticated as the Antikythera Mechanism, but to an average person, they were probably more impressive. Someone once called Hero the Leonardo da Vinci of Alexandria, but if anything, it was the other way around. Hero was a vastly better engineer.

Hero's devices weren't unique, either. An ancient barber turned engineer named Ctesibius (also from Alexandria, natch) invented a self-playing organ, and the water clocks he built remained the most accurate timepieces in the world until the 1300s. The poet Pindar claimed that the hundred-foot-tall Colossus of Rhodes, one of the Seven Wonders of the Ancient World, could move somehow, animated like a robot. And while we've all heard Mark Antony's funeral oration from *Julius Caesar* ("Friends, Romans, countrymen, lend me your ears ..."), in historical fact, it was less Antony's words that fired up the rabble that day and more the animatronic wax dummy he commissioned and displayed during Caesar's funeral. At first, the dummy Caesar lay quietly on a bier. But halfway through Antony's speech, it sat up, looked around, and began oozing blood from its stab wounds. This whipped the crowd into a righteous, riotous fury. No disrespect to Shakespeare, but it wasn't sweet rhetoric that doomed Caesar's assassins, but the work of anonymous craftsmen, a few "rude mechanicals" who'd mastered the art of the automaton.*

Given all these examples, why did it take historians so long to recognize how clever ancient engineers were? For one thing, seeing is believing, and no robots from antiquity have survived to the present day. (Like the other Antikythera computers, they were probably melted down for metal.)

Derek de Solla Price detected another factor: snobbery. For all Hero's genius, he built mostly playthings, trifles for amusement. This exasperated modern scholars who studied Serious Ideas. As Price put it, they felt "somewhat peevish discontent because the most ingenious mechanical devices of antiquity were not useful machines but trivial toys." Especially after the Industrial Revolution, the ideal inventor was someone like James Watt or Robert Fulton, who used steam and pneumatic power to *do* things: mine ore, manufacture goods, power ships. Meanwhile, Hero had the poor taste to become a Hellenic Willy Wonka. Scholars felt betrayed.

Now to be fair, however silly it looks to scold Hero, those scholars do have a point. It is odd that he (or someone after him) didn't at least attempt to build something more useful than a whirligig that poured wine. The standard explanation for this neglect is slavery. The ancient

* We don't know when the first Greek automatons appeared. Homer discusses them in his poems, including gates that shut themselves, self-steering ships, and tripods on golden wheels that rolled around of their own volition. There's no evidence that anyone ever built these machines, but perhaps these stories inspired Hero and others. If nothing else, these passages prove that the Greeks were thinking about automatons 2,700 years ago.

world was overrun with slaves, in Africa, Europe, and Asia alike. So why invest in labor-saving devices to dig a canal or whatever when you can just snap your fingers and have a dozen wretches do it instead?

That explanation seems incomplete, though, given that slavery and technological innovation can certainly coexist. (In the antebellum South, industries such as sugar production were highly mechanized.) In reality, ancient engineers like Hero probably just had different priorities than we do today. Amusement was perhaps enough. Indeed, it's possible that even the Antikythera Mechanism was merely a toy for some rich, smug jerk. But that doesn't make it one iota less marvelous.

Hero is a bit of an exception in the historical record in that we know his name and can credit him with certain innovations. All too often, the genius behind a new tool or technology vanishes forever. Sometimes that's understandable: Given how much time has passed, we'll never know who knapped the first stone blade or honed the first spear. Other times, as with toggle harpoons, issues of credit are more complicated—and fraught. As odd as it sounds, the origins of the toggle harpoon remain murky because it grew too ubiquitous too quickly. And unlike the Antikythera Mechanism—a plaything for elites—this weapon had its roots in the grim realities of life and death in one of the harshest environments on earth.

Imagine a whale hunt in the *Moby-Dick* era of the 1840s, with a few salty tars pursuing a whale in a boat. As they pull alongside, one of them—heavily bearded, with sun-scorched skin—leaps to his feet and flings a harpoon. It's connected to the boat via a line (a rope), and when it strikes home, it punches through the whale's skin and blubber to the flesh beneath. Now it was time for what they called a "Nantucket sleigh ride": The whale snorts and takes off. The line tightens with a jerk, and the boat springs forward. The hunt is on.

At least for a bit. Due to drag, the boat is pulling backwards on the harpoon, which threatens to tear free. To prevent this, the harpoon has barbs: rearward-facing points that dig into the flesh. But however effective in theory, barbs often failed during hunts. The harpoon head was simply too sharp, and as the whale bucked and thrashed, it often cut itself loose, allowing the harpoon to slip free and the whale to escape. Hunt after hunt ended this way. No matter the skill of the crew, each pursuit was a spin of the roulette wheel.

The toggle harpoon changed that. A toggle head is asymmetric, with a barb on one side only. More importantly, the head swivels. So when the backward drag began, and the single barb got caught in the flesh, the head felt an asymmetric force and pivoted 90 degrees, forming a T shape. At this point, it would tear free only with great difficulty, because the rotated head had a far greater surface area than the entry wound. The harpoon was effectively locked in place.

One whaling expert I spoke with recounted an experiment he runs for schoolchildren to drive home the power of toggle harpoons. He wraps two bananas in duct tape to simulate the anatomy of a whale: The duct tape is the whale skin, the banana peel the blubber, and the banana fruit the flesh beneath. He jabs one banana with a miniature version of a regular barbed harpoon. It can support around seven pounds of weight before the harpoon rips free. Not bad for a banana. Then he jabs the second one with a mini toggle harpoon. It can hold up to 70 pounds. Little kids could dangle from it.

Credit for inventing the toggle harpoon generally goes to Lewis Temple, a blacksmith who worked in New Bedford, Massachusetts, the whaling capital of the world in the 1800s. Temple was born a slave in Virginia around 1800; he either earned or bought his freedom and moved to New Bedford around 1830. In addition to its whaling industry, New Bedford was a stop on the Underground Railroad, and Temple took an active role in abolition work. He almost certainly met Frederick Douglass during the latter's time there, and was once arrested for protesting a pro-slavery rally. Temple never went to sea, but when he opened his own blacksmith shop in 1836, he specialized in nautical wares: hooks, hinges, barrel hoops, nails, and especially harpoons.

American blacksmiths first experimented with swiveling harpoon heads in the late 1830s. But nothing took hold until Temple invented his toggling harpoon in 1848. The iron part of the harpoon stretched a yard long and weighed roughly five pounds; it was hafted to a wooden shaft and sold for around $1.25 (around $50 today). The business end, the toggle head, looked like a cross between a Nike swoosh and a knife blade—sleek and deadly. Whaling scholars still gush over its beauty. More to the point, the Temple harpoon proved supremely effective at sticking fast beneath the blubber, and became ubiquitous on whaling voyages. One scholar declared it "the most important single invention in the whole history of whaling, since it resulted in the capture of a far greater proportion of whales."

Even before Temple's harpoon, whaling was an important American industry. It employed 70,000 people, and the 650 whaling vessels registered in the United States outnumbered the rest of the world's fleet by threefold. (Whales were hunted largely for oil; our addiction to the stuff began long before the first cars.)* But after the Temple

* Whales were so closely associated with oil that, in the olden days, some sea captains swore that crude oil was whale urine that had sunk in the ocean, seeped through cracks in the continental shelves, and come to rest inland. Oil from whale blubber was superior to vegetable and other oils because it produced lots of light and very little smoke when burned in lamps. Oil from the head, the spermaceti, was also light enough to lubricate watch gears and other delicate machinery. People paid the modern equivalent of $100 per gallon.

harpoon, the whaling industry exploded, eventually growing into the fifth-largest sector of the U.S. economy. New Bedford became the richest city per capita in the nation.

New Bedford blacksmiths forged perhaps a hundred thousand Temple harpoons in the decades after 1848. Temple himself, however, never cashed in, largely because he didn't patent his design. He could neither read nor write, and would have needed a lawyer to file the claim. Perhaps he couldn't afford one, or perhaps he assumed a Black man would never win a patent. Perhaps he didn't realize he even could patent his work. Regardless, without patent protection, other smiths copied his harpoon. But while he never grew wealthy, Temple did prosper, purchasing the building next to his shop and becoming a celebrity within the whaling community.* All in all, it's a remarkable tale: how a man born a slave, with every disadvantage against him, rose to fame through the dint of his own genius and invented one of the most effective hunting tools in history.

Except, things aren't so simple. Before Temple, whaling was a fairly even fight between man and beast. His tool shifted the advantage decidedly toward humans, and made it so much easier to slaughter whales—some of the most majestic creatures on earth—that several species nearly went extinct. The story gets even more complicated when you realize that, despite the acclaim he won, Temple probably didn't invent the toggle harpoon. Most of the credit belongs to Arctic people.

---

* Temple's life ended sadly. In fall 1853, New Bedford built a new sewer line, and instead of providing a safe way for pedestrians to cross the construction site, city workers slapped a plank over the trench and called it good. Temple tried crossing one night and fell, injuring himself so badly he could no longer work. New Bedford agreed to pay $2,000 in lost wages (around $75,000 today), but dawdled about handing the money over. Temple soon died, and left his family in substantial debt, perhaps due to the construction of his new shop. It took his widow, Mary, three years of fighting to collect the payment.

The first modest toggle harpoons, for hunting seals, originated in northern Japan several thousand years ago. We don't know how or when they spread from there, but the technology reached its zenith in the Arctic. Native Arctic people had the most advanced hunting technology of any traditional society, for good reason. If you were a hunter elsewhere in the world and failed to snag any game one day, you could trudge back home and, however discouraged, plop down and fill your belly with grain porridge or roasted vegetables. You'd eat. Things didn't work like that in the far north. Crops didn't grow there, and if a hunt failed, there was no fallback meal. Arctic people needed sophisticated, reliable hunting tools or they'd starve.

Little surprise, then, that they eagerly adopted and improved the toggle harpoon. They likely started off hunting seals and walruses, but by A.D. 500 (and possibly earlier) they were regularly taking down whales, the largest creatures on earth. They crafted the harpoon blades from slate and mounted them on heads of dense walrus ivory; the shaft was driftwood. They also refined this design in various ways and combined it with other technologies. For instance, instead of attaching the harpoon line to their boat, they often attached it to a series of inflatable sealskin floats. These floats marked the whale's position, provided drag to tire it out, and prevented it from diving too deeply, all while keeping the boat out of harm's way. When you have no fallback meal, you have to get creative.*

It's not clear how Arctic toggles first permeated the West. Basque whalers were collaborating with their counterparts in Greenland by

* Some Arctic people still hunt with toggle harpoons today, albeit fired from guns. However deadly, bullets don't mix well with sea mammals, since you lose the carcass if it sinks. A merely wounded animal can also dive and disappear. A toggle harpoon, and the floats attached to it (red plastic buoys nowadays), eliminate those problems.

the mid-1600s, so perhaps they exchanged ideas. But the technology made no inroads among American whalers until much later. In 1835, an American whaleship named the *Ganges* strayed into the Kodiak waters in the Gulf of Alaska. American whalers had rarely hunted in Alaska before, but the *Ganges* encountered such a bonanza that many other ships followed. The crews probably didn't have extensive contact with Native people, given that American whalers often stayed at sea for long stretches, rarely touching land. But some exchange was inevitable. And is it really a coincidence that American crews first entered hunting grounds dominated by toggle harpoons in the 1830s, and that American blacksmiths began tinkering with pivot and swivel designs a few years later?

Some historians say yes. They insist that New Bedford was simply a hothouse of whaling technology, and that Lewis Temple invented his sleek, deadly toggle harpoon independently of Arctic ones. But people with Native heritage roll their eyes at such claims, if not grind their teeth. They insist that New England whalers stole their design without giving them credit.

It's not easy to untangle these competing claims. But regardless of how you apportion credit, it's not fair to disparage Lewis Temple. He overcame a lot in his life, and there's no evidence he was scheming against Arctic people. My best guess is that he heard stories from returning sailors, or perhaps even saw a few Arctic toggles and immediately realized how clever they were. (Genius recognizes genius.) Then he refined the design, just as Arctic people refined earlier Japanese toggles. If that's the case, then Temple deserves his fame; iteration is how technology advances. It could also solve another mystery. If he was indeed influenced by Native Arctic harpoons, that might explain why he never patented his work—because he knew it wasn't wholly original.

In 2011, Kevin Kelly made an audacious claim about technology on NPR's *Morning Edition.* Kelly, a futurist and a founding editor of *Wired* magazine, told radio host Robert Krulwich that "no species of technology ... has ever gone globally extinct on this planet." Krulwich balked at this. No technology has gone extinct? *Ever?* Kelly stuck to his guns. He insisted that technology is tenacious. It's an invasive weed: Once invented, it establishes a permanent, ineradicable foothold and never disappears completely.

Still not believing him, Krulwich appealed to NPR's audience online, challenging them to find counterexamples to Kelly's claim. People submitted 2,500 ideas, and Krulwich culled them to three, a trio of technologies he was certain no longer existed. They were: the corvus, a bridge by which Roman sailors boarded other ships during wars; ferrite jukebox cores, an old memory system for jukeboxes that used iron-oxide ceramics instead of semiconductors; and radium suppositories, a medical treatment that involved sticking slugs of radioactive elements you-know-where for a little health goose back in the days when people thought radioactivity was good for you.

Guess what. Kelly found contemporary examples of all three. The corvus is really just a gangplank, which ships today use all the time for loading and disembarking. And while not found in jukeboxes anymore, ferrite memory cores still find use in specialized fields of electronics. (Remember, Kelly wasn't claiming that specific *parts* never disappear, only that general species of technology don't.) As for radium suppositories, doctors still slip radioactive materials into people's bums to fight rectal tumors, which is darn close. Krulwich took three impressive swings, but struck out just the same.

Still, I don't think Kelly's maxim—that technologies never die—presents the full picture. Right now, we do live in an era when technologies persist, but that wasn't always the case. Sometime after the invention of the Antikythera Mechanism, geared computing technology vanished for centuries. And what holds now might not hold forever: If a global calamity ever struck our species, technologies could easily go extinct in the future. Things are more fragile than Kelly allows.

Moreover, given the vagaries of history and how close we came to never learning about the Antikythera Mechanism, perhaps we should be humble and admit that we might not know about every species of technology that ever existed—the proverbial unknown unknowns. To be sure, these missing technologies probably aren't that advanced; no one's claiming people had fusion jetpacks way back when. But our ancestors lived radically different lives and had much different problems to solve. So it's conceivable that some sort of device or tool that they found indispensable has now faded beyond our awareness.

That seems all the more likely given how prone we are to dismissing the technical achievements of the past. Ancient rock-knappers could produce obsidian blades with edges sharper than modern surgical scalpels. Ancient Polynesians could discover new islands across hundreds of miles of open ocean using nothing but observations of birds, currents, and clouds. Ancient Egyptians built pyramids that we'd still find challenging to construct today, using techniques to raise blocks that we remain ignorant of. None of them have received due credit. Even more sobering, people in the future will probably dismiss our technical prowess, too—digital computers, the Moon landings, the atomic bomb. Let's just hope we've inadvertently stashed a few Antikythera Mechanisms here and there for archaeologists to find in the year 5000, to time-stamp our achievements.

Then again, perhaps those future men and women will know our technologies all too well—and rue our cleverness. As we'll see next chapter, human beings have been ravaging our ecosystems for centuries, and our planet has already lost enough species under our stewardship. But in a twisted way, the best path out of this mess might be even more technology.

CHAPTER THIRTEEN

LOST SPECIES

Appropriately, Marjorie Courtenay-Latimer was reconstructing a dinosaur fossil when the call came. It was 9:45 a.m. on December 22, 1938, in the coastal town of East London in South Africa. A fishing captain had dredged up a mess of inedible sea creatures in his nets, and was calling to see if Courtenay-Latimer wanted to pick through them to find specimens for her museum. Courtenay-Latimer sighed. She wanted to finish working on the dinosaur, and considered telling the captain to dump them. But she had a duty to expand the collection, so she told him she'd be right down. She grabbed a grain sack, then hailed a cab outside the museum.

Courtenay-Latimer was 31 years old, with doey black eyes and wavy hair. Over seven years as the East London Museum's sole curator, she'd built its frankly pathetic holdings—some stuffed birds, some obviously fake stone tools, a six-legged pig fetus in a jar—into a respectable collection. Indeed, the museum had become her life. She'd been engaged once, but her fiancé deplored her "sissy" habit of shinnying up trees to examine birds, so she'd dumped the oaf. She later fell in love with the son of the owner of a candy factory, but he died of pneumonia. Since then, she'd poured her heart into the museum, and she hoped the new dinosaur skeleton would make a splash.

She also hoped to add more marine life to her collection. Upon arriving at the docks, she found the captain's 115-foot trawler and climbed aboard. A Scottish deckhand showed her the two-ton pile of unwanted catch: mostly sharks, with a smattering of starfish and other critters. They were oozing slime in the hot summer sun, but she gamely rolled up her sleeves and was soon elbow-deep in the muck.

Before long, she saw a flash of blue inside the mound, the color of dinnerware china. Muscling a few sharks aside, she unearthed a five-foot-long, 127-pound fish, mostly cobalt with white speckles. It was pug ugly and seeping mucus, and had that pungent fishy aroma that puts so many people off seafood. Its scales were thick and hard, like chain mail, and it had an unusual three-part tail, with a middle section like the bobbed tail of a puppy dog.

The Scottish deckhand saw her studying it. "I have been trawling for over 30 years," said he, "but I have nae seen its like." He drew special attention to some odd "fins" on its side; they looked more like stumpy lizard legs. He also mentioned that the fish had still been alive when it emerged from the water. The captain had actually tried examining it, and had nearly lost a finger when the brute snapped at him. Courtenay-Latimer believed it: The teeth looked vicious.

All in all, the fish would make an excellent addition to the museum, so Courtenay-Latimer hefted it into the grain sack. Initially, the waiting cab driver refused to allow the stinky creature in his car, but Courtenay-Latimer placated him by putting it in the trunk.

Back at work, she showed her prize to the museum chairman. He crinkled his nose and dismissed it as nothing special, a common rock cod. "All your geese are always swans," he chided. Although stung, Courtenay-Latimer decided he was wrong: The fish was special, she was sure of it. And to confirm her hunch, she rang up James Leonard Brierley Smith.

If anything, Smith was even more prickly than the museum chairman, a dyspeptic, high-strung man of 41 with spiky gray hair and a permanent frown. Courtenay-Latimer had met him five years earlier while collecting specimens on a beach. Although a chemistry professor by training, Smith was obsessed with fish: He often spent whole weeks on fishing boats, despite debilitating seasickness, just to see what they dredged up. And however prickly, he always made time to help small museums. Courtenay-Latimer felt certain her giant blue fish would pique his interest.

She called and left a message at his university in Grahamstown, 80 miles away. When Smith hadn't responded the next day, she posted a letter, along with a sketch of the fish.

Meanwhile, she could smell the fish starting to turn. Refrigerators were rare then, so she borrowed a cart from a neighbor and a bedsheet from her mother, and schlepped it over to the hospital morgue. The director refused her request to store it there—he couldn't have the bodies reeking like fish. A local grocer with a fridge also turned her down. Finally, she trundled it over to a taxidermist, who agreed to stuff it.

The innards surprised Courtenay-Latimer. The fish oozed oil from every pore, whole cups of the stuff. Its muscles were more like clay than flesh; she could knead them. And instead of a proper backbone, it had a tube of gristle filled with more oil. Courtenay-Latimer told the taxidermist to preserve every greasy bit, in case Smith wanted to examine them.

But even several days later, Smith hadn't answered her. So when the taxidermist called and complained that the innards were growing putrid, Courtenay-Latimer told him to toss them out. The whole situation left her dejected. Maybe the chairman was right, and the fish was worthless. At least she still had the dinosaur.

Unbeknownst to Courtenay-Latimer, Smith wasn't at his university at all. A nasty illness had laid him low that December, and he and his wife had escaped to a cabin of theirs a few hundred miles down the coast to allow him to recuperate. The roads to the cabin were primitive, and given the Christmas holiday, Smith didn't receive any mail there until January 3. When the bundle arrived, he retired to his study with his wife, grumbling as he flipped through the envelopes—junk, junk, junk. Then he spotted Courtenay-Latimer's handwriting. He liked and respected the young woman, and settled in to read her letter.

The first page puzzled him. What kind of fish could she possibly mean? Then he turned to the sketch—and his eyes nearly popped out of his skull. As he later said, "A bomb seemed to burst in my brain." He leaped to his feet, and images of ancient fish fossils began flashing through his mind like slide projections. "I told myself sternly not to be a fool," he recalled. But the thought was already burning in his brain. This was a coelacanth.

The oldest fossils of the coelacanth date back 400 million years. The fish fascinated scientists like Smith because of its anatomy—especially the two pairs of fins that looked like proto-limbs. The emergence of the first coelacanths also coincided with one of the most important transitions in the history of life, when sea critters began dragging themselves onto land. Given those proto-limbs, biologists felt certain that something like the coelacanth had eventually given rise to the very first creatures to scuttle onto shore and look around: the very first creatures with arms, legs, and lungs. Creatures like us. And Smith was now staring at a picture of one.

At least he thought so. According to the fossil record, coelacanths died out 80 million years ago. So how could one turn up in a fishing net? You'd be just as likely to stumble across a triceratops—*more* likely, since the triceratops died out "only" 66 million years ago. It didn't make sense.

While pondering all this, Smith became aware of a voice calling out to him, as if from a distance. Suddenly, the world of his study came rushing back, and he jumped to find his wife, Margaret, standing next to him, repeating his name. She looked concerned, and no wonder: She'd seen her husband rocket to his feet and freeze catatonically, staring slack-jawed at a drawing of a fish.

He started explaining about the coelacanth and its fin-limbs, how it went extinct 80 million years ago but had somehow turned up in East London. Margaret nodded sympathetically, touching his shoulder, and asked if he'd gotten too much sun that day. Smith scowled. He didn't know what to think, but he had to see the creature for himself.

Margaret then pointed to the letter's date, and Smith jumped again. Courtenay-Latimer had posted it 11 days ago. Given the terrific December heat, her coelacanth—if it was that—had almost certainly rotted by now, unless she'd taken heroic steps. Smith rushed from his study and sprinted to the local post office. He danced around impatiently until the employees sauntered back from lunch, then fired off a telegram to Courtenay-Latimer: MOST IMPORTANT, PRESERVE SKELETON AND GILLS.

The next morning, Smith rang Courtenay-Latimer up on the post office telephone—a call that left the employees gaping. Long-distance calls were ruinously expensive then, and Smith was throwing away whole fistfuls of cash to gab about some fish. When Courtenay-Latimer admitted they'd thrown away the gills and other organs, Smith was crushed. He asked her to track down the taxidermist's garbageman and find out where he discarded his waste; Smith was prepared to dig the innards out of the city dump, no matter how rotten. Courtenay-Latimer looked into the matter, only to learn that East London dumped its garbage in the sea. There was no hope of recovery.

Although disappointed, Smith told Courtenay-Latimer to guard the fish with her life; he'd visit as soon as he could. Due to various delays, including rainstorms that turned South Africa's already iffy roads into prehistoric mud pits, he couldn't make the trip until mid-February.

Those six weeks gave Smith plenty of time to brood. And the more he thought about it, the loonier the idea of a coelacanth seemed. All known coelacanth fossils were small fry, less than a foot. This one supposedly stretched five feet. And while he respected Courtenay-Latimer, she lacked training in ichthyology and might have made mistakes in her drawing. Or maybe something fantastical had happened: Maybe the fish had been encased in preservative mud at the bottom of the ocean for millions of years and recently been disgorged. Even that seemed more likely than its hidden persistence.

Courtenay-Latimer did send Smith a few scales, which reassured him—for a bit. But before long, doubts started clawing him again. He pulled out Courtenay-Latimer's sketch a dozen times a day, glaring at it, and began suffering nightmares about the fish when he fell asleep. Later, he even started having nightmares about having nightmares, and would wake up panting in the dark. It took his bedraggled mind several minutes to sort everything out.

At last, on February 16, a half-thrilled, half-terrified Smith arrived in East London to see the supposed coelacanth. At the museum, Courtenay-Latimer greeted him and led him to a table in back. The taxidermist had preserved the fish with formalin, which turned its metallic blue scales a muddy brown. But the moment Smith laid eyes on it, all doubt evaporated. "That first sight hit me like a white-hot blast," he recalled. "My body tingled." Indeed, Smith barely knew what to make of the strange emotion bubbling up inside him—joy. Courtenay-Latimer had made the zoological discovery of the century.

Scientists now consider the coelacanth a "living fossil," a creature that looks virtually identical to its ancestors hundreds of millions of years ago.* Imagine visiting a museum and seeing a creature on display there pop out of its rock and start running around; that's essentially what living fossils are. They sported among the dinosaurs, soared among the pterodactyls, swam with the plesiosaurs—leaping, splashing, howling links to some of the most ancient life-forms in our planet's history. Yet you can hold them in your hands today. The coelacanth is an especially important living fossil because its evolutionary stability can provide insight into the origins of the first landlubbers.

---

* Other living fossils include horseshoe crabs, ginkgo trees, sturgeons, and gars. At least some living fossils, including coelacanths, persist unchanged because they lack natural predators and escape the evolutionary pressures that transform other species. Another factor in slowing down evolution is DNA. Gars (pointy fish with crocodilian jaws) have extremely good DNA-repair machinery, which limits any mutations that could drive changes. Some species of gars that split 105 million years ago can still interbreed today—their DNA is that similar. Living fossils also tend to have slow metabolisms and long generation times, which further cuts down on mutations.

Incidentally, the coelacanth is an example of a "Lazarus taxon," a species that disappears from the fossil record for a stretch before reappearing later. Paleontologists also speak of "Elvis taxa" (look-alike species, named after Elvis impersonators) and "zombie taxa" (species whose fossils have broken loose from their original stratum and misleadingly reappeared in later ones).

Smith arranged with Courtenay-Latimer to transfer her specimen to his home in Grahamstown for further study; armed policemen accompanied him. For the next few months, he arose at 3 a.m. six days a week to work on it, toiling for several hours. Then, after a full day teaching chemistry at the university, he'd resume his coelacanth labors and not quit until 10 p.m. Before long, his entire house reeked. Even after being taxidermied, the coelacanth continued to ooze oil, which turned rancid. Coelacanth flesh also contains urea and waxy esters. The former smells like aged urine as it breaks down, while the latter would have added a sickly bouquet of rotten fruit—an eye-watering one-two stench that permeated everything Smith owned. His pregnant wife Margaret found it especially nauseating. Yet he told her and his servants that if a fire broke out at home, they were not to even think about retrieving their valuables. Let the heirlooms and family records burn—he wanted the fish saved at all costs.

Months later, Smith published a book about the coelacanth to great acclaim. Strikingly, it lacked a list of works cited: The coelacanth was so new, so unlike any other life-form, that there was nothing he even could cite. Smith named the species after Courtenay-Latimer *(Latimeria chalumnae),* and newspapers around the world greeted the announcement of this living fossil with gigantic headlines. One write-up appeared in the *Illustrated London News*—the same publication that had trumpeted the discovery of the Indus Valley Civilization and the Dorak-Yortan treasures from Anatolia. This fish story was every bit as important.

Smith spent the next dozen years trawling eastern Africa for more coelacanths. In every port, he distributed flyers to local fishermen with a picture of a coelacanth and the word REWARD emblazoned across the top. He was offering £100 for one—50 times Courtenay-Latimer's monthly museum salary.

Smith also hunted the fish himself at ports. He'd paddle out to the nearest reef with his wife, light a stick of waterproof dynamite, and toss it overboard. After it blew, a huge mass of foam gurgled up, along with scads of dead pisces. Smith then made Margaret dive in and collect them all; like a cat, he hated getting wet. But no matter how many flyers he handed out, no matter how many fish he bombed, no more coelacanths turned up.

He finally quit searching in late 1952. While returning to Durban by ship on Christmas Eve day, watching the city lights twinkle in the predawn darkness, he felt resigned—he'd done his best. But he also must have wondered whether the universe was playing a cruel joke. Had the coelacanth gone re-extinct? Had science really discovered it after 80 million years of silence, only to have it disappear again?

After the ship docked, Smith wandered up to the galley and sat down with a local reporter. During their conversation, a sealed telegram arrived. When the conversation hit a lull, Smith opened the message—and once again leaped to his feet. A fishing captain in the Comoro Islands, between Madagascar and Mozambique, had just caught a second coelacanth.

Several frantic days of telegrams and phone calls followed, as Smith exhausted his Rolodex trying to charter a flight to the Comoros before this second specimen rotted. Given the holiday, he couldn't reach anyone. Why did this bloody fish always turn up at Christmastime? Afterward, Smith hated Christmas for the rest of his life.

At last, Smith reached the prime minister of South Africa, who arranged for an air force flight on December 28. This was not the most well-thought-through mission, considering that it involved landing military aircraft on another country's soil without permission; wars have started over less. Things were so hectic that the crew took off without even knowing whether the Comoros had a runway long enough for their albatross of a plane to land on. And halfway there, the old doubts began creeping over Smith again. He hadn't even gotten a sketch of the supposed coelacanth this time. Had this random sea captain really found the rarest fish in the world?

After landing—the runway was short and pitted, but sufficed—Smith hurried to the wharf, and the captain cracked open a coffin-like box on his deck. There, wrapped in cotton, was another coelacanth. Smith dropped to his knees and caressed it. He noticed drops of water slipping down its scales and wondered if it had started to rain. Then he realized he was weeping, "quite without shame."

Several more coelacanths turned up in the Comoros over the next few years, and Smith and other scientists eagerly dissected each one. The species proved to have a few anatomical traits unique to the animal kingdom. These include the jelly-filled rostral organ in their nose, which allows them to detect other fish by "smelling" the electrical activity in their nerves and muscles. They're also the only living animal with a working skull joint: Their cranium actually hinges open to help their mouths gape wider when devouring prey.

Other traits make the coelacanth seem like the chimeras of mythology. They have the inner ears of frogs, and their squishy spinal columns resemble those of sharks, as does their urea-rich blood. Like mammals, they give birth to live young, and their teeth look like modified scales—proof, we now know, that animal teeth originally evolved from fish scales that migrated inward to our jaws. In a surprise, although coelacanths can weigh as much as an adult human, they have brains the size of grapes, giving them the smallest brain-to-body ratio of any vertebrate, just $^1/_{15,000}$. (Humans are closer to $^1/_{50}$.) But before you chuckle, remember: They've been around for 400 million years—a thousand times longer than *Homo sapiens*—so they're obviously doing something right.*

Most intriguing of all are two traits that we land animals hold dear. First, coelacanths have rudimentary lungs. As one observer noted, this puts them in the company of mermaids, with breathing organs up top and fishy parts down below. Second, coelacanths have four odd fins on their sides: one pair near the chest and one pair near the pelvis. Unlike most fish fins, these are muscular and fleshy, with bones inside analogous to the leg and arm bones of land animals. Amazingly, coelacanth fins even move in alternating fashion as they swim along, with the front left and back right ones sculling to and fro in unison, and vice versa—exactly how land animals swing their limbs when walking.

As wild as it sounds, on the evolutionary tree of life, human beings are more closely related to coelacanths than coelacanths are to salmon or cod or most other fish. When Smith arranged for his country's prime minister to view the second coelacanth he'd found, the politician squinted down and cracked a joke. The man was an ordained Christian minister, and didn't buy any of that malarkey about humans evolving from primitive ancestors. His eyes twinkling, he said, "My, it's ugly. Do you mean to say *we* once looked like that?" Smith played it off and answered, "I've seen people that are uglier." But as he later reflected, the true answer, essentially, is

* On a more meta level, coelacanths helped determine whether the field of paleontology was even worth a damn. Paleontologists have long used fossils to make inferences about the behavior of extinct creatures, but they feared that these guesses rested on shaky foundations. Could they really extrapolate so far from some dusty bones? Coelacanths provided a great test case because scientists could compare what they'd predicted about the fish from fossils alone, before its rediscovery, to how the fish actually behaved. And they were pretty close. Their work wasn't hot air.

yes. In the coelacanth's ugly mug, we can see a glimpse of ourselves as we once were.*

In 1997, a second species of coelacanth was discovered at an Indonesian fish market by a biologist on his honeymoon. (He spotted it on an old man's cart that had, of all things, a scarlet *A* painted on the side.) The Indonesian coelacanth is more golden-brown than its African cousin, but the two species have much in common. Both are nocturnal hunters that live 500 to 800 feet underwater on the bare slopes of volcanic islands. That habitat also explains the lack of coelacanth fossils after 80 million years ago. Fossil formation requires the presence of sand or sediment to bury the body, and coelacanths likely once lived in habitats rich with such material. Then at some point—possibly after the asteroid strike that wiped out the dinosaurs 66 million years ago—coelacanths shifted to underwater volcanic slopes, which are mostly bare rock that does not promote fossilization. Their seeming "extinction" in the fossil record was nothing but an artifact.

Sadly, no coelacanth has ever survived long after being caught, probably due to the stress, heat shock, and decompression woes that result from being snared and dragged to the surface. As a consequence, much about their behavior remains unknown. Even sadder, both species are staring down the barrel of extinction. After 400 million years, they might not last another 40—an icon of evolution destroyed by habitat loss and the overfishing of their prey.

Moreover, however amazing, the story of the coelacanth has had one pernicious effect: convincing zealots and cranks that other lost species are also out there awaiting rediscovery, if only they search hard enough.

* To be scrupulous, coelacanths are not the closest aquatic relative of land creatures; that's the lungfish. But coelacanths and lungfish are themselves closely related, and comparing their anatomies helps scientists understand what the first land creatures looked like and how they colonized the continents.

As James Tanner scaled the tree, he was tingling with excitement. It was March 6, 1938, his 24th birthday, and he was about to glimpse the rarest bird in the world.

He'd been scouting the woodpecker nest for two weeks, craning his neck and squinting skyward. It sat in a hollow 55 feet high in a red maple tree in Louisiana. There were two parents, mostly black and white, plus a fledgling that Tanner nicknamed Sonny Boy. A few minutes earlier, Tanner had watched the parents fly off to fetch lunch, and he suddenly decided he wanted to see Sonny Boy up close. So he started climbing, his enthusiasm swelling with every foot.

Unfortunately, Tanner never considered how Sonny Boy might view the visit: some huge, pink, huffing-puffing thing breaking branches and jamming its beak right into his home. Tanner barely caught a glimpse of Sonny Boy before the bird panicked and darted out to fly to safety.

The problem was, Sonny Boy couldn't fly yet; he was too young. Worse, this was a hefty species of woodpecker; even a fledgling like him was the size of a pigeon. So when he bolted from the hollow, Sonny Boy plunged straight down toward the ground, his wings thrashing uselessly.

Watching him fall, Tanner felt his stomach crater. Had he just killed the most endangered bird on earth?

Thankfully, no. Sonny Boy crashed into a tangle of vines, which cushioned his fall. Tanner scurried down the trunk to free him. And what happened next was kind of magical. Tanner wanted to snap some pictures of Sonny Boy, so he handed the bird to his guide. As if showing off, Sonny Boy began hopping around on the guide's arm, then scaled his back and perched atop his hat. There, he mugged for the camera.

Tanner had heard from other ornithologists that this species had a swaggering personality. (It inspired the cartoon character Woody Woodpecker.) But to see its charisma in person, and capture it on film, absolutely thrilled him. And he wasn't alone. Even today, this species fascinates people—the ivory-billed woodpecker.

You might remember a flurry of news stories about the ivory-billed in 2005, when reports emerged of a sighting in an Arkansas swamp, decades after its presumed extinction. It was a rare bit of sunshine in a year clouded by war and political strife—one good thing we could all rally around.

Unfortunately, that sighting was almost certainly bogus. In fact, after Tanner restored Sonny Boy to its nest, only a handful of other people ever caught a glimpse of one. And the worst part is, it didn't have to be this way. We had a real chance to save the ivory-billed woodpecker—and might well have, if not for Adolf Hitler. However crazy it sounds, this once-iconic American bird was one of the very last victims of the Nazi war machine.

The ivory-billed woodpecker had lots of nicknames, including the pearly bill and king woodchuck. The most common was the Lord God bird, because that's what people cried out the first time they saw one. *Lord God, what a bird.*

They had wingspans of 30 inches, and had mostly black bodies with white racing stripes and white tips on the wings. Plus an ivory bill, of course. Perhaps most noticeably, they had eerie yellow eyes, and the males had bright red crests atop their heads.

Ivory-billeds had a distinct way of signaling their mates: tapping a tree trunk twice in quick succession—knock-knock—then freezing to listen for a response—knock-knock. Their call, unfortunately, was not the Woody Woodpecker "ah-ha-ha-*ha*-ha." It was more of a honk, a squeaky clarinet. But however inelegant that sounds, they made up for it with their flight. They always soared above the forest canopy, majestically alone, not so much flitting between trees as sweeping over them like comets, in one long, graceful arc. Lord God, what a bird.

Its range extended from Florida to North Carolina, and as far west as Texas. Dixie, essentially. Its preferred home was a classic North American ecosystem, the longleaf pine forest—90 million acres of sturdy trees, every one of them as tall and true as a cathedral pillar. Unlike most forests, longleaf pine ones have little undergrowth and no thickets. You could ride a horse through them for days on end. In fact, the forests were so unvarying that people often got disoriented and never came out again. The city of Savannah fired a cannon every day at dusk, so people wandering around out there knew which direction to return home.

The ivory-billed woodpecker thrived in such forests, living in tree hollows and digging grubs out of the trunks. (They also ate pecans, wild grapes, hackberries, and, daringly, poison ivy seeds.) But two wars sealed the bird's fate.

The U.S. Civil War laid the South to waste and left the region impoverished. The North, meanwhile, had already chopped down most of its forests, leaving its mills hungry for timber. Both sides licked their lips at those vast tracts of longleaf pine, and 87 million acres came crashing down. This loss of habitat hemmed the ivory-billed woodpecker into smaller and smaller pockets, or pushed them into swamps where they struggled to find food. By the 1930s, things were dire.

James Tanner set out to save the birds. As an ornithology student at Cornell University, he began a three-year census across the South in 1937. He made this trek in a sputtering Model A Ford, putting in 45,000 miles and becoming an expert mechanic given its temperamental engine. Where the Model A couldn't go, he plunged into forests on horseback or waded through swamps, slapping mosquitos and dodging snakes. He often slept on an old tennis net strung between trees.

He found Sonny Boy in northeast Louisiana, and was thrilled to see his charisma up close. But beyond that, the three-year odyssey left Tanner depressed. In those 45,000 miles of travel, he saw not a single ivory-billed woodpecker outside the refuge where Sonny Boy lived. It was an 81,000-acre tract of forest owned by the Singer Corporation, which used the wood to make cabinets for sewing machines. Even within that tract, Tanner found just a dozen ivory-billeds. This land was their last holdout, their Alamo.

Back at Cornell, Tanner wrote up an urgent report. If we don't save the Singer Tract, he predicted, the Lord God bird will vanish forever. This warning caught the eye of the president of the Audubon Society, John Baker. It took some time, but Baker eventually lined up the support of four southern governors, including Louisiana's. They agreed to buy the Singer Tract as a nature reserve. U.S. president Franklin Roosevelt also signed on.

Next, Baker approached the managers of the Singer Tract. Although the sewing-machine company owned the land, Singer had signed over the logging and management rights to the Chicago Mill and Lumber Company, and board chairman James Griswold was eager to sell. With World War II ramping up, there was zero labor around: Every able-bodied logger was off fighting. Griswold figured he might as well cut his losses. He told Baker he'd sell the land for $200,000—nearly $4 million today.

That was an obscene amount back then to save a bird. But a determined Baker convinced the governors to pony up. Baker then arranged a meeting with Griswold in Chicago in December 1943. The ivory-billed woodpecker was one signature away from salvation.

But seconds into the meeting, Griswold announced that the deal was off—he wasn't signing. Baker was stunned. Why? What happened? That's when a gleeful Griswold told him about the Nazis.

The British had recently defeated the Third Reich in North Africa, but had no money to house or feed the many brigades of German soldiers they'd captured. So the United States stepped in, packing the Germans onto "liberty ships" and freighting them to America. Nearly 375,000 Nazi soldiers spent the balance of the war there—including 505 at a fairground near the Singer Tract. To make these men earn their keep, the War Department put them to work. Most ended up tending crops, wearing denim jumpsuits with armbands stenciled P.W. for "prisoner of war." Others were assigned different tasks, including cutting timber for Chicago Mill and Lumber.

Owner James Griswold was tickled pink—practically free labor, and he could sell the cleared land afterward to farmers. He flatly told Baker that he didn't care about any damn birds. "We're just money-grubbers," he proclaimed. "We're not concerned, as you folks are, with ethical considerations." The deal was dead.

Sadly, the Singer Tract got wiped out over the next few years—an all-American landscape clear-cut by Nazis. For their part, the Germans were overjoyed to help: Rather than fester all day in their internment camp, they got to sun themselves in the great outdoors, tramping around the woods. Before long, however, the Nazis grew to hate the work. They had instructions to chop down every tree they saw; many were felled and left to rot.* Nor did most of the lumber help the actual war effort. Some got converted into crates

* That's not the only thing that stunned the Germans. Upon arriving, they gaped at the Statue of Liberty, since propaganda back home had claimed that the Third Reich destroyed it. They were also baffled to learn that they, despite being prisoners of war, got to ride in the best train cars on their way to labor camps, while Black Americans—even Black soldiers—had to sit in inferior cars. Regardless, many Germans enjoyed their time in the United States so much that they moved back after the war.

for shells or other matériel, but the majority became tea chests for British officers. The Nazis were disgusted. To destroy one of the last stands of untouched forest in North America, just so Major Twittingham and Colonel Snokesbottom could have fresh Earl Grey? Even they had more ethics than that.

As the Singer Tract dwindled, conservationists made pilgrimages there to pay their respects to the last ivory-billeds. One, a wildlife artist, visited with his pigments and brushes right before the tract vanished in April 1944. He found a single holdout, a female with no mate and no chick. The endling. She lived in an ash tree in a grove surrounded by stumps. When he saw her double-tap the trunk—knock-knock—and listen for a response that would never come, it just about shattered his heart.

On his last afternoon, the artist declined to paint anything; he just watched her scything through the sky. Lord God. Then he heard a noise—and saw a tree crash in the distance. The Germans would be coming for the rest soon. Rather than see the bitter end, he turned for home. He wanted to remember the ivory-billed as she was, in her glory, not what she'd be reduced to.

Since 1944, there have been zero confirmed sightings of the ivory-billed woodpecker in the United States.* Even the 2005 sightings, despite all the hoopla, were probably bunk. The affair actually began in 2000, when an ex-lawyer turned New Age hippie named Mary Scott took a three-day excursion into a foggy wildlife refuge in Louisiana with some birding buddies. One knew a clairvoyant who insisted she'd been communing telepathically with some

* Although largely a continental species, the ivory-billed woodpecker did have a toehold in Cuba, and the last universally accepted sighting of the bird took place there in 1986. It vanished the next year.

ivory-billeds. On day three, during a cell phone call, the clairvoyant relayed the message that the birds were disturbed by the group's energy field; they'd been acting too much like the grubby squirrel and rabbit hunters who frequented the area.

So Scott wandered off alone. Before long, she noticed a tree with stripped bark, a potential sign of woodpeckers. As she recalled, she whispered a message to the birds: "I only want to see what you want seen." Then she opened her heart, and lo—after a short walk, an ivory-billed revealed itself unto her, streaking past her in the sky. To be sure, she was looking into the sun at the time, and the bird was obscured behind several trees. Oh, and she never caught sight of its most distinct feature, the ivory bill. But she had no doubt what she saw.

Depressingly, the refuge was clear-cut shortly afterward. But Scott continued to scour other parks, including the White River wetland in Arkansas. There, while exiting her car one morning in 2003, she looked up and—mirabile dictu—saw another ivory-billed. Or at least its back: Once again, she didn't catch its bill. And while she later claimed, "I never go anywhere without my camera," at that moment, she didn't have it on her. It was the darndest thing.

People nevertheless ran with her story. Fearing an invasion of birders, local conservationists kept things hush-hush: They code-named the woodpecker "Elvis." But word got around in early 2005, and thanks to the power of suggestion, sightings multiplied; some people even captured videos. But the footage is laughably grainy: It makes the Zapruder film look high-def. Plus, in every sighting, the bird is always masked behind trees, or beating its wings in the distance; there's never a clear shot. Things seem even more dubious given that another species of large woodpecker lives in that same wetland, the pileated woodpecker. Like the ivory-billed, the pileated is black with white stripes and a red crest, making it all too easy to confuse the two. People get a half-glimpse of some fluttering wings, and Lord God, their imaginations take flight, too.

The early 2000s sightings aren't even unique. Another person claimed to have seen an ivory-billed in 1950. Ditto 1955. '58, too. And '59, '66, '67, '71, '75, and—well, you get the idea. But every single claim crumbled. Thousands of birders have spent millions of hours scouring the South for ivory-billeds—and so far, no one has ever gotten a clear glimpse.

At this point, the ivory-billed woodpecker might as well be Bigfoot: a myth. But like all myths, this one resonates with people for a reason. It's a story of greed and hope, of near misses and well-meaning mirages. Above all, it's a story of two species in conflict—a charismatic bird whose ghost still haunts the forests, and the featherless primate with a fervent desire to keep those ghosts alive.

The quest to find the ivory-billed woodpecker is actually part of a larger phenomenon called cryptozoology—the hunt for hidden species.

Some cryptozoologists pursue fringy creatures that never existed outside their imaginations: yetis, krakens, the Loch Ness monster. (Every last one of the United States has had a Bigfoot sighting, albeit under different names.) More reputably, some cryptozoologists hunt for creatures that we know once existed and might still be holding on in small refugia somewhere. Even within this realm, however, there are degrees of plausibility. Claims of spotting an ivory-billed woodpecker earn far fewer eye-rolls than claims of spotting, say, a megalodon, a species of 60-foot shark that died out 3.6 million years ago. Arguably, the first cryptozoologist in history was Thomas

Jefferson, who sent Lewis and Clark into the newly acquired Louisiana Territory with instructions to keep their eyes peeled for mastodons, giant sloths, and other megafauna that he was convinced still roamed free there.

Today, beyond the ivory-billed woodpecker, the most commonly spotted cryptoanimal is probably the thylacine, a striped marsupial dog from Tasmania that was hunted to death as a pest. The last-known thylacine died in 1936, but people claim to spy them on a regular basis in the bush today: the Sonny Boys of Down Under. Within crypto-z circles, ivory-billeds and thylacines are sometimes referred to as OOTS, out-of-time species. More catchily, sightings of creatures in the wrong location—kangaroos in the American Midwest, octopuses in Oklahoma—are known as out-of-place species. OOPS.

Cryptozoologists defend their pastime by noting that every species was a so-called cryptid at some point. Gorillas, pandas, duck-billed platypuses—respectable biologists dismissed them all as myths until the first specimens arrived on their doorsteps. As for OOTS, the best rebuttal here is the coelacanth. If a five-foot-long fish eluded every naturalist in the world for centuries, why not other creatures?

More recently, there's the black-naped pheasant pigeon, which was declared extinct after its last known sighting in 1896. Then, randomly, one wandered by a camera trap in Papua New Guinea in 2022. The scientist who'd set the camera up was staggered. "Seeing those first photos," he said, "felt like finding a unicorn."

Still, if all creatures were cryptids at one point, the converse doesn't hold true—that every claim for a cryptid must represent a real creature. There are other gaps in the logic of cryptozoology as well. However tempting on the surface, the comparison to coelacanths is misleading, since coelacanths live near remote islands in water that's far deeper than humans normally venture. No wonder they remained hidden. (And in truth, they were "hidden" only to scientists; fishermen sometimes caught them, but always threw them back because their oily, urea-rich flesh tasted terrible and caused diarrhea.) Contrast that to, say, Bigfoot, a large terrestrial creature on a relatively well-populated continent that has never yielded a single scrap of evidence—no bones, no scat, no teeth, nothing—despite decades of searching.

Equally damning, cryptozoologists put far too much faith in eyewitness testimony, despite well-documented problems with such accounts: spotty memories, false interpolations, and so-called story creep, the tendency of people to exaggerate over time and spice up a tale with each retelling. Finally, many sightings take place under doubtful circumstances: in foggy woods, at dusk or even midnight, among sleep-deprived campers or hunters. And insisting on the integrity of the witnesses—saying they're honest people, and would never lie—is beside the point. People make honest mistakes. Overall, adherents of cryptozoology spend far too much time geeking out over the *crypto* part and far too little time worrying over the *ology*—the patient, careful sifting of facts.

The big question is why. Why do people believe that thylacines and ivory-billed woodpeckers and other creatures still exist? Confirmation bias certainly plays a role. Psychologically, people see what they want to see, and grasp at any possible evidence as proof. We all do it.

But that only pushes the question back a step: Why, then, do people want to find these creatures, want to believe they haven't disappeared? In part, because the hope of finding them keeps a sense of mystery alive in a world that all too often seems drab and predictable. Who doesn't enjoy wondering *what if?* For crypto bros and gals, the field also provides a sense of community and adventure. As one put it, "If nothing else, it's an excuse to spend time in the woods."

More poignantly, there's the hope of paradise regained. The hope that if only we can find the ivory-billed or thylacine again, maybe it will prove that human beings aren't just money-grubbers after all, trading pristine forests for cash. We'll get one last chance to right our wrongs. I agree with the writer who suggested, "There's a touch of cryptozoologist in each of us."

But the days of cryptozoology might be numbered. Given advances in biotechnology, the easiest course of action when a species disappears in the future might be to resurrect it.

The two species that cause the most buzz in "de-extinction" circles are dodos and woolly mammoths, albeit for different reasons.

Scientists have found mammoth remains throughout Siberia: hair, skin, tusks, bones, even a baby with mother's milk in its stomach.* Any of those scraps can yield DNA, and scientists have in fact already sequenced the mammoth genome—the first step in resurrecting one.

Next, scientists would compare that sequence to the DNA of the mammoth's closest living relative, the Asian elephant. They'd pay particular attention to genes involving adaptations for cold weather.

---

* Crazily enough, the Russian mafia has gotten tangled up in the mammoth trade. Tusks can go for $500 per pound, and scientists sometimes have to bribe a local Don Corleoneovich for access to choice carcasses.

(Mammoth blood, for instance, contained a special type of hemoglobin that shuttled oxygen around more efficiently in freezing temperatures.) They'd also look at genes related to skin and hair, since mammoths were shaggy and elephants are not.

With this list of differences in hand, scientists would then tweak the DNA of an elephant cell using a genetic-engineering tool like CRISPR—cutting out elephant DNA at the relevant spots and pasting mammoth DNA in. After that, they'd harvest a donor egg from an elephant, remove all its DNA, swap in the DNA they'd tweaked with CRISPR, and implant that egg in the womb of a surrogate elephant mother. Assuming the egg takes, in around two years, she would give birth to the first woolly mammoth to walk the earth in thousands of years.*

All the technology to achieve this exists today. But would the creature that results *really* be a mammoth, given that you're starting with an elephant template and using an elephant egg? The answer is, it depends.

On the one hand, the mammoth and elephant genomes are 99.96 percent identical, so the species are already near twins. On the other hand, given the huge amount of DNA mammoths have (four billion base pairs, more than humans), that works out to 1.4 million differences. So would you need to alter the genome in every last spot to produce a "true" mammoth? Some people insist yes.

Most scientists aren't so pedantic. They understand that some of these differences are inconsequential. Moreover, individual

---

* The company Colossal Biosciences is currently attempting to revive a woolly mammoth, among other creatures, and has already attracted $435 million in investment. It made a big splash in 2025 by "resurrecting" the dire wolf after just 18 months of work—although, as critics noted, scientists there altered only a score of genes in a regular gray wolf genome. It's therefore an open question whether such a light edit should "count" as de-extinction.

mammoths were varied in their DNA just as individual humans are—so you can never re-create *the* mammoth genome anyway.* As for how many of the 1.4 million changes are necessary, different people have different answers. I, for one, would never count a creature as a mammoth if it lacked those gorgeous scimitar tusks. Beyond that, if it had the same skin and hair, the same teeth, the same basic physiology for cold weather, then I'm satisfied that we've effectively resurrected one, pedants be damned.

The scientists working to resurrect woolly mammoths are doing so mainly for environmental reasons. Mammoths once played a critical role in recycling nutrients in northern landscapes, turning over the soil and spreading seeds. They also knocked over trees, which sounds awful at first, but actually increased the biodiversity of the terrain by giving grasses and other vulnerable plants a chance to catch some sunshine instead of wilting in the trees' shadows. The plethora of plants in turn attracted more herbivores, which then attracted new carnivores, boosting faunal diversity as well. What's more, trees absorb more sunlight (and therefore heat) than other plants, which leads to warmer temperatures—the last thing the far north needs right now.

Equally important, mammoths redistributed snow. Fresh, untrampled snow insulates the ground beneath it pretty well, but mammoths packed that snow down or plowed it aside as they trudged across the tundra. The resulting lack of insulation allowed the permafrost up north to undergo a deeper freeze each winter. The same holds true

* To test whether the DNA in mummified mammoth flesh remains stable over time, scientists have tried extracting DNA from freeze-dried beef jerky, which undergoes a similar dehydration process. Some scientists even tried extracting DNA from jerky that they'd dunked in acid, run over with cars, and blasted with shotguns, just to make sure that genetic material remains intact during stress. For the results of these experiments, see *samkean.com/books/the-museum-of-lost-things/extras/notes.*

for grasses: They insulate the ground less well than trees and thereby render the permafrost more permanent. This has environmental consequences because the permafrost traps a truly gargantuan amount of methane, a potent greenhouse gas. As one observer noted in *The Atlantic,* melting permafrost would cause as much global warming each year "as do all of America's SUVs, airliners, container ships, factories, and coal-burning plants combined." In several ways, then, bringing back tree-busting, snow-trampling pachyderms—whether you call them "mammoths" or not—could be vital to the future health of planet Earth.

For technical reasons, birds like dodos would be harder to resurrect than mammoths and other mammals. For one thing, we don't yet have the tools to transfer DNA into bird eggs. And with dodos in particular, their nearest living relative, the Nicobar pigeon, weighs a few dozen times less and doesn't resemble the dodo at all, so the DNA template would likely require excessive tweaking. Still, workarounds exist. And unlike with mammoths (which would require implanting the embryo into an elephant uterus), we can raise bird eggs in incubators, making that step of the resurrection process far easier.

The case for resurrecting dodos is less environmental than moral. Dodos lived on Mauritius, a once-uninhabited island east of Madagascar. They were essentially giant pigeons, two feet tall and around 40 pounds in weight. Dutch sailors began colonizing Mauritius in the late 1500s, and while they found these fowls laughably easy to hunt—you could just walk right up and club them—they didn't do so often, because their flesh was reportedly gamy and greasy, every bit as foul as fillet of coelacanth.

Much more devastating was the introduction of predators. Being flightless, dodos made their nests on the ground from palm leaves, and their fat, white, apple-size eggs made tempting treats for the pigs the Dutch brought as livestock, the macaques they likely brought as pets, and the rats who'd stowed away on their ships. Pigs also proved adept at hunting adult dodos, able to sniff them out in dense thickets. We don't know exactly when dodos went extinct, but the last confirmed sighting was 1662. Today, only a few dodo relics remain; the most "complete" specimen, in Oxford, England, consists of a skull, some swatches of skin, half an eye, part of a leg, and one lonely feather.*

Eyewitness accounts of dodos are equally patchy, with wild disagreement on even basic facts. Did they waddle around comically slow, or dart about, surprisingly quick? Depends on the source. Visually, they were depicted as either brown or gray, with either black or yellow-white wings. Some accounts gave them feathery manes, while others gave them feathery trunks down to their knees: avian capris. As for their call, the historical record is virtually silent. Did they coo? Warble? Sing the most beautiful arias? The latter seems unlikely, but you never know.

One thing most everyone agreed about was that dodos were dumdums, but this judgment seems unfair. Before the 1500s, dodos had zero predators on Mauritius, and the healthy fear instinct that keeps most animals wary of hunters had long ago vanished. In a classic case of story creep, this lack of fear got warped, year by year, embellishment by embellishment, into tales of folly and incompetence. Although

---

* Reportedly, one dodo egg still exists—housed at none other than the East London Museum in South Africa where Marjorie Courtenay-Latimer preserved the coelacanth. A ship captain supposedly gave it to Courtenay-Latimer's great-aunt when the latter was a girl, and she in turn bequeathed it to the museum at age 98. The shell is hollow, the yolk and whites having long since been drained. Scientists at the museum hope to remove a bit of shell for DNA testing someday to confirm whether it belonged to a dodo. Unfortunately, disputes over the egg's ownership have so far prevented that from happening.

they'd never seen a live dodo, European naturalists had no qualms about dismissing the bird as "clumsy," "lazy," "stupid," and "grotesque"; the taxonomist Carl Linnaeus even named the species *Didus ineptus*. The tales went so far that by the early 1800s, some biologists declared that the dodo never existed—surely no creature could be that stupid. They deemed the Oxford specimen a hoax, a chimera of a turkey and a vulture, and reclassified dodos as mythological beasts: the idiot counterparts of griffins and phoenixes.

Eventually, enough dodo bones turned up to convince biologists of their reality, including a mother lode in a swamp in Mauritius in 1865. Still, the publication of a book that same year cemented their less-than-flattering reputation. An English mathematician named Charles Dodgson enjoyed taking a family friend named Alice Liddell to view the dodo remains in Oxford. Dodgson also wove the dodo into a stem-winding fantasy tale he'd been working on, and he soon published the story, under the pen name Lewis Carroll, as *Alice's Adventures in Wonderland*. Dodgson saw the supposedly awkward dodo as a stand-in for himself, and the enduring popularity of *Alice* established the bird as the bumbling nitwits we know today.* In truth, a scientific reexamination of dodo bones over the past few decades has revealed a bird that was likely thinner and more agile than anyone back then realized.

The moral case for reviving the dodo is strong. Before the modern era, Western scientists had no idea that species could go extinct. They viewed nature as bountiful and infinite, and God in His wisdom would surely protect all His creatures. The demise of the dodo killed that idea.

* Given how valuable the Oxford dodo is—the only soft dodo tissue in existence—the staff of the museum that owns it shifts it to a new location every few weeks to deter theft. For ages, everyone assumed the bird had died of natural causes, but in 2018, while scanning the skull in a CT machine, researchers found a spray of lead pellets, meaning the bird had been shot. They have no idea why, nor who the culprit was.

We saw it go extinct, and moreover caused its extinction. To be sure, people initially took a fatalistic view of the matter: If dodos weren't fit enough to survive in the modern world, tough. Life goes on. Nowadays, when we're hyperaware of humankind's impact on the environment, we're much less sanguine. As with the ivory-billed woodpecker, resurrecting the dodo would give us a chance to right a cosmic wrong. If we killed the critter off, the least we can do is bring it back.

Plus, think of the psychological impact—bringing *the* icon of extinction back from the dead. What a surge of hope. Research into reviving the dodo and other lost species could also lead to improved IVF procedures, and might even produce artificial wombs that would give premature babies a better shot at survival. If nothing else, the genetic engineering and embryological insights could save other species we're driving to extinction (pandas, rhinos, condors) by giving us the tools to expand their genetic diversity and resilience.

All that said, even if there are moral and pragmatic reasons to bring back extinct creatures, their resurrection would introduce moral and pragmatic quandaries as well.

One is where to put them. With mammoths, there's plenty of space in Siberia, but what about dodos? It wouldn't make much sense to restore them to Mauritius if the rats and monkeys there would simply devour their eggs again. The same goes for the ivory-billed woodpecker. Where would Sonny Boy live? Another popular candidate for de-extinction is the Yangtze River dolphin from China, which essentially choked to death in polluted waterways. Reintroducing them into the same filthy habitat and letting them die all over again seems heartless.

Another consideration involves birth defects. In 2000, a species of Iberian ibex called the bucardo went extinct. A few years later, Spanish and French scientists took the DNA from some preserved bucardo cells and, using the technique outlined above for mammoths, created 208 bucardo embryos from the eggs of a related ibex species. But of those 208 embryos, just one survived in its surrogate mother—and it died less than 10 minutes after birth due to a severely malformed lung, making it the only species in history to go extinct twice. Now, perhaps the scientists simply got unlucky here: Birth defects happen in naturally begotten babies, too. But it seems likely that genetic-engineering techniques, at least for now, have high rates of attrition. How much suffering are we willing to put up with to revive a species?*

We also need to remember that animals aren't just genes; behavior matters, too. Many newborns rely on elders to teach them how to find food and avoid predators. The first resurrected litters of tomorrow would have no one to mentor them; there's no creature alive that knows how to be a dodo. Equally important, many animals are social creatures that crave the company of their brethren. Recall how scared and confused that last ivory-billed woodpecker was, knock-knocking for her mate and hearing only silence in response. The first revived mammoth or dodo would be no less solitary. Things would be even worse for hominins. Using the technologies above, we could theoretically bring back Neanderthals or other lost humans. But imagine how unbearably lonely that first resurrected man or woman would be. It seems cruel.

The idea of resurrecting lost species tends to split people along emotional lines. Some argue that bringing back iconic species would galvanize the public and introduce optimism into an environmental

* The basic technique outlined here can also be used to clone mammals—most famously, Dolly the sheep. Nowadays, the cloned critters are usually house pets and horses, and the rates of birth defects are indeed high. Nevertheless, if the animals are born healthy, they seem to live as long as naturally begotten creatures.

movement that often descends into gloom and apathy. Others worry about moral hazards, fearing that the ability to revive extinct animals will hand society a get-out-of-jail-free card and undermine current conservation efforts. More viscerally, some people hate the very idea of species resurrection, insisting that it's just wrong somehow, that we'd be "playing God." But as others have noted, we're already playing God in driving species to extinction, so perhaps it's morally wrong *not* to restore them.

Regardless, with the planet's environments changing fast, we'll need to make a collective decision about whether to utilize these tools. Sometimes there's a cost to doing nothing as well.

AFTERWORD

Geology might not seem like a field that would stir up a lot of anger. But over the past decade, there's been quite a brouhaha among rockhounds over a seemingly simple question: What geological epoch do we live in?

The traditional answer is the Holocene, which commenced with the end of the last ice age and encompasses all of recorded history. But a significant number of geologists have been demanding that we define a new epoch, dating from roughly the middle of last century. They argue that humankind has so remade our planet, so fundamentally transformed its features, that we need a new term to acknowledge this: the *Anthropocene,* after the Greek word for human beings. So let's imagine a gaggle of geologists digging in the soil a million years from now. How would they detect the Anthropocene in the ground? Several ways.

For one thing, those future geologists will notice that major rivers, which normally meander and change course on a regular basis, were suddenly rerouted or got a lot straighter, due to dams, dikes, and other projects. Another clue will be a spike in metals such as gold, platinum, lead, and chromium. These elements were once buried and scattered throughout many geological layers, but mining and other industrial processes have concentrated them in ours. There will also be traces of radioactive elements with long half-lives, especially isotopes of plutonium and curium, the result of atomic bomb tests and nuclear power plants.

Probably the best marker for the Anthropocene will be certain fossils, a so-called corpse signal. Beneath the Anthropocene layer, geologists will find the bones of megafauna, the mighty beasts that once bestrode every continent—shaggy mammoths, 20-foot sloths, bear-size wombats, and beavers so big you could have saddled and ridden them. Inside the Anthropocene layer, the fauna will be minier. In essence, fossilization is a numbers game: The more critters around, the better a species' chance of appearing in the fossil record. So while there will certainly be some hefty Holsteins in the Anthropocene layer, there will be far more sheep, goats, pigs, and turkeys. Plus, pets—the hundreds of millions of cats and nearly billion dogs that human beings have welcomed into our cities and homes. Overall, the mass of domesticated mammals on earth outweighs the mass of all wild mammals by roughly two dozen times.*

The animals most likely to be fossilized from our era are some of the nearly 80 billion chickens we butcher each year. It helps that, compared to their scrawny ancestors, modern broiler chickens essentially have gigantism, shooting up quickly from birth and packing on loads of muscly meat. As a result, chicken bones are thicker and denser than most bird bones, traits that prevent weathering and

* Future archaeologists could also tell that dogs and cats had higher status than other animals because we bury them in tidy graves. Meanwhile, we toss food animal bones into landfills helter-skelter. Plus, butchered animals often lack a head, which has been chopped off and dumped elsewhere. That rarely happens to dogs or cats.

promote the formation of fossils. So while you might think of the Age of Humans in terms of computers or skyscrapers, that's just pride talking. Over geological time frames, those things will crumble to dust. The future belongs to chickens.

That's more than a little humbling to acknowledge. I mean, look at all we've accomplished—our dominion over nature. Look on our works, ye mighty! But in the future, the geological layer marking the entire sum of human experience won't be any thicker than a ruler—and not the width of a ruler, the height.

Then again, we might not have to wait a million years to be humbled. It's an odd question, but I've often wondered whether the Manhattan Project will exist in the future. That is, will historians several thousand years from now really believe that scientists in the 1940s split the atom? After all, think of everything society lacked back then: integrated circuits, calculators, microchips. We didn't even discover atomic fission until 1938, nor plutonium until 1940. Yet we're supposed to believe that a few eggheads with slide rules built an entire atomic bomb, from scratch, a few years after the project started? C'mon.

It might seem more likely to future scholars that people in our time simply took some mundane event—a scientific gathering in New Mexico, say—and mythologized the whole thing. It's a powerful story, after all: exiles in the desert, a war looming in the background between good and evil, an apocalyptic mushroom cloud rising toward heaven. Furthermore, they might argue, if these people were so clever, why didn't they *do* anything with their fancy new technology? Why not stop burning dead dinosaurs for fuel and convert to clean atomic energy? Why not build nuclear-powered rockets to explore other planets? Is it really credible that the so-called wise apes, *Homo sapiens,* discovered something so profound, so potentially world-changing, yet did nothing more than build bombs and shake their fists at each other?

Similarly, will it really seem plausible to future generations that we spent so much effort to reach the Moon in 1969, then collectively shrugged and explored no further? Heck, a cabal of people *already* deny that we landed on the lunar surface. Arthur C. Clarke once argued, in reference to the Antikythera Mechanism, that if the ancient Greeks had only grasped the power of computing technology, the history of Earth would be quite different. He even suggested that humankind might have reached the Moon by A.D. 200 or 300, and that we'd be an interplanetary species today. It's a startling what-if. But maybe the Greeks would have reacted as we did and never bothered going anywhere else. At minimum, you can imagine how the existence of the Apollo mission or Manhattan Project might be a contentious point among men and women of learning in the future, debatable on both sides.*

But if that's the case, modern humanity will be in good company. Homer's Troy, the ancient Maya, the people of the Indus Valley Civilization—heck, probably even the Peking Men, Women, and Children—they all once imagined themselves to be the summa of existence, only to fade away over time. Despite vast differences in temperament, knowledge, and material culture, that's one thing we share with them all.

Loss, of course, is an absence: something missing. But it can have a paradoxical presence as well—a lingering ache, a gnawing emotion. Think of Nebamun's family returning to his lovely tomb in Egypt to find half his name smashed; they must have felt bereft all over again. Think of paintings missing from the walls of galleries, a glare of negative space framed by dust and discoloration. Think of refugees

* A few things could unequivocally prove to future archaeologists how much technological power we yielded—a runaway environmental catastrophe, a nuclear holocaust. But in that case, it's probably best that our achievements be forgotten. There are worse things than being considered simpletons.

of Genghis Khan and Nazi Germany, returning to their villages to find little but scorched earth after the rampage—their homes, libraries, churches, all rubble. For such people, loss wasn't a mere cavity; it filled them.

Loss can also be an active force—it can drive people. Sometimes this stems from personal anguish, the forfeiture of something dear. But the drive can reach beyond the personal. Rakhaldas Banerji resurrected a forgotten civilization in India because his people needed to be reminded of who they were, of the best of themselves. Heinrich Schliemann scoured the earth for Troy because he wanted to gaze upon the faces of his heroes, and glimpse a bygone age of chivalry. Jean-François Champollion and Michael Ventris wanted to commune with the dead in their own tongues, on their own terms, and Philippa Langley simply loved a king whom everyone else despised. There was nothing personal about the pearl each one sought—until they made it personal, made it everything. Even those kooky cryptozoologists, tramping through forests for extinct birds and other ghost critters, do so in large part to right our collective wrongs, as if they could redeem humanity itself.

The countless others seeking lost books and graves and relics are no less committed to their quests—despite the long odds, and despite the scoffs from others. Because they have something better: hope. Indeed, that might be the most powerful motivator of all. It's the thing that keeps even people who know better—people who realize, rationally, that what they seek has vanished forever—plunging into the fray time and again, just in case. I actually find it touching. It's such a deeply human act: The head knows it's defeated, yet the heart fights on.

Perhaps loss can even benefit us. There's an idea in literary theory called the "anxiety of influence": the weight of the past that poets feel in considering all that's come before them. Amid millions of other poems, what could they possibly say that's new? Or what could painters, musicians, and other artists compose that hasn't been done and overdone already? Maybe starting over fresh would liberate us. No one wants to endure another dark age, but what if a new Renaissance was waiting for us at the end?

And no matter what happens in a thousand or a million or a hundred million years—no matter if our collective culture is lost and forgotten like so many individual ones—it cannot diminish what we did achieve. A modestly sized featherless biped, not particularly strong or fast, really did build the only civilization in the universe as far as we know. That's special.

As we've seen in these pages, history has always been rife with loss. In fact, that's the reason I wrote this book: to acknowledge the sheer scale of that loss throughout the past. But in reflecting on these stories, I realize that it's also worth celebrating all we've accomplished. And especially all we've managed to hold on to.

A THANK-YOU AND A BONUS

I hope you enjoyed *The Museum of Lost Things.* If you want to learn more, I've compiled some bonus material at *samkean.com/books/the-museum-of-lost-things/extras/notes.* There are bonus photographs as well, at *samkean.com/books/the-museum-of-lost-things/extras/photos.* If so moved, you can also drop me a line at *samkean.com/contact.* I love hearing from readers …

ACKNOWLEDGMENTS

This book provoked a lot of reflection about loss and what it means to people's lives. I'd therefore like to take the opportunity to thank everyone I can while I still have the chance.

On the personal side, my parents, Gene and Jean, have always been my biggest fans. The support from my brother, sister, brother-in-law, and not-so-little-anymore niece and nephew, Penny and Harry, has been vital and unwavering. My friends in D.C. and across the world have been constant sources of joy. I'm lucky to know you all.

On the book side, I'd like to thank my agent, Rick Broadhead: Eight books in, and we're still going strong. At National Geographic, my editor, Hilary Black, has steered this book brilliantly throughout, from its conception to the final page proofs and beyond—I couldn't have had a better champion. And this book wouldn't be in your hands without the hard work and deft help of Tyler Daswick, strong art direction from Nicole Roberts, meticulous photo research and design from Lisa Monias, additional photo work from Meredith Wilcox, production direction from Michael O'Connor, copyediting from M. P. Klier, and proofreading from Jenny Miyasaki and Jen Noon Hess, among many other Nat Geo staffers. Thank you all.

Finally, dozens upon dozens of scholars, librarians, and archivists took the time to help me dig up not-quite-lost documents and other material. Thank you for all the rich details you supplied for this book, and thank you for your patience in answering my pestering questions.

If I've forgotten anyone, I remain thankful, if embarrassed.

WORKS CITED

CHAPTER ONE: Lost Graves

Amin, Osama S. M. "The Egyptian Tomb-Chapel Scenes of Nebamun at the British Museum." *World History et cetera,* July 26, 2016. etc.worldhistory.org/exhibitions/egyptian-tomb-chapel-scenes-nebamun-british-museum.

Chan, Tessa. "The Search for Genghis Khan's Tomb." *South China Morning Post Magazine,* 2016. multimedia.scmp.com/magazines/post-magazine/article/genghis-khan/index.html.

Craig, Erin. "Why Genghis Khan's Tomb Can't Be Found." *BBC Travel,* February 24, 2022. bbc.com/travel/article/20170717-why-genghis-khans-tomb-cant-be-found.

Drobyshev, Yu. I. "Funeral and Memorial Rituals of the Medieval Mongols and Their Underlying Worldview." *Anthropology and Archeology of Eurasia* 45, no. 1 (Summer 2006): 65–92. doi.org/10.2753/AAE1061-1959450104.

Jacobs, Frank. "Mongolia's 'Forbidden Zone' Is Guarding an 800-Year-Old Secret." *Big Think,* June 26, 2023. bigthink.com/strange-maps/genghis-khan-burial.

Koutonin, Mawuna. "Lost Cities #9: Racism and Ruins—the Plundering of Great Zimbabwe." *The Guardian,* August 18, 2016. theguardian.com/cities/2016/aug/18/great-zimbabwe-medieval-lost-city-racism-ruins-plundering.

Langley, Philippa, and Michael Jones. *Lost King: The Search for Richard III.* St. Martin's, 2023.

McCouat, Philip. "Lost Masterpieces of Ancient Egyptian Art From the Nebamun Tomb-Chapel." *Journal of Art in Society*, 2015. artinsociety.com/lost-masterpieces-of-ancient-egyptian-art-from-the-nebamun-tomb-chapel.html.

McKie, Robin. "Raiders of the Lost Art." *The Guardian,* January 3, 2009. theguardian.com/artanddesign/2009/jan/04/british-museum-egyptian-nebamun-tomb.

Vallejo, Irene. *Papyrus: The Invention of Books in the Ancient World.* Vintage, 2025.

Weatherford, Jack. *Genghis Khan: And the Making of the Modern World.* Three Rivers Press, 2004.

CHAPTER TWO: Lost Cities

Allen, Susan Heuck. "Frank Calvert: The Unacknowledged Mentor of the Mythic 'Autodidact.'" *Echos du Monde Classique* 42, no. 3 (1998): 603–25.

Blöedow, Edmund F. "'Finding the Walls of Troy': Response to Susan Heuck Allen." *Echos du Monde Classique* 42, no. 3 (1998): 627–44.

Blöedow, Edmund F. "Heinrich Schliemann: An Archaeologist in Advance of His Time?" *Echos du Monde Classique* 42, no. 3 (1998): 579–602.

Cline, Eric H. *The Trojan War: A Very Short Introduction.* Oxford University Press, 2013.

Hammer, Joshua. "In Search of Troy." *Smithsonian Magazine,* March 2022. smithsonianmag.com/history/in-search-of-troy-180979553.

Haughton, Brian. *Ancient Treasures: The Discovery of Lost Hoards, Sunken Ships, Buried Vaults, and Other Long-Forgotten Artifacts.* New Page Books, 2013.

Korfmann, Manfred. "Was There a Trojan War?" *Archaeology* 57, no. 3 (May/June 2004): 36–41.

Lahiri, Nayanjot. *Finding Forgotten Cities: How the Indus Civilization Was Discovered.* Permanent Black, 2005.

Perur, Srinath. "Lost Cities #3—Muziris: Did Black Pepper Cause the Demise of India's Ancient Port?" *The Guardian,* August 10, 2016. theguardian.com/cities/2016/aug/10/lost-cities-3-muziris-india-kerala-ancient-port-black-pepper.

Rose, C. Brian. "Assessing the Evidence for the Trojan Wars." *Archaeological Institute of America,* May 2004.

Schliemann, David A. *Schliemann of Troy: Treasure and Deceit.* St. Martin's Press, 1996.

Vallejo, Irene. *Papyrus: The Invention of Books in the Ancient World.* Vintage, 2025.

Winkler, Martin M., ed. *Troy: From Homer's Iliad to Hollywood Epic.* Wiley-Blackwell, 2008.

CHAPTER THREE: Lost People

Balter, Michael. *The Goddess and the Bull: Çatalhöyük: An Archaeological Journey to the Dawn of Civilization.* Free Press, 2004.

Connor, Patricia, and Kenneth Pearson. *The Dorak Affair.* Atheneum, 1968.

Corrochano Labrador, Eduardo, Monica Baggio, Elisa Bernard, Monica Salvadori, and Luca Zamparo, eds. *Anthropology of Forgery: A Multidisciplinary Approach to the Study of Archaeological Fakes.* Padova University Press, 2019.

Mazur, Suzan. "Dig of the Century: Getting to the Bottom of the Dorak Affair." *Scoop,* August 27, 2005. scoop.co.nz/stories/HL0508/S00224/mazur-getting-to-the-bottom-of-the-dorak-affair.htm.

Mellaart, Alan C., ed. *James Mellaart: The Journey to Çatalhöyük.* Oxford: Archaeology and Art Publications, 2020.

Mellaart, James. *Anatolia c. 4000–2300 B.C.* Cambridge University Press, 1965.

Rieth, Adolf. *Archaeological Fakes.* Barrie and Jenkins, 1970.

Zangger, Eberhard. "James Mellaart's Fantasies." *Talanta* 50 (2018): 125–82.

Zangger, Eberhard. "James Mellaart: Pioneer ..... and Forger." *Popular Archaeology,* October 11, 2019.

CHAPTER FOUR: Lost Relics

Allegro, John Marco. *The Treasure of the Copper Scroll: The Opening and Decipherment of the Most Mysterious of the Dead Sea Scrolls.* Routledge Revivals, 2023.

Atkinson, Kenneth. "Two Dogs, a Goat and a Partridge: An Archaeologist's Best Friends." *Biblical Archaeology Review,* January/February 1996: 42–43. library.biblicalarchaeology.org/article/two-dogs-a-goat-and-a-partridge-an-archaeologists-best-friends.

Collins, John J. *The Dead Sea Scrolls: A Biography.* Princeton University Press, 2012.

Goodacre, Mark. "How Reliable Is the Story of the Nag Hammadi Discovery?" *Journal for the Study of the New Testament* 35, no. 4 (2013): 303–22.

Kingsley, Sean. *God's Gold: A Quest for the Lost Temple Treasures of Jerusalem.* Harper Perennial, 2008.

Nixey, Catherine. *Heresy: Jesus Christ and the Other Sons of God.* Picador, 2024.

Robinson, James M. *The Discovery and Monopoly of the Nag Hammadi Codices.* Brill, 2014.

Robinson, James M. "The Discovery of the Nag Hammadi Codices." *Biblical Archaeologist* 42, no. 4 (Autumn 1979): 206–24.

Wise, Michael O., Martin G. Abegg, Jr., and Edward M. Cook. *Dead Sea Scrolls: A New Translation.* HarperOne, 2005.

CHAPTER FIVE: Lost Bones

Berger, Lee R., Wu Liu, and Xiujie Wu. "Investigation of a Credible Report by a US Marine on the Location of the Missing Peking Man Fossils." *South African Journal of Science* 108, no. 3–4 (January 2012): 6–8.

Boaz, Noel T., and Russell L. Ciochon. *Dragon Bone Hill: An Ice-Age Saga of Homo Erectus.* Oxford University Press, 2004.

Frängsmyr, Tore. "Peking Man: New Light on an Old Discovery." *A Master of Science History Essays in Honor of Charles Coulston Gillispie,* edited by Jed Z. Buchwald, 49–62. Springer, 2012.

Reader, John. *Missing Links: In Search of Human Origins.* Oxford University Press, 2011.

Shapiro, Harry L. *Peking Man.* Simon and Schuster, 1974.

Wayman, Erin. "Mystery of the Lost Peking Man Fossils Solved?" *Smithsonian Magazine,* March 28, 2012. smithsonianmag.com/science-nature/mystery-of-the-lost-peking-man-fossils-solved-166415409.

CHAPTER SIX: Lost Civilizations

Bhattacharya, Ashok. *Rakhaldas Bandyopadhyay.* Sahitya Akademi, 1999.

Cheng, Yinghong. "Is Peking Man Still Our Ancestor?—Race and National Lineage." In *Discourses of Race and Rising China*, 99–159. Palgrave Macmillan, 2019.

Corrochano Labrador, Eduardo, Monica Baggio, Elisa Bernard, Monica Salvadori, and Luca Zamparo, eds. *Anthropology of Forgery: A Multidisciplinary Approach to the Study of Archaeological Fakes.* Padova University Press, 2019.

Mishra, Phanikanta. *Rakhal Das Banerjee: Time, Life, and Achievements of a Forgotten Archaeologist.* CDC Printers, 2018.

Murray, Tim, and Christopher Evans, eds. *Histories of Archaeology: A Reader in the History of Archaeology.* Oxford University Press, 2018.

Pillalamarri, Akhilesh. "When History Gets Political: India's Grand 'Aryan' Debate and the Indus Valley Civilization." *The Diplomat,* August 18, 2016.

Ramaswamy, Sumathi. "Archaeology, Nationalism, and the Yearning for Civilisation in the Indus Valley." *Modern Asian Studies* 38, no. 2 (2001): 105–45.

Robinson, Andrew. *Indus Lost Civilizations.* Reaktion Books, 2015.

CHAPTER SEVEN: Lost Languages

Dolnick, Edward. *Writing of the Gods: The Race to Decode the Rosetta Stone.* Scribner, 2021.

Fox, Margalit. *Riddle of the Labyrinth: The Quest to Crack an Ancient Code.* Ecco, 2024.

Machulak, Erica. "Texting in Hieroglyphs: What Unicode Will Make Possible." *Humanities* 39, no. 1 (Winter 2018). neh.gov/humanities/2018/winter/feature/texting-in-ancient-mayan-hieroglyphs.

Mahadevan, Iravatham. "Full Text of the Indus Script." Harappa.com. www.harappa.com/script/maha15.html.

Price, Kate. "An Analysis of Failure and Success: The Decipherment of Linear B." academia.edu/6376004/An_Analysis_of_Failure_and_Success_the_Decipherment_of_Linear_B.

Robinson, Andrew. *Lost Languages: The Enigma of the World's Undeciphered Scripts.* McGraw-Hill, 2002.

Robinson, Andrew. *The Man Who Deciphered Linear B: The Story of Michael Ventris.* Thames and Hudson, 2012.

Schele, Elaine Day. "The Untold Story of Alberto Ruz and His Archaeological Excavations at Palenque, México: A Micro- and Macrohistorical Approach." Ph.D. diss., University of Texas at Austin, 2012.

CHAPTER EIGHT: Lost Knowledge

Casson, Lionel. *Libraries in the Ancient World.* Yale University Press, 2002.

Crocker, Sarah. "The True Story of the Fire That Destroyed the Library of Congress." *Grunge,* April 13, 2021. grunge.com/380961/the-true-story-of-the-fire-that-destroyed-the-library-of-congress.

El-Abbadi, Mostafa, and Omnia Mounir Fathallah, eds. *What Happened to the Ancient Library of Alexandria?* Brill, 2008.

Greenspan, Jesse. "When the British Burned Washington, D.C." History.com, August 22, 2014. Updated August 29, 2018. history.com/news/the-british-burn-washington-d-c-200-years-ago.

Hannam, James. "The Mysterious Fate of the Great Library of Alexandria." Bede's Library. bede.org.uk/library.htm.

Jochum, Uwe. "The Alexandrian Library and Its Aftermath." *Library History* 15, no. 1 (1999): 5–12.

MacLeod, Roy. *Center of Learning: The Library of Alexandria in the Ancient World.* I. B. Tauris, 2004.

Marlowe, John. *The Golden Age of Alexandria: From Its Foundation by Alexander the Great in 331* BC *to Its Capture by the Arabs in 642* AD. Gollancz, 1971.

Vallejo, Irene. *Papyrus: The Invention of Books in the Ancient World.* Vintage, 2025.

Weber, Tomas. "Inside the AI Competition That Decoded an Ancient Herculaneum Scroll." *Scientific American,* April 2024.

CHAPTER NINE: Lost Gold

Barker, Anne. "Yamashita's Gold Was a National Obsession in the Philippines." ABC News (Australia), August 19, 2022. abc.net.au/news/2022-08-20/philippines-imelda-marcos-and-the-missing-gold-statue/101295806.

Bovill, E. W. *The Golden Trade of the Moors: West African Kingdoms in the Fourteenth Century.* Markus Wiener, 2009.

Koutonin, Mawuna. "Lost Cities #9: Racism and Ruins—the Plundering of Great Zimbabwe." *The Guardian*, August 18, 2016. theguardian.com/cities/2016/aug/18/great-zimbabwe-medieval-lost-city-racism-ruins-plundering.

Oliver, P. James. *Empire of Mali: Mansa Musa and the Empire of Mali.* CreateSpace, 2013.

Oulhadji, Mohamed. "The West African Medieval Empire of Mali (13th–15th Centuries)." Master's thesis, Ahmed Draia University of Adrar, 2018.

Pallamary, Matthew J. *Picaflor.* Mystic Ink, 2021.

Seagrave, Sterling, and Peggy Seagrave. *Gold Warriors: How America Secretly Recovered Yamashita's Gold.* Bowstring, 2010.

Tschanz, David W. "The Lion of Mali: The Hajj of Mansa Musa." May 2012. academia.edu/1593503/Lion_Of_Mali_The_Hajj_of_Mansa_Musa.

CHAPTER TEN: Lost Art

Burke, Peter. *The Polymath: A Cultural History From Leonardo da Vinci to Susan Sontag.* Yale University Press, 2020.

Charney, Noah. *The Thefts of the Mona Lisa: The Complete Story of the World's Most Famous Artwork.* Rowman and Littlefield, 2024.

Day, Nicholas. *Mona Lisa Vanishes: A Legendary Painter, a Shocking Heist, and the Birth of a Global Celebrity.* Random House, 2023.

De Camp, L. Sprague. *The Ancient Engineers: An Astonishing Look Back at the Ancient Wonders of the World and Their Creators.* Random House, 1995.

Fiorani, Francesca. *The Shadow Drawing: How Science Taught Leonardo How to Paint.* Farrar, Straus and Giroux, 2024.

Isaacson, Walter. *Leonardo da Vinci.* Simon and Schuster, 2017.

Poirier, Agnès. "Saviour of France's Art: How the Mona Lisa Was Spirited Away From the Nazis." *The Guardian,* November 22, 2014. theguardian.com/world/2014/nov/22/mona-lisa-spirited-away-from-nazis-jacques-jaujard-louvre.

Wallace, Robert. *The World of Leonardo: 1452–1519.* Little, Brown, 1966.

CHAPTER ELEVEN: Lost Loot

Balter, Brian Haughton. *Ancient Treasures: The Discovery of Lost Hoards, Sunken Ships, Buried Vaults, and Other Long-Forgotten Artifacts.* Career Press, 2013.

Kolbert, Elizabeth. "Forever Amber: A Room Built for a King and Treasured by an Empress Haunts Two Countries." *New Yorker,* April 7, 2003.

Loudis, Jessica. "Haul of Shame—the 'Trophy Art' Taken From Germany by the Red Army." *Apollo,* January 6, 2020. apollo-magazine.com/red-army-trophy-art-germany.

Nabhan, Gary Paul. *Where Our Food Comes From: Retracing Nikolay Vavilov's Quest to End Famine.* Island Press, 2011.

Nicholas, Lynn. *The Rape of Europa.* Knopf, 1994.

Scott-Clark, Catherine, and Adrian Levy. *Amber Room: The Fate of the World's Greatest Lost Treasure.* Walker, 2004.

Shirer, William L. *The Rise and Fall of the Third Reich: A History of Nazi Germany.* Simon and Schuster, 1960.

CHAPTER TWELVE: Lost Technology

Bruderer, Herbert. "The Antikythera Mechanism." *Communications of the ACM* 63, no. 4 (April 2020): 108–15.

Budiselic, C., A. T. Thoeni, M. Dubno, and A. T. Ramsey. "The Antikythera Mechanism: Evidence of a Lunar Calendar," parts 1 and 2. British Horological Institute, 2020.

Freeth, Tony. "An Ancient Greek Astronomical Calculation Machine Reveals New Secrets." *Scientific American,* January 2022.

Jones, Alexander. *A Portable Cosmos: Revealing the Antikythera Mechanism, Scientific Wonder of the Ancient World.* Oxford University Press, 2017.

LaFrance, Adrienne. "The Most Mysterious Object in the History of Technology." *The Atlantic,* June 20, 2016. theatlantic.com/technology/archive/2016/06/antikythera-mechanism-whoa/487832.

Marchant, Jo. *Decoding the Heavens: A 2,000-Year-Old Computer and the Century-Long Search to Discover Its Secrets.* Da Capo Press, 2009.

Pollard, Justin, and Howard Reid. *The Rise and Fall of Alexandria: Birthplace of the Modern World.* Viking Penguin, 2006.

Throckmorton, Peter. *Shipwrecks and Archaeology: The Unharvested Sea.* Victor Gollancz, 1969.

CHAPTER THIRTEEN: Lost Species

Cheke, Anthony. "The Dodo's Last Island—Where Did Volkert Evertsz Meet the Last Wild Dodos?" *Proceedings of the Royal Society of Arts and Sciences of Mauritius* 7 (2004): 7–22.

Forey, Peter L. *History of the Coelacanth Fishes.* Chapman and Hall, 1998.

Heidt, Amanda. "Gars Truly Are 'Living Fossils,' Massive DNA Data Set Shows." *Science* 383 (March 8, 2024): 1041.

Lawton, Graham. "The Last Dodo." *New Scientist* 244 (December 21, 2019): 74–76.

Loxton, Daniel, and Donald R. Prothero. *Abominable Science!: Origins of the Yeti, Nessie, and Other Famous Cryptids.* Columbia University Press, 2006.

Quammen, David. *The Song of the Dodo: Island Biogeography in an Age of Extinction.* Scribner, 1997.

Shapiro, Beth. *How to Clone a Mammoth: The Science of De-Extinction.* Princeton University Press, 2015.

Smith, J. L. B. *The Search Beneath the Sea: The Story of the Coelacanth.* Henry Holt, 1956.

Steinauer-Scudder, Chelsea. "The Lord God Bird: Apocalyptic Prophecy and the Vanishing of Avifauna." *Emergence Magazine,* July 1, 2020.

Tyson, Peter. "Moment of Discovery." *NOVA,* PBS, January 2003. pbs.org/wgbh/nova/fish/letters.html.

Walker, Sally M. *Fossil Fish Found Alive: Discovering the Coelacanth.* Carolrhoda Books, 2002.

Weinberg, Samantha. *A Fish Caught in Time.* HarperCollins, 2000.

AFTERWORD

Behrensmeyer, Anna K., Susan M. Kidwell, and Robert A. Gastaldo. "Taphonomy and Paleobiology." *Paleobiology* 26, no. 4 (Autumn 2000): 103–47.

Bennett, Carys E., et al. "The Broiler Chicken as a Signal of a Human Reconfigured Biosphere." *Royal Society* 5, no. 12 (December 2018): 180325. royalsocietypublishing.org/doi/10.1098/rsos.180325.

Mirsky, Steve. "I Shall Return." *Earth,* April 1998, 48–52.

Plotnick, Roy E., and Karen A. Koy. "The Anthropocene Fossil Record of Terrestrial Mammals." *Anthropocene* 29 (March 2020): 100233. doi.org/10.1016/j.ancene.2019.100233.

Schmidt, Gavin A., and Adam Frank. "The Silurian Hypothesis: Would It Be Possible to Detect an Industrial Civilization in the Geological Record?" *International Journal of Astrobiology* 18, no. 2 (2018). doi.org/10.1017/S1473550418000095.

ILLUSTRATIONS CREDITS

Front cover, ridersuperone/Shutterstock; 188, Dr. Christian Prager; 190, "upended frog" and "toothache" glyphs courtesy of the Penn Museum; I-1 (UP), English School (15th century)/Private Collection/Bridgeman Images; I-1 (LO), Erich Lessing/Bridgeman Images; I-2 (UP), AP Photo/Ng Han Guan; I-2 (LO), Photo 12/Universal Images Group via Getty Images; I-3 (UP), frantic00/Shutterstock; I-3 (CTR LE), Universal Images Group/Getty Images; I-3 (CTR RT), brandstaetter images/Hulton Archive/Getty Images; I-3 (LO), ullstein bild via Getty Images; I-4 (UP), Roy Anderson/National Geographic Image Collection; I-4 (LO LE), Illustrated London News Ltd/Mary Evans Picture Library; I-4 (LO RT), Nathan Benn/GEO Image Collection/Bridgeman Images; I-5 (UP), Menahem Kahana/AFP/Getty Images; I-5 (CTR LE), Patrick Chapuis/Gamma-Rapho via Getty Images; I-5 (CTR RT), akg-images/Bible Land Pictures; I-5 (LO), David Boyer/National Geographic Image Collection; I-6 (UP), Bettmann/Getty Images; I-6 (LO), Archives Charmet/Bridgeman Images; I-7 (UP LE), from *The Modern Review,* January 1925, via Wikimedia Commons; I-7 (UP RT), National Museum of India, New Delhi, India/Bridgeman Images; I-7 (LO), National Museum of Pakistan, Karachi/© A. Dagli Orti/© NPL — DeA Picture

Library/Bridgeman Images; I-8 (UP), Fine Art Images/Heritage Images/Getty Images; I-8 (LO), George Holton/Science Source; I-9 (UP), Kenneth Garrett/National Geographic Image Collection; I-9 (LO LE), Randy Olson; I-9 (LO RT), Cogniet, Leon (1794–1880)/French/Louvre, Paris, France/Luisa Ricciarini/Bridgeman Images; I-10 (UP LE), British Museum, London, UK/Bridgeman Images; I-10 (UP RT), Express/Hulton Archive/Getty Images; I-10 (LO), David Parker/Science Source; I-11 (UP), Fine Art Images/Heritage Images/Getty Images; I-11 (LO LE), from the British Library archive, London, UK/Bridgeman Images; I-11 (LO RT), Spanish School (16th century)/Biblioteca Colombina, Seville, Spain/Bridgeman Images; I-12 (UP), Nick Hawkins/NPL/Minden Pictures; I-12 (LO), Cresques, Abraham (1325–1387)/Spanish/Bibliothèque nationale, Paris, France/Bridgeman Images; I-13 (UP LE), Chroma Collection/Alamy Stock Photo; I-13 (UP RT), Sergio Anelli/Mondadori Portfolio/Electa/Bridgeman Images; I-13 (CTR), Rubens, Peter Paul (1577–1640)/Flemish/Akademie der Bildenden Kunste, Vienna, Austria/Luisa Ricciarini/Bridgeman Images; I-13 (LO), PVDE/Bridgeman Images; I-14 (UP), SZ Photo/Scherl/Bridgeman Images; I-14 (LO), Antoine Gyori/Sygma via Getty Images; I-15 (UP), Science Source; I-15 (LO LE), AP Photo/Thanassis Stavrakis; I-15 (LO RT), Abbus Acastra/Alamy Stock Photo; I-16 (UP), Atsushi Sakurai/Nature Production/Minden Pictures; I-16 (LO LE), James T. Tanner/Science Source; I-16 (LO RT), Natural History Museum, London/Alamy Stock Photo.

INDEX

B

C

D

I

J

K

L

O

P

T

U

V

W

Y

Z

ABOUT THE AUTHOR

Sam Kean is the *New York Times* best-selling author of eight books, including *Dinner With King Tut, The Icepick Surgeon, The Bastard Brigade,* and *The Disappearing Spoon*. His writing has appeared in *National Geographic,* the *New Yorker,* the *New York Times,* and *The Best American Science and Nature Writing.* His work has also been featured on NPR's *Radiolab, Science Friday, All Things Considered,* and *Fresh Air,* and his podcast, *The Disappearing Spoon,* debuted at number one on the iTunes chart for science podcasts. He lives in Washington, D.C.